Penguin

Shooting

Day

A true account of the first weeks

living with brain injury

By

Pearl A. Gardner

Pearl A Gardner

Copyright 2013 Pearl A Gardner

eBook edition
ASIN: B00FRIO2ZO

Print edition
ISBN-13: 978-1495450181
ISBN-10: 149545018X

Printed by CreateSpace, an Amazon.com Company
Available from Amazon.com and other online stores.

Edition 2

The actual events recorded in this account are true. Unfortunately, because there is a certain amount of discrimination towards people who have brain damage, I have changed the names of my family members to protect their identities. Some locations, dates and small details have been changed for the same reason.

ACKNOWLEDGEMENTS

I apologise in advance to all my readers who know the correct terminology for the specialists and therapists I mention in this diary. I know I got some of them wrong.

I must also apologise to all the staff at Ryde Rehabilitation Centre in Sydney. You did a marvellous job, and I know you have many grateful patients and families who benefitted from your rehabilitation programme, but it wasn't right for Simon at that time.

I have to say a huge thank you to friends, neighbours and family in Australia and in UK, who helped in so many ways while we struggled in Sydney. Special thanks go to hospital staff at the Royal Prince Alfred Hospital in Sydney, (who are too numerous to mention), and of course to Simon for allowing me to take this diary to publication.

Finally, I dedicate this book to my brave daughter. During the initial days after the accident and throughout her husband's recovery she was, and still is, an inspiration to us all.

You kept us strong my darling, even when your heart was breaking; you found the courage to uplift us with your tireless positive attitude. I love you.

FOREWORD

I kept this diary for a number of reasons. Firstly, my nature is to put everything down on paper, from shopping lists to seating plans. Secondly, I needed to channel my emotions. Setting it down in black and white helped contain the threatening avalanche of emotion, and made it easier to focus on what might lie ahead. Thirdly, it was going to be a bloody long flight, and if I didn't do something, I would be out of my mind before my jumbo got off the ground.

I was about to set out on a familiar 30 hour trip, but this time, I didn't have the anticipation and flurry of pretty butterflies in my tummy to shorten every minute of that journey. Instead, the lonely, panic filled, hours stretched endlessly before me, and I felt as if a dozen fruit-bats with scratchy claws were doing aerobatics in my insides. I had no one to share my distress with and couldn't face idle chit chat with fellow travellers who were innocently going away on holiday.

Over the following weeks, my diary became my confessor and confidant, my dumping ground for sorrow and a place to share the joys and laughter when there was no one else around. It became the saver of my sanity, and I hope it will now give hope and maybe a little inspiration for others who may find themselves in a similar situation.

Pearl A Gardner

TABLE OF CONTENTS

ACKNOWLEDGEMENTS..4

FOREWORD...5

WEEK ONE: Panic & instinct.....................................7

WEEK TWO: Confusion & explanations 80

WEEK THREE: Delusions & laughter....................112

WEEK FOUR: Hopes & uncertainties...................160

WEEK FIVE: Visitors & fixations...........................202

WEEK SIX: Move to rehabilitation.......................246

WEEK SEVEN: Frustrations & temper 283

WEEK EIGHT: Home at last 310

WEEK NINE: Objections & arguments.................327

WEEK TEN: Promises of help 335

NOVEMBER: Five weeks on 337

POST SCRIPT: Five years later 339

ABOUT THE AUTHOR 342

MORE PUBLICATIONS 343

CONNECT WITH THE AUTHOR 346

WEEK ONE: Panic & instinct

DAY 1 Sunday 29th June 2008 (written on 30th June)

Paul and I were in the attic office room in our tiny home. At 11am, the phone rang, and I answered it brightly, expecting to hear the voice of our youngest daughter, Katy. Instead, it was the phone call from hell.

'Hello, Mum. It's Natalie.'

'Natalie?' I could tell from my eldest daughter's trembling voice that something was terribly wrong. I fleetingly registered the time of the day being odd too. (With the time difference, it was much later than usual for her to be calling us from Australia.)

'Something awful has happened, Mum.'

'What is it, love?' I asked, trying to sound normal but hearing my croaky nervous frog voice coming out of my mouth. Paul glanced over, questions forming on his lips. I managed to flick the phone to loud speaker so Paul could hear first-hand what our daughter had to say.

Then the words that shook our world came over the line.

'Simon's had a car accident, he's...'

I heard her take a strangled breath. She sounded something like a gulping guppy stranded on a dry bank. It was a chilling sound for us to hear.

'Okay, Natalie.' I swallowed hard and tried to keep the frog in my throat under control. I had to be strong to give my daughter the courage to tell me the worst. 'Tell me simply. How bad is it?'

Paul was huddled beside me now, concern on his face, fear shadowing his eyes. I knew my face held the same terrified look.

He reached for my shaking hand and clasped it firmly as we continued to listen.

'It's pretty bad, Mum,' I heard her take another choking gasp before she rushed on, 'He's fractured his skull, he's in a coma.'

Time froze. The edges of my vision blurred, and I barely drew a breath. My chest tightened as I listened to her listing his injuries in a monotone voice that didn't seem real. I was too shocked to take it in.

'…And so he has multiple fractures,' she paused, 'these are all fixable,' she hastened to add. Then before I had a chance to comment, she continued, still speaking in that brisk, matter-of-fact tone, punctuated by guppy gasps to steady the shaking in her voice. 'But the worst is his head. His face is smashed up. He has a small fracture to the front of his skull and a large one at the back. They've put him in a coma, and he's on a respirator.' She ran out of steam then, and all we could hear was her rasping breath.

My mind went into overdrive.

I took a deep shaky lungful of air and blinked the tears away quickly. 'Okay, Natalie. Let's see what we can do.' I glanced at Paul, knowing that whatever I said, he would back me up one-hundred-per-cent. 'Where are you now, Natalie?' My mothering instincts took over and I went into autopilot, organising the practicalities in my mind, finding out the facts, skipping ahead in my brain to plan what I would have to do next to help.

'We're at Byron District Hospital,' Natalie told us, 'but they're going to airlift him to Brisbane because he needs care from a specialist neuro-team and they don't have the facilities here.'

It's Penguin Shooting Day

My brain was busy making the calculations of what that would mean to Natalie. Brisbane is a three-hour drive from their home near Bangalow. It would be a nightmare to travel back and forth to the hospital, for the amount of time he would have to be there. Natalie would need help with looking after Ruby, the animals and zillions of other things. Then I realised that my little granddaughter hadn't been mentioned.

'Where's Ruby?' I asked, desperate to know that my little grandchild was safe. At almost five months since her first birthday, I'd only seen her twice in her short life. The first time when she was three-weeks-old, and again when she was ten-months-old at Christmas when I felt I'd cuddled her to within an inch of her life and got to know her better. I was already making plans to spend more time with her. I knew I'd have to go and help to take care of her. What I didn't begin to understand was how I was going to do that! It was more than twenty-five years since I looked after a small child, but the how was far from my thoughts in these first few minutes of the half-formed plan in my head.

'Martin took her home and put her to bed. One of the other neighbours is staying over at our place. She's in her own bed and settled. Martin came back to the hospital to be with me.'

Martin and Sally are their nearest neighbours who live just a five-minute walk away. Natalie and Simon don't live in the outback, thank goodness.

'Natalie, listen to me.' I looked at Paul and flapped my arms, motioning to him that I was going over.

He nodded and ran a hand over his face.

I took a steadying breath. 'I'm going to see if I can get a flight.'

The words were out and hung in the air between us like a dark fog. Paul's eyes darkened, and he pressed his lips together, but he didn't interrupt me. We'd have lots to discuss when I put the phone down.

'I can't ask you to do that, Mum. It's going to be a long haul with Simon. You'd have to give up your job and...' then her voice broke on a sob. She was overwhelmed.

'I can and I will!' I surprised myself at how strong and firm my voice sounded, as my whole body was trembling with shock. 'You listen to me,' I demanded of her. 'You need help. I can look after Ruby, help with the animals and be there for you. Whatever you need. Whatever it takes. I'm coming!'

'Oh, Mum!' She sounded so relieved. I sensed her body sagging as it drained of tension. 'Thanks,' she said quietly.

'Listen, love, I don't want to waste a second.' I wanted to start making arrangements. 'I'm going to start looking for a flight now. I'll ring you when it's booked. Go back to Simon now and try not to worry. I'll be there with you just as quickly as I can.'

We said our goodbyes and I turned to Paul. We both held the tears back as we hugged.

'Oh, God!' and, 'Oh, no!' Paul kept saying as we tried to draw strength from each other.

When we eventually drew apart, I asked him, 'Can you start looking for flights? I'll ring Katy to tell her and John the bad news.'

I felt I was in the middle of a nightmare. I've had a

few bad dreams since our eldest daughter left home. All about the worries that a parent would have when a child is far from home and the television news fills their heads with murders and muggings of travelling youngsters.

Natalie went to work in Australia a few months after the millennium celebrations, hoping to see the Olympic Games in Sydney. We thought she'd be home again in England after a year when her work sponsorship expired. That was the plan, but it was not to be.

Her sponsorship was extended, and she met Simon during a business trip to Melbourne. They fell in love, said they were soul mates, and we flew to Australia to meet him before they got engaged on Valentine's Day.

A year later, Natalie accepted a position in her company that meant she had to move north. Simon is a skilled construction worker, and soon found a job in northern New South Wales. They moved close to Bangalow, a small town just inland from Byron Bay.

They found a beautiful property in the countryside with acres of land, a pool and a four-bedroom house. They bought their dream home and held their wedding ceremony on top of the hill overlooking the house in September of 2005. Paul and I, with our youngest daughter, Katy, travelled out to Australia to attend the wedding.

They are so much in love it's a joy to watch them together. The term, soul mates, is overused and often misunderstood, but it fits them perfectly.

I had no worries about my eldest daughter and her future happiness with the man of her dreams in a place they adored.

Simon and Natalie travelled back to England to stay

with us in June 2006 so we could introduce him to all the family here. We had a big party that ended in the small hours as we talked and laughed together.

Katy was in the middle of planning her wedding to John, whom she'd met shortly after returning from Natalie's wedding. Dresses and shoes, flowers and food, were top subjects of conversation between my two girls. Natalie was to be Katy's bridesmaid, so she and Simon planned to travel back to England the following year to join in the celebrations.

Fate intervened, and Katy had to find another bridesmaid because Natalie discovered she had conceived while visiting us, and their daughter, Ruby May, was born in early March of 2007 shortly before Katy got married here in UK.

We were sad to have Natalie and Simon missing from Katy and John's celebration, but Natalie sent a video of our first grandchild and an e-mail that she asked me to read at the wedding reception. The video arrived on the morning of the wedding, making me late for my hairdresser's appointment as I couldn't drag myself away from the TV screen.

The e-mail brought tears to many eyes at the reception as I read Natalie's words full of love and laughter and Katy's eyes were the wettest of all.

Life could not have been better for my daughter, and her husband, Simon, in Australia.

I flew out to meet my granddaughter in April. Paul couldn't take time from work, but I was determined to go see my first grandchild as soon as possible.

I went again at Christmas with Paul, Katy and John.

So I can't complain that I never saw my eldest child. We have been very lucky to see her so often.

Did I worry about Natalie's happiness? Not a bit. She was blessedly happy. She had everything she could ever want and more. Was I happy for her? Of course, I was. Was I happy for me? Not at all! My daughter lived on the other side of the world and now my baby granddaughter was growing up so far away.

The realities of it hurt like a nagging toothache sometimes, but we can talk on the phone and with the computer we can videoconference and see each other in real time on screen. The world is a much smaller place now, flights are so easy to arrange, and we work hard to afford them as often as possible. So we make the best of things.

I always had a niggling fear, though, which seemed to deepen after Natalie married an Australian and made it clear that England would never be her home again. I agonised constantly about all those, what if's. Every parent must worry about them.

'What if,' is the start of nightmares when dropping off to sleep and sometimes the really terrible 'what if's' carry into waking dreams.

I had some nasty dreams in the months after Natalie and Simon's wedding. They were the kind of dreams I had to shrug off as I saw them as a manifestation of an irrational fear.

I'd see a train or plane disaster on television, and my thoughts would drift to, 'what if?' What if something like that happened to Natalie or to Simon? What would I do? They are so far away! How could I be there to help my child if the, 'what if's,' happened to them in real life?

At 11am on Sunday the 29th June, 2008, the, 'what if's,' had happened, and my worrying dreams began to play in real time.

Thank goodness we are experts at organising Australian travel. We'd done this many times since Natalie made her home there, but not always with such urgency. The most recent was Christmas 2007 when Katy and John came with us.

I'm blessed that my family get on well with each other. John and Simon share an interest in motor racing. They are both more than fans, they live and breathe Formula one and Michael Schumacher is their hero.

When Natalie and Simon came to England to stay with us, in June 2006, we went to see the races at Silverstone together. That was the year the heavens opened over the main race. When I saw the weather forecast, I packed a roll of black plastic bin liners, and I recall the kids scoffed at my forward planning as we set out that morning in the sunshine.

They didn't laugh when I started handing out black plastic sacks when the rain came down. We poked holes through them for our arms, wrapped them around our legs and heads as the rain poured down. We had a great time, despite the weather and enjoyed an exciting and slippery race. My whole family stood all afternoon in the torrential downpour, looking like a pack of drowned black plastic rats and I couldn't have been happier!

Katy! I had to ring her. She is Natalie's younger sister by three years, and they are as different from each other as the day and night. Katy has a Mediterranean look about her, goodness knows where those genes came from in our ancestry, with flowing auburn hair and skin that tans easily. She's a whirlwind of fun, but she's quick to bite and slow to back down.

Natalie is a natural blonde with a pale, transparent quality to her skin. She's slow to fire up but once roused; she'll fight like a she-cat defending kittens. To look at her, you'd think she was a fragile and delicate creature who would be rocked off her feet at the slightest puff of trouble, but you'd be so far off the mark!

Katy's home is neat and uncluttered, where Natalie's is an untidy happy jumble. We survived many battles between them when they both lived at home.

Their love-hate relationship veers much more toward love, when they're thousands of miles apart. Closeness causes friction, because of their very different personalities, but their underlying love for each other is undeniable. This was the call I had to make next.

'Katy, it's Mum. is John with you?'

I didn't want to beat around the bush but would have preferred that she wasn't alone when I told her. She was sobbing before I'd finished explaining what I knew.

'We're coming over. See you soon.' She barely got the words out before she hung up.

Paul was cursing the computer. 'I can't find any damned flights. These bloody sites are useless!'

He stabbed aggressively with one finger at the keyboard. 'Why do I have to put in all my details first? I get all the way through the bloody forms then they tell me there are no bloody flights!'

Poor Paul. He was so distraught he couldn't think straight and was getting cross at the frustrations of surfing the Internet. He is the computer specialist of the family and can fix most software and hardware problems, but due to the stress of our situation; he was finding it difficult to do the simplest of tasks.

I turned to my computer. We have his and hers computers, in our home office, in the attic of our small bungalow. I surfed to the travel website I'd used before and within seconds I had a screen full of flights.

I clicked through to check availability to find there were no seats until Wednesday. So I decided to ring and speak to them directly to see if they could help due to our special circumstances. I got through to speak with one of their representatives. He was brilliant! He listened to my shortened and emotionally edited version of why I needed to get to Australia as soon as possible and he began to search in earnest.

Within a few minutes, he had found me a flight with Singapore airlines that left from Manchester at 10am in the morning of Monday, the 30th June, and arrived in Brisbane on Tuesday evening! Manchester is a couple of hours drive away, so I booked this immediately and organised a return date of 25th September, taking the full three months allowed on a tourist visa. I knew that I could change the departure date later if I needed to.

Katy arrived in the middle of the phone call, but she waited until I put the phone down before hugging me and bursting into tears.

Katy wears her heart on her sleeve and couldn't hide her emotions if she tried. We held hands and I told her as much as I knew. She wanted to come to Australia too, to help in whatever way she could, but I reassured her that it wasn't necessary.

Natalie would love her sister to be there for the first

day or so, but sparks would fly between them before a week went by, and that wouldn't help any of us.

'You look after Dad for me,' I told her. 'That will be help enough for now.'

She nodded and turned to John for a cuddle.

I was still operating in autopilot and going through what had to be done, like a robot. I didn't let myself dwell on the emotions tying my stomach in knots.

'I need to ring Natalie to tell her when I'm arriving.' I picked up the phone and dialled her mobile number. Her phone rang for a while before she answered it.

'Hi, Natalie, it's Mum. How's he doing?'

'They haven't got a bloody bed in Brisbane!' she cursed, her voice full of pain and anguish. 'They're flying him to bloody Sydney!' Natalie doesn't normally swear unless she's really angry, so I knew she was stressed to the limit.

'Don't worry,' I tried to calm her. 'I'm arriving in Brisbane on Tuesday night. I can get an internal flight to Sydney and meet you there.'

'Oh, Mum! I can't take Ruby to Sydney. It would be too much for her. I don't want her to see all the upset. I'll just have to go home to look after her and let the medical people look after Simon. I can't do anything for him anyway!' She sounded so upset and angry.

'We'll all go to Sydney when I get there. We'll work it out. You concentrate on Simon now. Do what you have to do for him and we'll arrange things as we go along.'

We talked more about arrangements and difficulties and possible solutions. She asked me how I planned to get from Brisbane airport to Bangalow. Trains stopped running before my plane landed. We discussed a few alternatives and then I realised I was keeping Natalie away from Simon. She needed to be with her husband and I could work out the details of my journey from here.

'Don't worry about it now, Natalie.' I told her. 'I'll get to you somehow. We'll organise it from here and find out as much as we can from the Internet. You concentrate on Simon. I'll see you real soon, honey.'

'I'll be really glad to see you, Mum,' she said quietly.

We said our goodbyes and I fought to keep my calm composure. She had admitted she needed me, and that was so hard to hear. She was always my strong and independent child. She never needed me in the way most children need mothering. She always wanted to do things her way, in her own time, and I constantly had to watch her struggle.

I had memory flashes of Natalie obstinately feeding herself at ten months old, porridge dribbling from her hair to her toes, struggling to fasten shoe buckles at three-years-old, changing a wheel on her first old banger at seventeen, walking away from me at the airport when she left England for good.

She wanted so much to do everything her own way! Now she needed me, and it was such a double-edged sword! I wondered if I were up to the challenge. Could I really fulfil all the needs she would have of me? It was too late to worry about that now. I would find out soon.

John made us lunch at 2pm as we hadn't eaten since an early breakfast, but it was like forcing cardboard down. We sat quietly around the table, gulping tea and chewing without tasting. Each of us seemed lost in thought, too scared to give voice to them; too afraid that if we mentioned what we were thinking, it might come true.

We were all worried about the kind of damage Simon's body had suffered, and were concerned about the disabilities he might be left with. When we did speak, these subjects were briefly touched on, but it seemed there was a silent agreement not to discuss those topics in depth. We'd start a sentence and words would dry, and the sentence would be left hanging.

'How bad is the skull fracture?' Katy asked.

'Bad enough to need surgery.' Paul shook his head.

'That's the worst thing, isn't it?' John looked at Katy. 'How will he…?' He didn't finish his sentence, and no one offered to finish it for him.

In the silence, I wondered how they would survive this as a family. Then I thought about the accident. What had caused it? Was anyone else involved? Was anyone else injured, or worse than that, was anyone killed?

'Wonder how it happened? Do you know?' John asked, seeming to read my thoughts.

'Did Natalie say?' Katy asked.

I shook my head. 'Don't think she knows yet.'

'It's irrelevant now, anyway.' Paul sighed, closing another thread of jilted conversation. He turned to me. 'What else do we have to do?'

Katy helped me pack while Paul organised my visa and insurance. The Internet is a wonderful thing. How else could we have all the paperwork organised so quickly, on a Sunday in the UK?

Katy did a sweep of the bathroom collecting my toiletries, pills and potions. I grabbed the clothes I thought would be practical. Sydney in July could be cold, but it could also be very warm. I pulled out vests and sweaters. Layers would be suitable.

'I don't want to sound pessimistic, Mum,' Katy hesitated, looking uncomfortable, 'but do you think you should take something black, just in case?' She was biting her lower lip, and tears were glossing her eyes.

I grabbed my black skirt and threw it in the suitcase without a word. I couldn't speak. I hadn't thought of that scenario. Simon had to live. He just had to.

'What about your phone?' Katy changed the subject tactfully. 'Is it fully charged? Does it need a top up?'

I gave her my old-fashioned pay-as-you-go phone. It gave her something useful to do, and off she went to the shops with my top up card, after putting my phone on charge.

Meanwhile, Paul was in a tizzy about my Australian Visa. He'd made a mistake when filling in the form online and the application had been rejected. He was advised to e-mail the correct details to the head office in Western Australia. We had to wait for the office to open before they could start to process the application. The office opened at 2am our time! I was due to fly at 10am, and it can take twenty four hours to process a Visa. Talk about cutting it fine! We could only wait and pray it would go through in time.

When everything was ready, I felt I needed to know more about Simon's condition. Katy had put the thought into my head that he might not survive, and I needed some reassurance. I decided to ring the hospital and see if I could talk to someone in authority who could tell me about his condition in more detail.

After looking up the number on Google then going

through the hospital switchboard, I got through to intensive care. I put the phone on speaker so Paul and Katy and John could hear too.

First I had to explain who I was and why I wanted the information. I told them all they needed to know and added that I didn't want to keep bothering Natalie as she was distressed enough. Amazingly, I got through to speak to the consultant in charge of Simon. She was very kind and answered all my questions fully.

She listed his injuries for me as I couldn't remember them all from my first conversation with Natalie. He had a broken nose and cheekbones, a broken shoulder blade, badly broken femur, and a broken heel-bone on the foot of the same leg. His other leg had a dislocated ankle and the foot was badly crushed. The most serious injury was a depressed fracture of his skull, on the left side, which was why he was being transferred to Sydney.

I asked if his injuries were life-threatening.

She answered honestly. 'He has a very serious brain injury and we can't predict the outcome of that at this stage, but he is doing very well so far.'

I pushed for clarification and asked if there were any danger of him actually losing his life.

'I can't say,' she said. 'It is always a possibility in these cases, but he is holding his own so far and doing well.'

I thanked her for her time and her honesty. She had put our deepest fears into words, and we realised there was a real chance Simon might die before I got there. Even though the consultant had sounded positive, there was still the nagging doubt. No one could be sure of the outcome for Simon.

We'd all seen enough television hospital programmes to know what kind of problems can arise from an injury to the brain. It was no use speculating. She said he was doing well, so we clung to that and hoped he would continue to do well.

Katy and John went home in the early evening. They could do no more. Paul and I spent the next few hours ringing and e-mailing everyone we thought should know.

I rang my boss. I was leaving him in the lurch, when he really needed me to be at work, but he didn't hesitate. 'Go, she needs you,' he told me. 'Don't worry about us! Keep in touch and let me know how he goes.'

All our family and friends were informed by 9pm, and we were still sitting in our attic office, not knowing what to do next. We continued waiting for news, talking in hushed tones, speculating on a very uncertain future and hoping for the best.

Sunday 9.30pm 29th June for us, Monday 30th June 6.30am for Natalie.

Paul and I were still sitting by our computers when Natalie called us on Skype. She was back in her home near Bangalow with Ruby, and we had a videoconference. Simon had just arrived in Sydney and was stable. She was going to call the Royal Prince Alfred Hospital, at 10am her time, for more news.

She told us they were keeping him in a coma, but between medications he was rousing and trying to remove the respirator.

The doctors told her that was a good sign.

We grasped at this good sign as a drowning man grasps at a twig near the riverbank. It was something positive. It gave us something to hold on to, no matter how fragile.

'Is anyone there with you?' I hoped she wasn't on her own. She looked so drawn and tired on my screen. Her pale blonde hair merged with her even paler face, and the computer screen gave her the appearance of having a halo. Her eyes were like dark saucers, and I felt I was looking at a ghost.

'No, I sent everyone home. I need some space to get my head around all this.' She cast her eyes down, and I knew she was hiding tears from me.

We could hear Ruby in the background. She was laughing and squealing with delight.

'Ruby sounds happy, what's she doing?' I asked.

'Playing with the dogs, she's chasing Max down the hall, and he's growling at her. It's a game they like to play all the time.'

Max is a big black Labrador. He's gentle and obedient. He's a perfect playmate for Ruby. Their other dog, Sasha, is a huge brown and cream mongrel with one brown eye and one pale-blue one. Sasha mothers Ruby at every opportunity, licking the mud from her legs after a fall, nosing her away from the stairs to the garden, and keeping her safe. Natalie also has three horses a cat and twelve chickens. This menagerie was more responsibility that she had to cope with and organise care for.

'Did you get any sleep?' I asked.

'Not much,' she admitted. 'There's so much going on in my head. They're talking about waking Simon to see how he goes, but I need to be there for that.' She lifted dark glistening eyes to look at the screen. 'Oh, Mum! I don't want him waking up to strangers. I need to be there, Mum, but how can I?' She was so distressed.

'Go to Sydney,' I told her. 'It's as simple as that, Natalie. Get the next flight down there. You need to be with him.'

'What about Ruby? I can't drag her down to Sydney, into the middle of all this.'

'Leave Ruby with the neighbours. She'll survive, and I know Martin and Sally will be happy to look after her for you. I'll be there soon to take over. I can look after her at your place, or I could bring her to Sydney to be with you. But your priority now has to be Simon. Ruby will adapt.' She'll have to, I thought.

'Okay.' She looked so forlorn. 'I'll see what the neighbours say when I ring them later.'

'Try to stay hopeful, Natalie. Ring us when you know anything or leave a message on Skype for us. We're going to try to get some sleep, we have an early start.'

'Okay, Mum, will do.'

'Love you, darling.' Paul and I chorused.

'Love you too, Mum and Dad.'

Day 2 Monday 30th June

We spent the next few hours tossing and turning beside each other in bed. We both occasionally dropped off. I heard Paul snoring softly when I woke, with a start, to remember what had happened.

At 3.30am, I couldn't stay in bed any longer and got up to check the computers. We had an e-mail to say my Visa had been granted. I had a small uplifting moment of relief as I printed the confirmation and moved to Paul's computer to see the Skype messages on his screen.

Natalie had left a few messages for us. She'd been busy while we were trying to sleep.

Emma and Alan, Simon's sister and brother-in-law who live north of Brisbane had volunteered to collect me from the airport and take me down to Bangalow.

It would be a round trip of over seven hours for them, and I was so pleased to hear that they were doing this for me. It would save me a lot of time and hassle.

Natalie had already left for Sydney, leaving Ruby with Sally and Martin. She planned to organise some accommodation down there, and I was to fly down with Ruby when she was ready for us. My brave girl was finding her inner strength and doing all the practical things she needed to do to get through this. All I needed to do was get there.

We were impatient to leave, and Paul wanted to beat the rush-hour traffic into Manchester, so we made it to the airport by 6.30am. It was a quiet drive. We had so much to say, but we couldn't find the words to express what we felt. We were both dreading the parting. I hated to leave him behind to worry, and he didn't want me to face it on my own.

I've been writing this in the airport after saying goodbye to Paul. I don't know when I'll see him again, and our parting was a huge wrench.

He wanted to hang around until I boarded, but after a coffee, I couldn't stand looking at his strained and worried face any longer.

'Let's not put off the inevitable,' I told him, 'Go home and get some sleep, you look like hell.'

'Thanks!' He smiled at me gently. 'You've looked better yourself!'

We hugged fiercely, both of us determined not to cry and I watched him leave before I went to join the queue to go through to the departure gates.

I bought a notebook from the newspaper kiosk and I'm filling in the waiting time by writing it all down. Maybe I'll continue to write and make this a diary. Maybe I'll be too busy once I get there. Who knows, one day I might look back at this with interest, or maybe I'll just throw it away. I'm sure it will read like the demented scribbling of a tormented mother. For now, it's helping me. I have no one to talk to, and I need to dump all these thoughts somewhere. I have to prepare myself for the journey ahead and think about how best I can help when I get there.

Now, my plane is taxiing to take off. With no idea of what lies at the end of this trip, I'm certain of one thing, I'll be doing everything I can to help my daughter and her small family get through this.

DAY 3 Tuesday 1st July, 6am Singapore time

I'm now sitting in Changi airport in Singapore, waiting for my connecting flight to Brisbane. I'm over halfway through my journey, but still have so far to go. I'm so tired I feel spaced out. When I move my head too quickly, I go dizzy. It feels like being drunk without the bonus of feeling happy and carefree. I've barely had any sleep for the last forty-eight hours.

Time seems meaningless. I'm caught somewhere between UK and Australia, and feel as if I'm in no-mans-land, a bit like Simon is by the sound of things.

I turned my phone on when I got inside the terminal, eager for news, but dreading it at the same time. I had four messages. Two were from Katy, and two from Paul.

The messages from Paul were typical of him. He'd been watching the flight details online and knew I had landed safely. *'Glad u r landed safe. Nxt flight on time. Kat has txt u bout Simon.'*

I clicked to the next message. *'U av 2hrs to kill in Singi. get onto the free Internet I'll be online lets try to talk on MSN'*

I remembered where the banks of free computers were from the last time I journeyed via Singapore to Australia when Ruby was born, but because my brain was fogged by tiredness, I couldn't remember my log-in details and passwords to get onto MSN. So I sent him a text by phone instead. A brief text conversation followed. He didn't know much more, but said that Katy had found some information, and had sent a text to me. He told me to stay safe, and to try to sleep on the next flight. Some hope!

Katy's texts were more practical, as expected. *'I've talked to Nat. Simon had brain surg. hav to see how much brain swells post op. Nat reckons Simon in Sydny for few weeks.'*

Nothing in this text was unexpected, but it touched me deeply. I suppose because I was so tired and strung out, I cracked. Changi airport has many restrooms, and one became my refuge for a few minutes until I managed to pull myself together. I then leant against the locked cubicle door, to read Katy's second text.

'Been on the net to look up local Bangalow news to find details of crash. Simon ws overtaking lost control an skid into gum tree. Took 20 mins to cut him out. No other

cars involved. Look for Byron Shire Echo online to read it. Tke care, x K'

I was relieved there were no other casualties, but the brief facts that Katy had given me didn't begin to answer my many questions. I decided find the story myself. I dried my eyes, splashed my face with cold water and went back to the computers. I had to stand in line, to wait for one to come available, but within a few seconds of searching I found what I was looking for.

Extract from the Byron Shire Echo (online)
Crash victim fights for life
30.06.2008

A 38 year-old Clunes man is fighting for his life after crashing into a gum tree on the outskirts of Bangalow last night.

Police sergeant, John Brodey said the man suffered life-threatening injuries in the accident, which occurred on Bangalow road near the intersection with Friday Hut Road at 5.20pm.

Sgt Brodey said the driver was heading south along Bangalow Road when he overtook another driver heading in the same direction.

He said it appeared the driver had lost control of the ute he was driving soon after he had crossed back to the correct side of the road.

Police rescue rushed to the scene of the crash and used the Jaws of Life to cut the man from his vehicle.

It is believed he was trapped in the car for twenty minutes.

He was taken to Byron District Hospital where his condition remains critical.

If his condition does not improve overnight, it is expected he will be airlifted to a Brisbane hospital this morning. Police are investigating the cause.

Well, they didn't print his name, and they got the name of his hometown wrong. Clunes is about fourteen kilometres from Bangalow, but there was no doubt it was Simon's story. It didn't answer all my questions, but reading the news report helped me absorb the sobering facts of the crash. Simon was very badly hurt and would probably need hospital care for many weeks.

What was he thinking of? A tiny part of me was angry with Simon. Was it his fault? Immediately I'm angry with myself for thinking like that. How could I blame him? But how did it happen? What caused him to crash?

It may remain a mystery how or why he lost control of the ute. Was the road slippery? Was there a fault with the car? I'm looking for excuses, or reasons, but I guess we'll never know for sure unless one day Simon will be able to tell us himself.

I found a quiet spot in the concourse to sit and send a text to Natalie. I had no idea what time it was in Australia as my brain wasn't functioning well enough to work it out. I didn't want to wake her with a phone call in the middle of the night if she were managing to sleep.

'Im in Changi. Kat txt 2 let me no bout Simns op so I no its a waitin game. Will do as u want wen I get ther, eg bring Ruby to sidny. C u soon x mum.'

Natalie text back immediately. *'ok thanx mum will talk wen u get here.'*

I have another hour until boarding time, then a seven and half-hour flight. It will take approximately three-hours to drive to Natalie's place. So I have about another twelve hours to go. I'll be so happy to see Emma and Alan waiting for me at Brisbane. I'll be even happier to see Ruby. Hope she likes me and accepts me as her carer. She doesn't have much choice.

Neither do I and I must admit to being afraid of the responsibility. What does she eat? How often? When does she nap? What about changing nappies!!! How will I manage that? How many times a day? What should I pack for her to take to Sydney? Will I need to take a car seat, the pram, toys? How will I manage with Ruby and all that baggage on a plane? Help!

Day 3, or 4, early hours of the morning, Australia time. (Can't work out what date it is, I'm too jet-lagged!)
I'm at Natalie's house at last. I'm so desperately tired, but only managed an hour of sleep before waking again. I close my eyes, but my mind won't shut down, so I'm writing, hoping to dump these thoughts on paper so I can get some peace, and sleep some more before dawn.

I arrived at Brisbane and met Emma and Alan. Poor Emma looked dreadful, with a blotchy face and dark circles under her eyes. I must look the same. We hugged and cried. Emma and I are about the same age. Simon is her little brother, and she was so upset for him.

During the three-hour drive, she told me what had been happening with Simon's family. He is the youngest of seven brothers and sisters and all of them are very worried about him.

His parents are in their eighties and desperately want to go see Simon, but his mum is so frail that Natalie has said it's not a good idea just yet for her to travel to Sydney. The shock of seeing him might literally kill her.

Carol, the oldest sister and her husband, James, were staying with Simon's mum at their home in Geelong at the time the accident happened, thank goodness. So his parents weren't alone when they received the news. Natalie had phoned Carol first to make sure she was still there with Simon's mum. That's so like Natalie to be thinking of others, even when she was so desperately upset.

Carol is a retired nurse and is explaining all the technical medical terms in words they can understand.

Carina and Gerhard, Simon's mum and dad, emigrated from France to Australia shortly after the Second World War. They still speak with heavy French accents and speak French to each other at home, but the children are Australian to the core.

The large family are spread throughout the east and south coast of Australia, and if they were all to keep ringing Natalie, she wouldn't get a minute to be with Simon. Emma told me that her eldest sister was acting as the go-between, so Natalie doesn't have to talk to all the brothers and sisters.

Emma also told me how upset her mum was. 'She is desperate to see him. He's her youngest and Simon has always been special to her.'

I know Simon is especially close to his mum. They

have an exceptional bond. They talk on the phone for hours, and he would do anything for her.

She is a lovely lady, full of love and fun. I only met Carina a couple of times, but I can see why her children adore her.

Even when Simon's mum can go to see him, it will mean a long and tiring journey by car and plane to Sydney from her home in Geelong on the south coast.

Emma and Alan made good travelling companions, and we had plenty to talk about on our journey south. We made good time and arrived at Natalie's place a few hours ago. Sally and Martin were waiting for us, and the two dogs came out to greet us too, licking my hands and wagging their tails. Ruby was in bed and fast asleep, so obviously was none the worse for being abandoned by her mum.

Martin and Sally are such good people. They have been taking care of Ruby and the animals.

Sally has cleaned and tidied the house and bought supplies for Ruby; nappies and snacks for my journey to Sydney. Martin made tea, and we shared some chocolate cake that Natalie had made earlier on the day of the accident. As we ate, Martin filled in some missing pieces of the jigsaw.

The utility vehicle that Simon was driving had gone off the road and ploughed into a gum tree at speed. It launched into the air, turned on its side and continued to bump along some uneven ground, taking down a fence.

No wonder he was so badly injured.

We discussed all kinds of scenarios, but still had no answers why it had happened, or what had caused him to lose control. We hoped we would eventually know, but realised that the truth may never come out.

After our tea, Emma and Alan set off on their long journey home. I thanked them, but it could never be thanks enough for what they had done for me.

'We couldn't do any less,' Emma assured me with a hug, 'and it's nothing compared with what you have done.'

I didn't feel I was doing anything special. It was instinctive to fly to my daughter's side. I think any mother would have done the same.

Martin and Sally needed so many thanks I didn't know where to start. Their sixteen-year-old daughter, Janine, had been helping too. She'd been having fun entertaining Ruby.

'She's such a placid happy baby, so full of smiles and giggles.' Sally grinned at me. 'She's a real pleasure to look after.'

I know she was giving me encouragement, knowing that I would have to look after Ruby from now on.

Martin and Sally are staying overnight at Natalie's place too, so I can get some sleep and they will be here in the morning to give Ruby some familiar faces to wake up to.

My body clock is still on UK time, and I'm not at all sleepy now, despite only snatching the odd nap since Sunday morning. It's the early hours of Wednesday, and I really will have to try to sleep. I have a very long day ahead of me.

Day 4 Wednesday 2nd July

I'm writing this in Sydney in the small hours of day five

as I didn't get the chance to write yesterday. Ruby and Natalie are sleeping in the next room, but I'm restless and sleepless yet again. So much has happened, and I have no room in my head for everything juggling for position in it. My mind is here, but my body still feels as though it's back in UK. Jet lag is bad enough on its own, without all this emotional turmoil to add to it.

Yesterday morning I woke in Natalie's bed in Natalie's home after only a few hours' sleep. It was still dark and silent in the house. I was wide-awake and knew that more sleep would be impossible, so I got up at 5am. I quietly shut myself in Natalie's computer room and began to send some e-mails.

By the time I had finished letting everyone know where I was and what I knew, I heard Ruby stirring. Every fibre of my being wanted to go and pick her up and hug her close, but as I would be a stranger to her, I didn't want to scare her. She thinks I'm the funny lady in a pink dressing gown on the computer screen from our Skype calls.

So I stayed in the office and let Martin go to her, and didn't emerge until I could hear her chattering to him in the kitchen. When I entered the dining room, her face was a picture of wide-eyed surprise! She was amazed at this new stranger in her life! She went quiet and shy, put her head down and looked at me from under her hair. I smiled and said good morning to Martin and hello to Ruby, and then went to make myself some toast and coffee.

Martin and I chatted while we ate breakfast, and I included Ruby in some of my general questions.

'Have you fed the dogs, Martin?' was quickly followed by, 'where are the doggies, Ruby?'

Then when I directed a question at Martin, 'Where is Sally?' Ruby pointed to the door.

Martin explained that Sally had left earlier to check on things at home and would be back later this morning. It seems I'm not the only one finding it difficult to sleep!

After a while, I started to get some smiles from my little girl, and in an hour or two we were the best of buddies, chasing each other around on the back lawn. By that time, I knew that I had to create a bond with her quickly. I was taking her to Sydney that afternoon!

I had spoken to Natalie during the morning. She'd got us an apartment, with help from a welfare worker, only a few minutes walk from the hospital, and Simon's company had offered to pay for our accommodation.

Simon's boss also arranged flights for me. I just had to look at the schedule and let him know which flight I wanted to take. Within an hour, everything was organised.

Martin offered to take us to Ballina airport to get the flight to Sydney. All I had to do was pack. I'd written a list to Natalie's e-mailed instructions.

"Grab everything from the top drawer in Ruby's room, some nappies, towels, more pants for me, shoes and her coat. Her sleep suit needs a wash; can you do it before you come down?"

The instructions went on. They were long and detailed, and it was clear she'd had time to think about what she would need for Ruby and herself in Sydney.

I packed and then I re-packed twice more, taking things out and adding items. There was so much stuff, and I only had two arms! I left half my things in a heap on Natalie's bedroom floor. I could always buy more clothes in Sydney if I didn't have enough.

Sally made us all a sandwich at lunchtime. Then I practiced putting the pram up and down, unfolding and making it safe, refolding it and trying again until I was sure I could do it quickly enough.

I have three overnight bags, one large and heavy suitcase, one weighty and bulky pram, and Ruby. The pram is an all-terrain monster, bought because they live on farmland, and it is very heavy.

Martin arrived at 3.30pm, and we loaded the car and set out to the airport. We got a coffee in the tiny departure lounge, and Martin enjoyed more cuddle-time with Ruby.

When the plane eventually arrived I was shocked. It was a tiny, thirty-seat aircraft with a propeller on each wing! It looked so small and fragile! I was used to flying with the comfort of jumbo jets, how was I going to cope on this puny little kite?

Martin hugged us and had a tear in his eye as he said goodbye to Ruby. His eyes were full of compassion as he wished us luck and a safe journey. I took Ruby through into the tiny departures gate, and she ran to the window. She was excited about her adventure. I wished I could share her enthusiasm. She was so full of energy she started toddling all over the place, very interested in all the passengers, their bags, and her surroundings. That quickly changed when we boarded the plane.

We were placed right at the back of the tiny plane, and thankfully there was a spare seat beside me to allow us some space on the two hour journey.

Ruby was fine until I had to strap her to me with the seat belt. She hates to be confined and began to wriggle and squirm and cry. She continued to fuss and moan on and off for the next two hours! I had help from the lady who sat in front of me. She kindly played peekaboo with Ruby for a little while. Then I played peekaboo with my little angel, using one of her soft toys. She was happy to be distracted, but only for a few minutes at a time.

One of the stewardesses came to see if she could help, and asked if I had a connecting flight in Sydney. I tried to explain our situation, but the stewardess got confused. She had presumed that Ruby was my child, and thought it was my husband in the hospital.

'I'm her grandma,' I explained. 'This little one doesn't know me from Adam, no wonder she's so upset.'

The stewardess looked even more confused, so I tried again, 'I flew in from England last night. My daughter is in Sydney with her husband. She had to leave this little one with neighbours, and now...'

I gasped for air as the awfulness of it enveloped me and the avalanche that I had been controlling until that point, came tumbling down in a torrent. I struggled to stop the raw emotions, for Ruby's sake and for the poor stewardess who looked mortified. I rummaged for a tissue in my bag while I stifled my sobs. I wiped my face and blew my nose quickly.

I hate to have others pitying me, so I gave myself a good mental telling off. I shook myself, blew my nose again and assured the stewardess I was fine. With a tight smile, I apologised for my unexpected emotional outpouring, and got on with the business of trying to keep Ruby happy.

As we neared Sydney, the pilot announced that due to sixty-mile-per-hour winds at the airport, we had been put in a holding pattern. We wouldn't be landing for at least another forty-five minutes. Oh no, poor Natalie will be going out of her mind. This delay is all I need, I thought!

However, because of the winds, the flight became a very unpredictable roller coaster ride and Ruby loved it! While the stewardesses struggled to supply passengers with fresh sick bags, Ruby and I were giggling and squealing with delight at the back of the plane.

After a particularly bumpy landing, the baggage collection was daunting. I held tightly to Ruby, balancing her on my hip with one arm around her waist, as I struggled to pull the pram, my very large suitcase and the smaller bags from the carousel.

I had a heap of bags around my feet, and there were so many people milling around that I daren't let Ruby out of my arms.

I turned my phone on before trying to think how I was going to get from the baggage claim area to the taxi rank. I needed to let Natalie know we had landed. We were so late, and I knew she'd be very worried about us.

When my phone lit up, I had a text from Paul.

'Whre r u?'

I couldn't try to answer him at that point, but I tried to phone Natalie. I couldn't get through, so I tried again. The signal dropped out.

Thankfully, the crowds had thinned as I had to put Ruby down while I erected the pram. I needed two hands to unfasten the locking mechanism and to shake it upright. I watched in horror as she toddled away from me at the speed of light. I fixed the pram by Braille, with my eyes glued on Ruby, not looking as I kicked the footplate down to secure the brake. Then I ran to get Ruby, leaving all our precious bags to fate. If they were stolen, the thieves could have a field day, I was past caring.

Ruby had toddled about thirty feet away from me, but I soon caught her and returned to our rag-tag pile of belongings. She was quickly installed in the safe cocoon of her pram. With Ruby safe, I collected the rest of the bags from the floor, hanging the smaller ones from my shoulders and pulling the big one behind me. I felt like Sherpa Tensing but I had an awful feeling that Everest would have been an easier journey than the one I was facing right now.

I had pre-booked a taxi with a child-seat, but of course because of the delay, it was not there. A very kind gentleman offered to help me. I explained that I needed a taxi with a baby-seat and he took charge of arranging it for me.

'Follow me,' he said, taking my large suitcase and pulling it from my hands.

He took me to the front of the queue then went to speak to a security guard. He came back to me and said, 'Don't worry, doll. The guard will get you sorted, no worries.'

I thanked him warmly. I'm always uplifted by the kindness of strangers, and he'd called me "doll"! How very quaint and Australian.

I phoned Paul. I didn't have the patience to text. I told him I couldn't get hold of Natalie and asked him to let her know we had landed.

The call was short as the taxi pulled up while we were talking. We loaded everything into the cab, I gave the driver the address that Natalie had given me, and within five minutes, we were on our way.

After the fifteen-minute drive, Natalie was waiting outside the apartment block when we pulled up. She was shivering in the blustery wind, shoulders hunched around her ears. She gave me a small, brief smile and turned on a huge grin for Ruby.

Ruby looked at her mum through the cab window and quickly looked away. Her mum's big false grin didn't fool her. I let the driver take care of unloading the luggage and stepped out to give Natalie a quick hug.

'How is he?' I asked.

She shrugged, her face blank.

'Still with us?' I asked, tentatively.

'Oh, yes!' She smiled, seeming to realise that I had no idea whether he was alive or dead.

'Let me get Ruby for you.' I turned back to the taxi, unstrapped Ruby and placed her in Natalie's arms.

'I can't believe the plane was so late. I thought it had crashed and I'd lost you and Ruby too.' Natalie hugged her child tightly, and I could see that Ruby would be staying safe in her mummy's arms, so I loaded the smaller bags into the pram.

Natalie pushed the pram and carried Ruby and I pulled the heavy suitcase.

Our apartment was on the top floor of a four-storey block, which thankfully had a tiny lift. The apartment is small, but has everything we need. Natalie has bought some basic supplies; food, toiletries, nappies and tea.

We unpacked and Natalie got Ruby ready for bed

while I made toast and tea. I hadn't eaten since lunchtime, but toast was all I could face. Natalie's phone rang a few times through the evening, and each time she answered with enthusiasm and a cheery voice.

'He's doing well.' She told Simon's family. 'He's hanging in there for us.'

When she explained to them that I had just arrived with Ruby, they didn't chat for long. I listened to Natalie's side of the conversation, picking up bits of information. Her main concern was for Simon's mum. She advised Carol that it still wouldn't be good to bring his mum to Sydney.

'It would kill her, Carol. She couldn't take it,' she was saying, and I realised that Simon can't have been doing so very well after all.

Thankfully, after the call from Simon's oldest sister, the phone stayed silent for the rest of the evening and we had some peace to talk. Natalie had bought a travel cot for Ruby, and after some cuddle time and a light snack, she was soon snuggled in and fast asleep after her tiring and stressful day.

I was to sleep in the combined living and kitchen room on a large sofa bed. Natalie had unfolded the contraption and made it up, and we huddled under the duvet with a cup of tea to warm our hands. We were cold in Sydney, and the apartment had no heating.

I wanted to know the truth about Simon. She had told all the callers that he was doing well, but it was clear to me that she was holding something back. I asked Natalie to tell me what had been done for him so far.

'The worst injury is a crush fracture, or a compressed fracture of his skull.' She touched a spot just above her left ear. 'They think it was something that was loose on the back seat of the car that flew forward and smashed him in the head. It could have been anything from a tool to a toolbox. We don't know. Even a box of tissues could have caused the fracture, travelling at speed. Just shows it's better not to carry anything loose on the back seat or parcel shelf of any car.'

I sipped my tea, listening to her, hearing the steady tone of her voice. I was reassured that she sounded so firm and confident.

'Anyway, a five-inch circle of the skull has been splintered and cracked and pushed into his brain.' Then she added really quickly, 'But only a little bit, and they pulled it out and cleaned it up underneath, and that's all fine now.'

I realised that she was emphasising the positive aspects, and I found that encouraging. My girl is still being very strong and optimistic.

'The front of his head, or his face, has a fractured nose and his sinus bones are broken, but these are clean breaks and he can have plastic surgery later to fix them if he needs that. His top lip is torn, and that's a full thickness tear, but they stitched it and it doesn't look too bad.

'His shoulder blade is broken, and a lot of the little wing bones on his vertebrae are fractured, but they'll heal too and shouldn't cause any problems.

'His right femur has a metal rod holding it together now. On one foot, his heel bone and one other bone in there are broken, and his ankle is dislocated. On the other foot, all the small bones have been fractured into tiny pieces, but they pinned them all and the surgeon said they should heal well. He might need plastic surgery on his face, but that can be done at a later stage.'

Her voice was still strong and confident. I couldn't help but be encouraged by her positive energy until she told me the rest.

'His blood gases were high in carbon dioxide today, so they needed to increase his respiration, and he had two blood transfusions. They were worried he might be bleeding from somewhere internally, not sure where, or it could be due to the swelling. The fluid could be collecting in his tissues because he's inactive.'

I knew she was searching for the positive angles, and looking for best-case scenarios to tell me. I realised at that point that things must be much worse than she was admitting to me or even to herself.

I talked to her of the future, but sketchily, not in detail, just skimming the surface of what might lie ahead for her. I asked what kind of recovery he could be expected to make and how long might it take.

'We can get the best physiotherapist and chiropractor for him when he's ready for that. We already know of one or two back home from when he had his motorbike accident a few years ago.'

She was thinking a long way into the future with that plan, but I let it go. Simon's injuries from a motorbike accident were simple breaks and mended quickly. What he was facing now was much more serious and far more complicated.

'How will you manage financially?' Paul and I had discussed the possibility of having to help in this way, but I wanted to know what they already had in place.

'We'll be okay for the first six months, Simon's work

insurance will pay his wages and then after that he'll get the government handout. But if he can go back to light duties after six months, we should get the government money topped up to his full pay.'

Again she was talking of the best possible outcome. Then she faltered, her eyes sliding away from mine.

'But if his brain function is compromised it might be different.' Then she sniffed, seemed to straighten her shoulders and said, 'But as it stands, I think we'll be okay.'

I realised that she had just revealed the chink in her armour. Simon's physical injuries were bad, but could be fixed, however, his brain injury could be the worse thing ever to happen to them, and was something he might not recover from.

I followed her lead and didn't make a big fuss about this condition. Although I wanted to discuss it further, I understood that it was too early for that, so I simply nodded and told her we'd help as much as we could, and certainly as much as they needed us to.

'And I'll be staying in Australia until you or the Australian government kick me out, whichever happens first.'

We hugged, and Natalie went to her own bed in the same room as Ruby. I slept like a dead woman for an hour until a nightmare jolted me awake. I'd picked up a phone and heard the words, 'Mum, Simon's had an accident. He's in a coma...' Now my dream is continuing in real life beyond that call, but my brain can't tell the difference.

Day 5 Thursday 3rd July
Ruby woke before the sun was up. She was full of life and very inquisitive. As we got breakfast then showered and dressed, Ruby explored her new surroundings. She found the cutlery drawer and stood beside the kitchen unit proudly brandishing a carving knife almost as big as her, looking very happy with the discovery. I rushed to take it from her and then set to work rearranging the kitchen area, making sure all the sharp and dangerous items were out of reach.

She followed me into the bathroom when I went to brush my teeth and promptly put her hands into the water at the bottom of the toilet pan. It quickly became clear to me that I would have to 'up' my game plan to keep a step ahead of her.

Natalie's plans were to go to the hospital, and I was determined to go with her. I needed to see Simon, and Ruby needed to see her daddy. We left the apartment at 7.30am just as the sun began to lighten the sky. As we walked to the hospital, I tried to take in my surroundings and remember landmarks so I could navigate the unfamiliar streets on my way back later.

Natalie led us into the lift in the hospital, and we descended into the basement of the building. We walked through a rabbit warren of old-fashioned tiled corridors with doors leading off to rooms full of very ill patients.

There was a hush in the place, interrupted by beeps and buzzes from various machines surrounding the beds. This place freaked me out, so goodness knows what it did to Ruby, taking it in with great interest from the comfort of her pram.

Natalie stopped outside a corner room. 'He's in here,' she told me, and stepped inside to let the staff know she was there before turning to beckon me in.

I pushed the pram into the room and took my first look at Simon. I was pleasantly surprised. After imagining all kinds of facial scars, I was relieved to see his face looked smooth and clear. He was very swollen, and the severe swelling made him look like he'd eaten lots of pies in the last few years and put weight on, but he still looked like Simon. His head was swathed in wraps of linen, just like an Egyptian mummy, and the stitches in his lip stood out like black spider legs against his pale skin. The breathing tube was taped to his mouth. His eyes were closed, and he looked peaceful.

His neck, shoulders and arms were swollen too. He had wires attached to his chest. A narrow, folded sheet protected his modesty. His legs protruded from the sheet and were encased by bandages that matched his head. He had tubes running into his arms with a bag of blood slowly dripping into him, which was clearly another transfusion. Another tube led from his modesty sheet into a bag containing yellow fluid. A bank of monitors beeped quietly beside the bed.

Natalie introduced herself to the two staff members who were hovering over Simon, adjusting tubes, taking readings and writing notes. (I presumed they were new staff that she hadn't met yet. I was right.) They filled us in on his progress overnight.

'He's doing okay, but still needs more blood,' one of them said, pointing to the bag hanging from a hook just above the bed.

'The neurosurgeon is due any minute.' The other one told us.

We stayed with Simon for a few more minutes. Natalie took Ruby from the pram and stood by her husband.

'Daddy is sleeping, Ruby,' she tried to explain to her little daughter, but Ruby wasn't interested.

She didn't connect the man in the bed with her daddy, and she squirmed to get down.

When the doctors arrived, we left to sit in the family room, along the corridor, to wait. We allowed Ruby to run around the tiny room as we agonised over the transfusion and what it might mean.

'Could he be bleeding from somewhere else that they haven't looked at yet?' I asked.

'He's had so many scans, Mum. They'd know if he had more any internal injuries, let's wait and see.'

I realised that Natalie's way of coping with everything would be to find the positive in every situation and cling to it. She didn't think in any other terms, so I had to back her up.

'You're right, Natalie. If it worries them so much, they'll do more scans, won't they?'

'Yes.' She nodded, staring at the floor.

Ruby was getting restless and was banging on the door to be let out. Natalie picked her up and cuddled her, but Ruby didn't want to be cuddled, she wanted to escape! She began to moan and struggle, but when Natalie set her on the floor she began to cry.

'She's tired.' Natalie told me. 'She has a nap every morning about a couple of hours after breakfast, and another sometime in the afternoon.'

'I'll take her back to the apartment and put her to bed, shall I?'

I didn't want to leave Natalie, but Ruby was becoming too much of a distraction when all that my daughter wanted to think about, was Simon.

'Thanks, Mum.' She gave me a small smile. 'Can you remember how to get out of here?'

'I can ask if I get lost.'

I picked Ruby up and put her in the pram. She didn't want to be strapped in again, but thankfully she didn't fight against me too much.

'Ring me if you need me, I have my phone.' I told Natalie.

'Bye-bye, Ruby.' Natalie gave her child a wave.

Ruby moaned, but didn't cry, as I pushed her out into the ICU reception area.

I found my way back to the apartment without getting lost, and gave Ruby a drink and some sultanas, her favourite snack, because she didn't want to go to sleep. She moaned and cried so I turned on the television, hoping to use it to lull her to sleep, and I held her in my arms on my sofa bed. I sat with her for a long time as she sobbed and kept turning her head from one side to the other.

I guessed that she was searching for her mum, and she began sobbing more when she realised that Natalie wasn't there. It was so obvious to me, why my granddaughter was upset. She couldn't talk and couldn't tell me, but I knew she thought she would never see her mum again. She was distraught.

I held her tightly and began to sing as she struggled to get out of my arms. Eventually she relaxed against me and finally fell asleep. I think she realised it would be the only way to stop the awful noise. I sang the folk song, 'Where have all the flowers gone,' through all the verses four times before she gave in. I was the only pupil in my school to be refused a place on the school choir, so I guess Ruby was very tolerant of my awful racket. I gently eased her onto the bed and covered her with the duvet.

I gathered some laundry from the floor in Natalie's room, added my pile of worn clothes and put it all into the washing machine in the bathroom. It didn't take long to work out how to use the unfamiliar contraption. I soon had our dirty smalls swishing around in soapy water.

I finished unpacking the large suitcase, placing all my belongings into the old chest of drawers that acted as our television stand in the corner of the living room.

Now I'm catching up with this diary as Ruby continues to sleep. I haven't heard from Natalie yet, and have no idea when I'll see her. Maybe I'll make some sandwiches and take them for lunch to the hospital when Ruby wakes.

DAY 6 Friday July 4th

Yesterday, Ruby woke from her morning nap at 11am. Natalie had phoned to say that Simon was awake, could understand what was said to him, and was responsive.

I was so pleased to hear this news and couldn't wait to go and celebrate with Natalie. I told her I had made us a picnic lunch, and went to the hospital to meet her.

When she didn't show at the ICU security entrance, I asked the receptionist if I could go through, and she let me in. I navigated my way through the busy wards to find Simon's door closed. I listened for a few seconds and could hear voices. I could tell that there was a lot going on in there, so I walked down to the family room and took Ruby out of her pram. I had remembered to bring her some toys, and we played for a few minutes, making cow noises and looking for Ruby's tickles in her tummy.

A member of staff came in to ask who I was, and she explained that Natalie had left a short while ago. I stood to leave too with the intention of finding her, but the lady touched my arm.

'You should know that the next few days are going to be very harrowing for Natalie. Simon is awake, but he's in a lot of pain. Seeing him like this will bring her down. He's so helpless and angry, and there's nothing she can do for him.'

My heart sank as I listened to her describing the reality of what I'd believed was good news.

'The good thing about this,' she continued, 'is that Simon won't remember any of this afterwards, so it won't matter if Natalie is with him or not. She needs to take a break from all this. She hasn't left his side since she got here except to snatch a few hours' sleep.

'She has to be here for him for the long haul, and she can't afford to wear herself out in these first few weeks. Simon will need months, if not years, of support from specialist, and from Natalie.'

'I understand what you're saying.' I swallowed hard. 'But you try to tell that to Natalie. She feels she has to stay with him and to help him through this. She's always been the strong one.'

'She's being too strong. We've all said so. She will

reach breaking point at some time. We've been expecting it for days. She needs to think of herself, too.'

The lady was very kind and obviously had spent a lot of time with Natalie to know her situation so well. My phone rang. Natalie was looking for us outside the reception area.

'I'm on my way, stay there,' I told her.

I picked Ruby up and held her in my arms as I pushed the pram to the door.

'I'll talk to her,' I told the kind lady, and went to meet Natalie.

Natalie looked dreadful. Her face was so pale she was almost see-through, and her eyes were circled by dark shadows. Tension tightened her features, and her shoulders were hunched. I handed Ruby to her, hoping the closeness of her child would bring her some comfort.

'Come and sit down, Natalie.' I led her to a row of sofas. 'Tell me what's happened.'

She explained that Simon had the breathing tube taken out, and his meds lowered. 'He became agitated, and squirmed around so much that they had to tie him down. He's so strong he can get out of bed, pull his tubes out and damage himself. He doesn't know how badly injured he is.'

I took the wriggling Ruby from her arms so she could concentrate more on what she was telling me.

'The first thing he did was to yank out his catheter, and that really would have hurt like hell as it was held in by an inflatable collar!' She shook her head, staring at the floor. 'He's in so much pain, Mum.'

I reached to hold her hand, but Ruby started trying

to get down. I got a biscuit from my bag to keep her quiet, and let Natalie continue.

'They asked him where it hurt, and he said, "All over". He looked at me and said, "Natalie! Oh, fuck"!'

'So he recognises you?' I glimpsed a ray of sunshine through the horror of what I felt as she continued to explain what had happened throughout the morning.

'I asked him where it hurt most, and he pointed to his left side. I asked if he meant his hip. He said, "No". "Your wrist"? I asked him. He said, "Yes". He's crafty. His wrist is about the only place he didn't damage! I told the nurse that he thought we'd take off the manacles if he said his wrists hurt.' She smiled briefly. 'So he's thinking properly and reasoning things out. His brain can't be that bad, can it?'

'That's good news then, isn't it?' I was helping her to clutch at straws, and I knew it.

'Then he started to shout at me. "Shoot me"! He was screaming in agony. "Fucking shoot me"! His pain is so intense he can't stand it. But they can't do anything about it. They say he has to learn to cope with it. Oh, Mum. He turned to me with this look on his face as if to say, you of all people should be on my side!'

Natalie had continued talking to him, trying to explain things to him, and trying unsuccessfully to calm him, but eventually the doctors persuaded her to leave.

'They say he has to endure this for a few days until his body gets used to the level of pain. They can't keep him sedated as he can't breathe for himself if they give him enough painkillers to keep him pain-free. It's a fine balance, and he has so much pain that he needs a lot of painkillers, so they had to make the decision to lower the dose. They need him to stay conscious now so his body can adjust to the pain and his mind can begin to understand everything that's happened to him.'

I tried to talk to her about the positive signs, that he was conscious and that he recognised her, and seemed able to reason. I brought up every little piece of evidence that proved his brain function was good and tried to get her to concentrate on those details.

'He's come back to you, Natalie. Simon is going to be all right.'

I could see my words were falling on deaf ears. Natalie had a different look about her, and I could see she was fighting to keep control. I know my daughter well enough to realise that she would never lose her cool in front of Ruby, so I started to play with my grandchild, chasing her up the hospital corridor, away from her mum, to allow Natalie some space to collect herself. When we'd finished our game of chase Natalie had regained some of her composure.

'Let's go find some fresh air,' I suggested. 'There must be a park around here where we can have our picnic.'

Natalie led us out of the hospital, and we walked around the perimeter of the university next door.

Eventually, we found an area of green grass with a play park in the middle of it.

We took Ruby out of her pram, and she set out at a run across the wide-open space. We strolled after her, discussing Ruby and how she loves to be outside. She was inquisitive, and stopped at every fallen twig and leaf to inspect and pull it apart before moving on to the next interesting piece of nature in her path. We sat on a bench to eat, watching Ruby play.

Every few minutes she'd come back to us, begging for a piece of sandwich, but when it was in her mouth she'd toddle away quickly to investigate more park debris.

I suggested taking Ruby down to the swings after we'd packed the remnants of our picnic away. Neither of us had eaten much. Just as we were nearing the play park, Natalie's phone began to ring. It was one of Simon's work colleagues. He was here in Sydney, to see a sick friend, and wanted to see Simon too. He was already on his way to the hospital.

'I'll have to go back and meet him there. Will you be all right with Ruby, Mum?'

'Go, Natalie. I'll see you later.'

I watched her leave. She didn't even stop to say goodbye to Ruby. I knew it was going to be difficult to make Natalie take time for herself. She just wanted to be at Simon's side, and his work colleague had provided her with the excuse she needed to go back to him.

I decided to take Ruby shopping. I let her play on the baby rides for a few minutes, and when she got tired of that, I put her in the pram and set out for the shopping centre. Natalie had told me there was a large shopping complex farther down the road, so I started walking towards where she'd pointed.

We needed a few things, and I thought I could manage to buy them and carry them back to the apartment on the pram. We needed a baby bath as there was only a shower in the apartment, and Ruby didn't like showers! We needed a heater. We had been very cold during the night. Paul had called to suggest that I buy a Sim-card for my mobile phone as it would be a cheaper way to keep in touch if I called him from an Australian network. I could also get some supplies to make a few simple meals.

After a couple of wrong turns, I saw what I was looking for. The Broadway shopping centre held everything I needed, and two hours later I was on my way back. The pram had a shopping tray under it which was now crammed with my purchases. I had a heater balanced inside a baby bath on top of the sturdy pram hood, and although it was a heavy load, it was stable.

I faced a long walk, and it was mainly uphill, but Ruby had fallen asleep, so I was in no rush. When I arrived at the apartment my phone was ringing. I answered it as I got into the lift, but the call dropped out. When the lift arrived on my floor, Natalie was there in the corridor with Bob, Simon's workmate.

'I was just trying to ring you.' She laughed. 'You have the only key.'

'Oh, sorry.' I fumbled for the key. 'I didn't realise.'

'You look as if you've been busy.' Natalie took charge of the heavy pram. 'This is Bob.'

We exchanged greetings as Natalie let us all into the small apartment.

We had a cup of tea and chatted about Simon's progress, speculating about how soon he might be able to get back to work. We were talking of months, not weeks. We knew it was going to be a long time.

After Bob left us we had a good long chat, and Natalie was on the brink of tears again, but as before,

Ruby was playing happily at our feet, and Natalie refused to give in to her feelings.

I unpacked the shopping and got Natalie to assemble the heater. As we worked, I broached the subject of counselling. I told her that she and Simon would need the services of a good counsellor at some stage to help them deal with all of this. She agreed with me, and said that she would look into it at some time in the future, but she didn't think she needed it yet.

'You are too strong, love. No one expects you to handle something like this without a few tears.' I began.

Natalie glanced at me, but quickly looked away.

'You will have to learn to give in to your emotions, or they'll burst like a dam when you least expect it. Once that happens you won't have any control, and you'll find it twice as hard.'

Natalie wouldn't look at me, and she concentrated on fixing the castors on the heater.

'Let go, Natalie. Do it now!' I insisted, knowing how close to tears she was and knowing how much she needed to let it out.

'I can't,' she said, quietly, glancing at Ruby playing with some plastic spoons.

'Okay. Maybe not right now. I can see you don't want to upset Ruby.' I smiled gently at her. 'But will you promise me you'll talk to someone at the hospital?'

She looked at me questioningly. I told her about my earlier conversation with the lady in the family room. I explained everything that she had said to me.

'She told me I had to try to persuade you to take a break, Natalie. She didn't need to tell me. I can see it myself. You're close to breaking point, and you need to let go. You need to stop being such a bloody rock!' I could see she was listening to me, and her eyes glossed with unshed tears.

'The whole team that are looking after Simon are worried about you. They think you're very brave and strong, but they want you to find a way to cope with all this tension and emotion.'

Natalie stared at the floor, so I went on.

'Ask them for help. They're expecting you to break at any minute, and if you can't find the space to do it here because of Ruby, do it with them. They are waiting for it, and will be able to help you through it.'

She nodded, sniffed, straightened her shoulders and got to her feet.

'Can you feed Ruby and put her to bed for me? I have to go to the hospital.'

'No problem.'

I watched her leave, and felt useless. She should have been able to let go with me. I should have been able to offer her comfort and support, but because Ruby was there, she couldn't lean on me. She wouldn't give in to her emotions in front of Ruby. She wanted to protect her child from all the upset, just as I wanted to protect Natalie, but couldn't.

Luckily for me, Ruby was not a demanding baby. She was happy for me to feed her and play with her until bedtime. She loved her new bath, and we splashed and giggled until she was ready for her supper.

After her yogurt and a drink of water, she settled in her bed with only a few minutes of half-hearted crying in protest of being left alone.

I prepared some dinner for Natalie and me, and

waited for her to come home. It gets dark early in Sydney. It's the middle of winter here and night falls at around 5.30pm, so I worry about Natalie walking home alone in the dark city streets. It's another small concern on top of everything else I constantly worry about.

When she came back, I could see she had been crying. Her face was puffy, and her eyes, nose, and lips were red and swollen. She'd had a real meltdown! I gave her a hug, but she shrugged me off after a few seconds.

'Don't set me off again.' She tried to smile, but didn't quite manage it. 'You were right, they were expecting it, and they were fantastic.'

I was glad, and I said so, but I couldn't help feeling a failure. I should have been able to help my daughter, but I knew that if she'd broken down with me, I would have been useless. I would have cried with her, and wouldn't have been any good at giving her the kind of support that she needed.

I let her tell me what they said, and allowed her to explain how they'd helped her while I served our meal.

Over dinner, she told me about the telephone numbers she'd been given to contact some counsellors.

'I know I'll need them at some point,' she said.

She told me that Simon's medical team had called for a social worker to come and sit with Natalie once the tears started to flow.

'She was brilliant, Mum. She let me sob my heart out before she said anything, then she told me I should have done it sooner. She said I shouldn't feel so guilty every time I left Simon. She knew exactly how I felt.'

I thought I knew how she felt too, but I kept quiet and let Natalie tell me the rest.

'She reassured me that although Simon is in great pain, he wouldn't remember any of this, so I mustn't feel guilty that I can't be with him one-hundred-per-cent of the time. She told me I needed to take time away from him to recharge my batteries and that seeing Simon like this will just drain me.'

'I agree totally, Natalie.' What more could I say? 'What else did she suggest?'

'She said we should go out tomorrow. We should go somewhere like the zoo or the harbour.'

'That sounds like a good idea. Ruby would love that too, wouldn't she?'

'They have my telephone number, and I can always get back to the hospital quickly if I need to, can't I?'

I couldn't help but smile. 'You have to take a break, Natalie! No hospital tomorrow. Simon won't remember if you're there or not. You have to think of yourself!'

'I am doing, Mum.' She looked at me. 'Simon might not remember if I'm there for him or not, but I'll remember. I need to be with him if he needs me, whether he remembers me being there or not.'

'I understand, Natalie. I know how much you want to be there for him.' I tried to be as gentle as I could. 'But Ruby needs you too, and you need her. Try to spend just one day with her, to reassure her that you're still in her life, and...'

'I will, Mum. We'll go somewhere tomorrow, but I'll have my phone switched on just in case.'

'I won't ask for any more than that.' I gave in gracefully. I knew it was a battle I wouldn't win.

We cleared away the dinner things and Natalie's phone rang. She spent the next hour taking calls from

Simon's family, telling them the good news, and explaining in simple terms that he was out of the coma.

I lay on my put-up bed, listening to her, and realised how brave she was. She was offering reassurance but stressing that Simon's condition was still far from good. She didn't want to give them false hope, but she was sparing them the awful details. I knew she was an emotional wreck inside, but the callers would never have guessed it from the tone of her voice. I was so proud of the way she was handling the family. She was compassionate but firm. They were asking to come and visit him, but she was refusing them in such a kind way.

'He would hate for you to see him like this. I have to be his advocate. He has no dignity just now, and he is so vulnerable. You know how proud he is…' and so she went on, protecting Simon and keeping his family informed, but shielding them from the fears that she has faced through every minute of every day since this awful nightmare began.

When it seemed the phone had finally stopped ringing, we sat together on my bed. Natalie was slumped, hugging herself with her head in her arms. I put my arms around her shoulders and hugged her close.

'This is just one day, Natalie.' I tried to find some positive things to say to her. 'I feel we've reached a milestone, don't you?'

'Yeah, I guess so,' she said quietly.

'He's awake, and we have so much to be thankful for. It hasn't been a good day, and we'll probably have more bad days in store, but we'll get through them, just as we got through today.' I squeezed her gently. 'At least he's awake. He can only improve from here, can't he?'

'I hope so, Mum.'

We went to bed early. We were both physically and emotionally exhausted.

Ruby woke before the sun again. I'd been awake for hours already; sleep still seems impossible for me. I know it's jet lag, but the constant whirl of thoughts in my head makes it worse. I can't switch off. Natalie got Ruby's breakfast ready, and I realised that 6am was a good time to call home as it was 9pm last night in UK, so I phoned Paul to give him the good news about Simon coming out of the coma.

While Natalie fed and dressed Ruby, I told Paul how responsive Simon was and that his brain function seemed good so far as we could tell. We'd both been so worried that Simon would be brain damaged and cabbage-like for the rest of his life. Awful enough for poor Simon, but a fate worse than anything we could imagine for Natalie. In our eyes, this latest proof of Simon's brain function was enormously important and fantastic news. I knew Paul would be relieved.

I handed the phone to Natalie so she could tell her dad all the technical and medical details, then I took the phone back to chat of mundane things.

I asked him things like, 'Have you fed the fish in the pond?' 'Have you watered the greenhouse plants?' 'How are you coping?' 'What did you have for dinner?' 'Are you eating well?'

I told him of the outing we had planned. We'd decided to go to the Botanical Gardens for some space and fresh air. He agreed that it would be good for Natalie to spend time away from the hospital. He told me he was missing me, and we discussed the possibility of him coming to visit once Simon could be transferred to a hospital nearer to home. I think just the thought of coming to join me helped to cheer him.

By the time Natalie and I were showered, dressed, and organised, Ruby was ready to go back to bed for her morning nap. Once she was in bed, Natalie insisted on going to see Simon.

'I'll only stay a few minutes. Just to see how he is. Then we'll go out, I promise.'

I knew it would be pointless to try to persuade her not to go. She loved Simon. He was her husband, and I knew if it were Paul in that hospital bed, wild horses would not have kept me from his side, never mind an interfering mother.

Natalie was gone for an hour, and Ruby was just waking when she got back. There was no change in Simon, and Natalie looked very low. We ordered a taxi with a child seat and went to the Botanical Gardens.

The sun was out, and the sky was blue, but it was cold. Ruby had lots of space to run around. The Botanical Garden is full of peaceful walks through plants and trees and open lawns. We walked all the way down to the water of Sydney Harbour area.

We stood in front of the famous Sydney Opera House and looked across to the harbour bridge behind it. I never thought about how I would feel if I ever stood in front of this impressive building, but if I had, I could never have imagined feeling as I did.

I felt flat. I felt weary to my bones, and I felt as useless as a chocolate teapot. I had come all this way to help my daughter, but I could do nothing to help the way she felt. I couldn't take her pain away. I couldn't make Simon better. I couldn't sleep, and my tiredness was so draining. I had no energy to look after Ruby properly. I just let her play and amuse herself most of the time.

I took my camera from my bag, and we unenthusiastically took some photos of each other near the steps of the Opera House.

'I don't know why we're bothering,' I told Natalie as I clicked away. 'We look like a couple of bag ladies, and the bags are under our eyes.'

We stopped for lunch in a cafe and then let Ruby wander where she wanted as we strolled along aimlessly behind her. The afternoon became warmer, and we shed our coats as Ruby chased the white cockatoos and pigeons on the lawn. Natalie took her phone out and told me sheepishly that she wanted to check on Simon.

'Go ahead.' I grinned tiredly at her. 'You've done well to last this long without calling.'

They told her he was talking more today, and he was insisting that they let Natalie know where he was. He couldn't remember that she'd been there that morning. This forgetfulness is normal, we'd been told to expect it, but we also know there is a chance that it might be permanent.

When our legs grew tired, we ordered a taxi and went back to the apartment. Natalie was eager to go back to the hospital, so when Ruby went to sleep for a late afternoon nap, she left.

Ruby is still asleep. All the sunshine and fresh air must have tired her out. I'm still light headed with the jet lag, and would love to take a nap, but I need to write this diary. It helps me cope. I don't have the hospital staff to comfort me. I don't need them, but I do need the cathartic release of this diary. It really helps me to put everything down on paper.

Ruby had her meltdown this evening. It started when she was woken suddenly by a loud bang outside in the corridor. I was just nicely getting her back to sleep when Natalie came back, and disturbed her again.

She didn't settle at all after that, and continued to cry until late into the evening. Occasionally she would come around for a few minutes, and we'd coax a smile or two, but then she'd dissolve in tears, and cry broken-heartedly in Natalie's arms.

We both thought this was the result of all the upset in her life. From being dumped with neighbours, the disappearance of her daddy, and mum spending so much time away from her. Added to this, she now had a stranger looking after her.

The change of environment and a routine that had gone to pot was more than a seventeen-month-old baby could take. Having her nap disturbed twice was the last straw. It was all too much for her little brain to cope with so she blew a gasket and we knew about it!

Patiently, we allowed her to get it out of her system, even when she threw herself on the floor, kicking her feet, and banging her head on the carpet, screaming at the top of her lungs, we let her. For Ruby, the world had become a nasty place, and she was letting us know that she didn't like it one little bit.

Eventually we could give her the dinner, bath and bed routine, and although it took a lot more cuddle-time than usual, she did settle down to sleep, and at last Natalie could tell me about Simon's day.

We are freezing in the apartment. The heater I bought isn't nearly efficient enough. So we snuggled under the duvet on my sofa-bed in the lounge.

'He's more responsive,' she began, 'and he's more aware of things other than his pain. He asked if he'd had his dinner, but he's not eating proper food yet. I guess he must be feeling hungry.'

I smiled, and took her hand as she talked.

'It all got too much for him at one point, and he said, "Fuuuuuck"! He said it really slowly, opened his eyes and saw the nurse and then said, "Sorry". He apologised for his bad language!' Natalie giggled. 'The nurse told him it was all right and said he could swear as much as he liked.'

These little snippets were huge steps forward to us. Simon was coming back to us. The gentle caring side of Simon was still there inside.

Natalie told me that Simon is still heavily sedated, but rouses every half hour or so for periods of lucidity and pain. She is very good with him. She could have been a nurse. She's so patient with her patient. She calms him, reassures him, and convinces him to relax.

She's been down this road with him before. Simon was knocked off his motorbike a few years ago by a thoughtless driver who didn't look where she was going. He hit the car windshield, somersaulted and landed on his knees. He had a couple of fractures, and a badly bruised spine, but thankfully the temporary paralysis soon disappeared. He was in hospital for a week or so, and this was followed by months of physiotherapy, but he made a full recovery.

I offered to fly to Natalie's side at the time too, but I wasn't needed then. This accident happened before they were married.

So Natalie knew how to handle Simon this time. She'd dealt with his worries about disability before, and knew that his worst fear would be about mobility. He would hate to be so physically damaged that he couldn't live how he wanted to live.

He's an extremely fit young man. At thirty-eight-years-old he still surfs. He was a keen snowboarder, and in his youth he was a real daredevil. Sports and dangerous activities are his lifeblood! Doctors said that his level of fitness was a huge contributing factor to his survival. A less fit man would have died of the injuries he sustained.

Simon's lung capacity was an amazing six breaths a minute while sedated. It was so low they had to double-check his oxygen levels to see that he was getting enough, but he was fine. His resting heart rate was an incredible forty-four beats per minute, again, due to his level of fitness. So Simon's survival was mainly due to him being so fit and strong.

As well as owning acres of paddocks and land that has to be mowed, cleared of weeds, and managed, Simon works for a large building company. His job involves manual labour, climbing scaffolding and manoeuvring heavy loads. Bob told us when he was here that one of the fitness tests they have to do involves squeezing a ball as hard as they can. This tests their hand-strength. Simon burst the ball!

His strength and fitness were never in question, but it's easy to see that because of this, Simon fears becoming dependent. Natalie can understand this more than anyone and knows the importance of reassuring Simon at every opportunity that he will recover. He needs to know that his pain will be temporary and that he will be back to normal eventually.

'I told the nurses how important it is to tell Simon that he will get better. I asked them to put that into his notes, so all the staff will know to reassure him even when I'm not there.'

'Well, let's hope they can all remember to read the notes!' I said.

'They'd better.' She smiled softly. 'He needs a goal. If he knows he'll get his mobility back, he'll work toward it. He'll do as he's told, and he'll know he will improve. I said they couldn't tell him how long it might take. He wouldn't be able to handle that. A few weeks would be bad enough, but if he thinks it might be months, he'll be so lost, he'll give up.'

'What did you tell him?' I was interested in how she was handling him and guiding him through this.

'I just told him he had a goal and that goal was to get back to normal. I said that if he could endure this awful bit, the pain and the frustration, that normality was waiting there in the future for him. Then I told him to relax. To try to sleep.'

I could almost hear her telling him. "Do it for me, honey." We all might think we have a good relationship with the person we love, but with Natalie and Simon it's always been more than good. Sure, they have their rows; fiery and passionate shouting matches, with screaming and swearing at each other. I've only witnessed this once, but Natalie tells me it happens occasionally. However, their love for each other is stronger than most couples I've known.

On their wedding day, they wrote their own vows, and read them to each other in front of the guests who gathered to watch the ceremony on top of their hill at home. As Max, their dog, lay at their feet, they stared into each other's eyes and spoke of their love. There wasn't a dry eye on the hill. The phrase, soul mates, is often used, but only rarely describes a relationship truly. In Natalie and Simon's case, it is the only phrase to describe them. They are soul mates in every sense, which makes it doubly agonising to watch Natalie fighting for his recovery as much as he would have to fight for himself.

It is also rewarding, to hear that he is responding to Natalie, listening to her and doing as she asks. Even though the effort it takes to relax is so very hard for him, when his body is screaming in agony, he tries because he loves her and because she asks him to.

DAY 7 Saturday 5th July

Despite our intimate chat last night and the wine I'd bought to help us unwind, I still found it hard to sleep. I can't blame jet lag any longer as I should be over that by now. It has to be the stress of watching Natalie dealing with this and the worry that never leaves me. I can't switch off the nightmare thoughts that torment me as I desperately fight for sleep.

How long will it take Simon to recover? What kind of life will they have in the future? How will his brain function be compromised? How will their marriage survive this tragedy? What effect will all this upset have on my little angel in the long term?

Despite her distress last night, Ruby is adapting to the situation, but what kind of future will she have if she has to live with a brain damaged daddy? How many more meltdowns might she need to cope with that? What about Natalie? How could she live with a very different Simon to the one she had promised to love forever?

My thoughts stray into the future imagining all kinds of scenarios, and each time I have to give myself a mental shake and drag my mind back to the present. I was doing no good lying awake and worrying about things that might never happen. I need to sleep at night so I will have the energy to cope with my days.

I force my mind to go blank, thinking only of blackness and silence, but soon the stray niggles that contribute to my anxieties drift across to illuminate the blank screen, and I have to try to push them away again.

It is an endless battle, and when Ruby woke at 5.30am I'd already been awake for three hours. I know Natalie is struggling with sleep too. She looks so tired.

Natalie has gone to the hospital to see how Simon got through the night, and to ask the doctors what progress he is making. I'm killing time writing this while Ruby has her morning nap. The plan is to go shopping today, change the inefficient heater, buy more food, and get back to the apartment in time for Ruby's afternoon nap. Natalie will then go back to the hospital and return in time to put Ruby to bed before our dinner. We're trying to set a routine for Ruby. We want her to feel secure, and for our little angel, security is in the details of her routine.

There could be a fly in the ointment, though. Our accommodation was arranged in a hurry, and the apartment manageress told us that we might have to move to a smaller apartment as this one was pre-booked weeks before to someone else. We don't want to move, especially as Ruby is familiar with this place and another change won't be good for her, but whatever happens, we'll cope. We'll have to.

One good thing in our favour is the fact that Simon's boss at the construction company rang Natalie to tell her that he will cover all our accommodation costs for as long as we have to be in Sydney, no matter how long that might be. At hundreds of dollars a week, this news is very welcome.

SAME DAY next entry
Natalie had a beaming smile on her face when she came back from the hospital. When she told me why, I smiled with her. She told me that when she walked into Simon's room he was awake. He smiled at her and said, 'I love you.'

She answered, 'I love you too, honey. Can I give you a kiss?'

He puckered his lips to accept it.

'Oh, it was so good to see him so peaceful, and he was looking so happy to see me.'

I was so pleased for her and encouraged her to tell me more as we set out on our long walk to the large Broadway shopping centre.

'The nurses undid his manacles for a few minutes, and the first thing he did was reach for my hand. He raised it to his lips and kissed it. He was so sweet!'

I knew their love was strong, and this news really gave me a lift. This was proof that Simon's love for Natalie was still there, and as strong as ever.

Ruby was snuggled into her pram, and as it was still so cold, we bypassed the park on our way to the shops. Natalie continued to tell me how the morning visit had progressed. She could reassure Simon once again that everything was going to be okay as he fiddled with her fingers in his hand.

'He always tickles his fingers through mine when we hold hands. It was so good to feel him doing something so familiar.'

The nurse came in then, and asked Simon, 'Do you know where you are?'

'Yeah, The Gold Coast, or The Sunshine Coast, or somewhere.' Simon said confidently.

'No, you're in Sydney.' Natalie told him.

'Nah, I can't be in Sydney.' He sighed and drifted off to sleep again.

Simon was in and out of consciousness every few minutes, but the greatest thing for Natalie was that they were managing to control his pain.

'Do you hurt anywhere?' she asked him in one of his wakeful moments.

'No, I don't think so,' he answered, then seemed to concentrate for a few seconds. 'No, no pain,' he decided.

He was asking questions each time he woke, and some of them made no sense at all.

He asked, 'Was anyone else there?'

He asked, 'Was Richard okay?'

Natalie told him his friend was fine, and explained that Richard hadn't been with Simon when he crashed.

Simon then told Natalie to remember to pick Ruby up from school. He was confused, and Natalie tried to explain that Ruby was seventeen-months-old, but Simon was asleep again before she could finish. The nurse told her that this confusion sometimes happens, and could be due to the drugs he was taking.

Natalie came back to the apartment when he fell into a deep sleep, knowing he wouldn't miss her for a few hours while we did some shopping.

We had lunch in the shopping centre and bought more supplies. We both bought some warm trousers as we didn't have enough warm clothes with us, and we exchanged the poor excuse for a heater for a fan assisted one.

That afternoon when we got back we plugged in the new heater and felt warm for the first time in days. Ruby soon settled for her nap and we settled down on my bed for a rest. The shopping centre was a long walk, and we were both already exhausted through lack of sleep.

I was surprised to wake two hours later to the sound of Ruby squealing in the next room. We felt much brighter, and Natalie sneaked out to go back to Simon while I distracted Ruby with a snack, but as soon as my little angel realised her mummy was gone she became agitated. She went to the door and banged on it. She started moaning and sucking her thumb.

I entertained her, playing peekaboo, playing chase, asking her to show me her tummy, and then chasing her to tickle her. It was tiring, but if I stopped, she was back at the door with her thumb in her mouth looking so forlorn and upset.

Natalie came home in time to give Ruby her bath and enjoy some playtime with her before bed. While Natalie was enjoying her quality time with Ruby, Katy and Paul both rang, and I gave them the latest news.

I enjoyed hearing their voices, they reminded me of everything I'd left behind, but it was good to know that they were supporting Natalie from afar, sending the good vibes of their love to her and Ruby and Simon.

They both feel so inadequate, and both expressed concern for me as well as for Simon and Natalie. Even though I reassured them I was okay, I know they heard the tiredness in my voice.

I really need a good night's sleep, but so far haven't been able to snatch more than a few hours before waking and staring into the darkness, tossing and turning with my uncomfortable thoughts in my even more uncomfortable bed. I swear I've slept on more comfortable floors!

When Ruby was in bed, Natalie and I had dinner and shared a bottle of wine. We settled down to talk of Simon's progress today. She told me Simon had eaten proper food for the first time, half a ham sandwich, with the speech therapist present to make sure his swallowing reflex was working properly.

Natalie was surprised to learn that Simon had a small break in his jaw, which we weren't aware of before now, and that could have caused problems with chewing. Also, as he was bleeding so badly from his cut lip at the scene of the accident, they had difficulty inserting the breathing tube, and this has left him with a grazed and sore throat. So due to these extra difficulties, they had to make sure he could chew and swallow without any problems.

He did fine, and later enjoyed some lamb and vegetables. Natalie was told he ate lots of this dinner, and I smiled with her, remembering what a great appetite he had for good food. Natalie is a really good cook and loves nothing more than to be in her kitchen baking or making a lovely meal.

Then she told me the downside to this good news. After his first solid food, he would have to be monitored carefully to make sure it went through his digestive system correctly. There was a danger his insides wouldn't function properly. It was another small thing to add to the list of things to worry about.

Natalie then told me that, in the next few days, they would start to do some neurology tests on him. They explained that they will repeat the test every day over a period of time. This will assess his memory, both long and short term. They have to wait until the dosage of the drugs can be lowered enough to be sure they're not affecting the outcome of the tests.

Natalie is dreading the results of these tests. It's easy to stay positive about his lapses of memory and his confusion when drugs can be used as an excuse. These tests will either confirm the drugs as the cause, or could set Natalie on a whole new path of possibilities. A path she has no idea how to travel. If Simon does have severe memory problems, it could mean a whole different future for them, and one I wouldn't wish on either of them. That is the future that keeps me awake at night.

We know now that we'll be in Sydney for a long

time. The plastic surgeons want to operate on his facial bones while we're here. They won't do that until he's well enough, then he'll have to recover from the operation sufficiently before he can be flown to a hospital closer to home.

So we discussed longer term plans for our stay here in Sydney. How could I get access to more money for me? How could Natalie pay her bills and keep things ticking over at home from here? We made a list of phone calls that we would need to make, to get more information.

Natalie took a few calls from friends and family during the evening, and was positive when telling each of them about Simon's improvements. She played down the worrisome concerns and emphasised the positive things. I was happy to hear her laughing with Emma, and it became obvious to me that she had a special bond with her thoughtful sister-in-law.

Natalie told her about the tender moments she'd shared with Simon earlier, and she started giggling. I understood from listening to one side of the conversation that Emma was helping Natalie to remember other times when he hadn't been so tender, and even suggested that Simon might be more thoughtful after his brains had been shaken about. Natalie laughed and sighed and was totally immersed in her conversation, and I watched with envy as her eyes sparkled and her lips smiled. I wished I could lift her spirits in the same way.

We went to bed in a happier mood. We were feeling positive and had plans in place to get things organised the following day.

People have been generous with their offers of help, and over the last few days some calls have been very touching and heart-warming. However, some have also been harrowing, so I'm going to write about two of those calls here.

One of Natalie's friends has a mum who does house-sitting for people who go on holiday. She offered to come and stay at Natalie's house, to look after the animals for a few weeks, to give the neighbours a break. Natalie rang her to take her up on her kind offer, and they discussed the practicalities of where things are kept, and what to feed the animals. Natalie told her she would organise the farrier to come to clip the horses hooves, and even though she's not confident with horses, this lady said she would hold them if the farrier needed her help. She insists she doesn't want payment for her time. She just wants to help.

This morning Natalie phoned the tow-truck company who took Simon's ute from the scene of the accident. She wanted to ask what she needed to do about the insurance people and to see if she could organise someone to collect his belongings from inside the wreck. The chap she spoke to was hesitant.

'What's the state of play?' he asked as if he were afraid to ask how Simon was.

When Natalie explained his progress, the chap was relieved and admitted that he thought Simon had been killed. He'd never seen a worse wreck in all his years of business, and didn't think it was possible for the driver to have survived it. We were reminded how lucky Simon had been.

Then Natalie told me the details of the night of the crash. Simon had been working overtime that Sunday, and Natalie had a call from the police station. They'd had their car broken into a few months before while parked at a tourist spot near Byron Bay, and the police had recovered some of their belongings. The police wanted Simon and Natalie to identify and collect them.

She'd called Simon, and they arranged to meet at the police station at 4.30pm. After collecting their belongings, Natalie set off in her car with Ruby, and Simon followed her in the ute. Somewhere on the journey, a slow-moving car moved out between them from a junction. On a long straight stretch of road, they became separated as Natalie drove to the speed limit, and the slow-moving car held Simon back.

Natalie looked in her rear-view mirror before she rounded a bend in the road and saw Simon pulling out to overtake. She said there was plenty of room for him to do this. The road was long and straight, and there were no other cars around.

She continued home, fed Ruby, fed the horses, rang Simon to see where he was, but his phone went to answer-phone. She left a message asking him to let her know where he was.

She gave it a few more minutes, and she rang again as it was unusual for him not to ring her back within a few seconds.

'If you've called at Richard's place, let me know! I'm worried. For all I know you could be dead in a ditch somewhere!'

'You actually left that message?' I asked, and she nodded. 'Well, I suppose it's what we all think isn't it, when someone is a few minutes overdue, but we don't believe it will ever happen, do we?'

'I knew something was wrong, Mum. You just know sometimes, don't you? I knew.'

She put Ruby back in the car and set out, driving slowly, checking the dark shadows at the side of the road. It was dark by then, and as she got closer to town the blue flashing lights in the distance stood out starkly against the black sky.

'At first I thought the police had pulled someone for speeding. You know how you try to convince yourself that it's okay and that it's nothing to do with you?'

As she got closer, she saw the fire truck and began to think the worst. She pulled over to her side of the road and got out to check it wasn't anything to do with Simon, but when she saw the red canopy of his ute, she couldn't deny it any longer. She ran over the road and pushed her way through the rescue people and vehicles, screaming Simon's name.

'Where is he? Where's Simon?' she yelled.

She said her legs went then, and she found herself on the ground, but she realised the ute was mangled and empty, and she quickly got to her feet, ran to the ambulance and yanked open the door.

'Simon, are you in there?'

A policeman grabbed her and asked who she was.

'That's my husband in there, let me go!'

She struggled with him, but he pulled her gently away and told her that Simon was all right.

'Listen to me,' he asked her, 'he's doing okay. He's conscious, but you have to let them take him to the hospital now.'

By this time, Natalie tells me, she was freaking big-style. She was shouting and screaming for Simon. The policeman was trying to calm her, telling her that Simon had been talking to him and was conscious throughout.

Then he said, 'Are you okay to drive?'

'Yeah,' she told him without thinking. 'Yeah, of course I can drive.'

A nearby paramedic told the policeman, 'Look, mate, that's her husband in that ambulance. If you don't want another RTA on your hands, I suggest you get someone to drive her to the hospital.'

Arrangements were made for a policeman to drive Natalie, with Ruby, to Byron District Hospital. Once there, she had an agonising wait while they worked on Simon. Eventually she was shown into a family room where a doctor and a chaplain sat waiting to talk to her.

'I knew it wouldn't be good news when the chaplain was there, but when they told me he was alive, it was all I could hear. It took awhile for it all to sink in, and they asked if they could call anyone for me. I could only think of Martin at first, and well, you know the rest.'

WEEK TWO: Confusion & explanations

DAY 8 Sunday 6th July

It's Sunday morning as I'm writing this, exactly one week since the accident that happened at 5.20pm local time. Natalie is with Simon at the hospital, and Ruby is taking her morning nap. It's 9.45am, and the doctors should have done their rounds by now.

Maybe Natalie will have more news when she gets back. She doesn't always remember everything to tell me, but as various people ring her throughout the day, I get to overhear more bits of the jigsaw as she relates pieces of news to the many callers. Last night was different. Last night we could talk properly.

We shared another bottle of wine and had a good long chat. Wine has become our relaxation medicine, and we have indulged almost every night. I've found a bottle shop on the high street close to our apartment, and it is the second place I stop on my daily walkabouts. The first is always the supermarket to buy mundane supplies.

With Ruby in her oversized pram, it is no easy task to navigate the narrow supermarket aisles, especially with her little hands reaching out to grab things from the lower shelves. One morning I was half-way back to the apartment before I realised that Ruby had a large jar of pickled onions on her lap. I know I hadn't paid for them!

After Natalie had told me the details of that awful night, we were able to lighten our spirits and laugh as she told me about the things Simon had been talking about at the hospital. When questioned by nurses, he remembered he was married to Natalie, but thought

Ruby was seven-years-old. He thought he'd travelled to Sydney with Natalie and Ruby and me. He remembered he'd been told that I was there, although he hadn't seen me, as yet.

We were able to laugh, but lurking behind the laughter was the fear that his confusion might be permanent. Natalie wasn't ready to face this fear yet, so we talked of other things. We discussed our family back home in UK, and Simon's family. We talked of how funny and how strange family relationships can be, and how great it was to have so much love and support from them all. We enjoyed a good night, a bonding session between mother and daughter, with a glass or two of wine to ease the stress.

SAME DAY next entry

Natalie came back at lunchtime with not much news. Simon is still confused, which is beginning to worry her more. According to Simon, today he is in Coraki, a small town in the area where he works. He remembered the two dogs they have, and asked if they were missing him.

'Oh, and according to Simon, Ruby is eleven months old.' Natalie smiled. 'So I told him he was a bit closer to her age today.'

It was a relief that he'd stopped thinking of his daughter as six years older than she was, then Simon asked her what she meant.

Natalie asked him, 'Ruby had her first birthday a few months ago, don't you remember the party?'

'Nah.' He shook his head, not concerned about Ruby or her party. Then he asked, 'Why am I here?'

Natalie explained about the car crash, about the broken legs, the bang on his head.

'My head?' He looked puzzled.

'Yeah, you had a bit of a bump.'

'How bad?' he asked.

'Pretty bad,' she told him. 'That's why you're so confused.'

'Oh,' he said and drifted off to sleep.

It's easy to understand why Natalie is even more worried now.

After lunch, we went out. We bought a map of the area at a local newspaper shop. We used it to find a park closer to home and took Ruby there to play. She loved the sandpit and the slide, and was happy to toddle around and watch the other children playing.

We are falling into a routine, living our lives around the hospital and Ruby's naps and feed times. We are finding our feet in Sydney and now know where the closer shops are, where the newspaper shop, bank, post office, Internet cafes and pharmacists are.

Today, we both realised we'd soon need more prescription medications. Natalie needed birth control pills. Not that it will matter if she doesn't take them for a while, there's not much chance of her conceiving just now. I needed more pills for my stomach problem. I had enough for a month or so, but I would need to get more pills if I stayed here longer.

We were taking some breathing space from Simon and concentrating on our needs, and assessing the practicalities of our life here in Sydney.

We got a small respite from our landlady. She

stopped us on our way out told us she had done some juggling with the apartments and we can stay where we are, for the time being at least.

Natalie is back at the hospital now as I write this, and it's getting close to Ruby's bedtime. I'll give her a bath and play with her and hope Natalie can make it back to put her to bed. I love to play with my little angel. I love to cuddle her when she's tired, and she is accepting me more and more as her primary carer, but I know she's happier if her mum is there to put her to bed at the end of the day.

DAY 9 Monday 7th July

I'm writing this at night. It's been a long day. Ruby and I have been cooped up in the apartment as it's been raining heavily, non-stop, for twenty-four hours.

Natalie didn't get back last night until Ruby was fast asleep. She didn't want to leave Simon, and he took a long time to settle. His temperature spiked at 38.8 degrees, and now the doctors are concerned that infection may be starting somewhere. He's already taking antibiotics, so we have to wait and hope this won't be significant.

The doctors are going to reduce his medication today, to see if that helps with his confusion and memory issues, we think he seems to be improving, but the progress is erratic. He thought his daughter was called Grace today. He has a niece called Grace, so we can understand where the name comes from, but he's still very confused.

He has now started to have the neurology tests every day to assess his memory functions. He can remember his name and his date of birth with no trouble at all, but other things evade him. He doesn't know what year it is and answers differently every time he's asked. For Simon, it can be anywhere from 1977 to 1994, and has answered 2006 once, which is closer, being only two years ago. He just doesn't know, and seems to say dates at random, instead of admitting he doesn't have a clue.

His short-term memories are improving. From having to be reminded every thirty seconds that he has broken legs and can't get out of bed, he now seems more aware of his condition. From getting agitated each time he wakes, and pulling on his restraints angrily and forcefully, he now wakes and tugs gently and seems to realise and understand why they are there.

So we think he remembers small details from one day to the next, which is a huge improvement. However, Natalie then told me that she watched him eat a good dinner tonight, and he snoozed while they cleared the plates away. He came awake briefly as she was about to leave, and asked her, 'Will you bring me something to eat next time you come? They don't feed me here.'

We see the funny side and laugh without looking into each other's eyes. We know this won't be so funny if it's permanent.

Last night and this evening, Natalie had lots of calls from family and friends. I got to hear more details of Simon's condition through her conversations with them.

I had formed the impression that Natalie could talk with Simon quite normally. I began to understand, as she was describing Simon's conversations in more detail, this was not so. Because of his confusion and problems with his short-term memory, their talk is no more than disjointed sentences. He's placid and compliant, doing what he's told without argument. This is worrying because this isn't like Simon at all!

Bob rang to say he was coming to Sydney again soon and asked if he could bring anything down for us. I'd left my walking shoes on Natalie's bedroom floor in my packing frenzy before coming to Sydney, and was hobbling around in high heels or sand shoes. I'd packed the lightest footwear to carry and hadn't thought about my comfort. He kindly offered to collect them for me from the house.

Simon's brother, David, asked to come and see him, and Natalie tried to stick to her guns, protecting Simon.

'He won't want you to see him like this, David. He's so weak and vulnerable, and he has no dignity.'

Then after listening to David she burst out laughing.

'You've got me there!' She giggled.

She told me later that David said, 'He can't expect to take a slide down the Tarmac and hold on to his dignity at the same time!'

So David will arrange to come to Sydney soon to see his little brother. I was pleased to hear this. I know that Natalie will benefit from seeing more friendly faces. She needs normal conversation about ordinary things in her life, and I can't give her as much of that as she needs.

I know little about her life here, or her friends. I know some details, but not enough. Maybe that will change over the coming weeks as we spend more time together.

After the phone had stopped ringing tonight, we sat quietly, digesting the day. The little-to-no improvement in Simon's mental state was worrying us both, but we agreed that it was early days. At just over a week since the accident, we decided that maybe we were worrying too soon.

'I miss him, Mum.' Natalie said, quietly. 'I miss his conversation, his feisty self. I can't help thinking…' her voice trailed off, and her shoulders slumped.

'Don't go down that road yet, love. We just said that it's only been a week. Give him a chance.' I struggled to find the words that might make her feel better, and tried to give her some hope. 'He could come back to you soon, or it might take a few months, but he's worth waiting for, isn't he?'

I was rewarded for my efforts with a small smile, but I shared her fears. What if? What if his short-term memory doesn't improve? We are only glimpsing bits of what kind of effect this might have on their future, but it is enough to scare the pants off us and ensure another sleepless night.

DAY 10 Tuesday 8th July
Not much change today. Simon is still making no sense. The psychologist came to assess him and asked the same series of questions.

'How old are you, Simon?'

'Err, forty-five?' he answered uncertainly. He is only thirty-eight-years-old.

'What year is it?'

'Err, seventy-eight?'

He's thirty years out. He was guessing. He doesn't know answers to the most basic of questions. He can't hold a conversation. I don't wonder that Natalie is so worried about him.

When she came home from the hospital, Bob was with her. He'd brought my walking shoes from Natalie's house. At last I could walk in comfort! He also brought get-well cards from work and a cheque to pay our accommodation bill. Bob was in Sydney to see another sick friend and also wanted to check on Simon. He left his bag with us and arranged a time to call back later.

Natalie was dead on her feet. I wasn't the only one finding it difficult to sleep. Ruby had an unsettled night. We'd been awake every few hours trying to soothe her. Natalie had eventually taken her into bed with her, and although that helped Ruby to sleep, it made it hard for Natalie to do the same. I offered to take Ruby for a long walk, to give Natalie the chance of a nap.

I pushed the pram up the backstreets intending to avoid the busy, traffic-filled roads, and I discovered a gem. A tiny park was just around the corner from our apartment block.

Ruby was delighted with our find, and I played with her on the swing and the slide for a time. We saw lots of magpies, and she chased them, giggling as they flew up to settle in the branches above us. When she got tired, she didn't complain when I put her back in the pram and set out for King Street and our nearest shops.

I walked the whole length of this very long shopping street twice, and found another supermarket where I bought more food; a different bottle shop where I bought more wine, and finally called at the Internet cafe where I sent e-mails to all my friends while Ruby conveniently slept.

I was proud of myself as I headed back towards our temporary home. The skyline of Sydney hung in the near distance, and I could see the famous Centre Point Tower standing tall above the skyscrapers. The scene was as alien to me as the surface of the moon, but I was finding my feet in this unfamiliar place. The strangeness of life in Sydney is becoming more normal, and I'm just getting on with it, doing things without worrying *how* I was going to do them.

The pram and I were loaded down with my purchases as I walked slowly back through the tiny streets, exploring a different way to get home.

The backstreets of New Town, the area we are living in, are quite picturesque, and under different circumstances I might have taken some photographs of the quaint and pretty architecture. Tiny, multi-coloured houses with Parisian style wrought-iron balconies compete side by side with modern apartment blocks. The streets are narrow with high paving on either side. These high walkways are obstructed every few yards by old knurled trees that grow at odd angles across the paths. Sweet scented flowering shrubs tumble over terraces, filling the air with fragrance, and the foreign sound of Australian birdcalls filled my ears.

When I arrived at our apartment block, I pressed the button to call the lift and Bob walked into the foyer behind me. He took the bags from the overloaded pram, and we rode the lift together.

He stayed for a few minutes, telling us of the gossip from home. He told us of the birth of a baby, a new team member in Simon's work gang. He said there was to be a retirement party for one of the men at work, and it was a shame that Simon would miss it. Bob also told us of the latest report in the Byron Shire Echo that had everyone fired up at work. The report read something like, 'Local man in a fight for life after a car crash, is now recovering well and is expected home within the week!'

'That's great news.' Natalie laughed. 'Wish they'd told me that.'

When Natalie came back from the hospital this evening, there had been another worrying development. Simon's heart had begun to race at two hundred beats per minute. So he's been prescribed more drugs to regulate this, but every time they lower the dose, the heart races again. They think the injury might have affected the part of his brain that regulates heartbeat and temperature as his temperature is still spiking too.

Natalie thinks there might be a possibility that Simon's personality has changed. He's placid and calm, despite being confused. This is not like the Simon we know. He would be angry. He would normally be shouting and demanding to know what was going on. This calm acceptance is totally out of character for him.

His speech is irrational. He can only manage snippets of conversation at best.

Bob reassured Natalie on one point that had confused her, though. Simon had kept repeating that he'd been in Coraki, and Natalie was sure he'd not been near the place. Bob told us that Simon was sent to Coraki on the day of the accident to do some work there. We were relieved to realise that Simon's insistence was indeed, grounded in solid fact.

DAY 11 Wednesday July 9th
Ruby had another unsettled night. She was awake every

few hours, so Natalie is really tired again today. We had a lazy morning, and I took charge of Ruby while Natalie stayed in bed for a while. I gave her breakfast and changed her dirty nappy, something I can't do easily. I nearly lose my breakfast every time I deal with the smelly mess.

'How did you manage with us, Mum?' Natalie laughs at me from her bed as I hold my nose and retch.

It's so long ago I can't remember, but I think I was the same. I've never been good at handling bad smells. I managed to get the job done without losing my breakfast, and continued to dress Ruby.

We played tea parties for an hour. She seemed fretful and puked her breakfast but didn't seem too upset by it. I had some cuddle time with her before putting her back to bed for her nap. She may be coming down with something, so I'll keep a close watch on her.

When Ruby was asleep, Natalie rang the policeman who attended the accident. She needed to ask his permission for someone to collect Simon's belongings from the wreck. She also had some questions about the crash. We still didn't know any details about what had caused the accident, and we were eager to know whether this policeman could throw any light on it for us.

He was very kind and very thorough. He told her that plenty of witnesses had seen Simon overtaking the slow-moving car; however, the car appeared to speed up, and Simon seemed to change his mind about overtaking and pulled back behind the car. Then the car in front unexpectedly braked hard, too early for the bend, and forced Simon, in the utility vehicle, to brake harder. The back end of the ute began to fishtail up the road, and when the back wheels hit gravel, Simon lost control completely and spun off to hit the tree.

Apparently, the other driver did not stop and has not come forward to offer his side of the story.

The policeman advised Natalie not to attempt to see the ute as it would be too distressing. Simon lost a lot of blood, and the inside of the cab makes for gruesome viewing. He told her that because Simon was losing so much blood, he was in danger of bleeding to death from the wounds on his head and both his feet. The firemen had problems in freeing his trapped legs, and the paramedics were discussing the decision to amputate his legs to save his life. The firemen were given a few more minutes, and mercifully managed to free him in time.

The ute hit the tree with the right side, slamming the headlight and the entire front wing up into the driver's seat. The mangled car then rode up the tree, flew through the air, turned over and landed on the left side, leaving Simon hanging from the seat belt.

The policeman said that in his opinion if Simon had hit the tree head on, he would have died, or he would have lost his legs for sure. It was a sobering thought, for Natalie. She was clearly shocked as she relayed the graphic details of this conversation to me.

The policeman also asked about Simon's drinking habits. Would he have had a drink? Natalie assured him that Simon might have had one with his workmates at the end of the working day, but would never drive with more than two beers inside him. Then she added that it would be unlikely he'd had anything to drink as he had left work early to meet her at the police station. She wasn't worried when the policeman told her Simon's blood had been sent for testing as a matter of routine. She knew that Simon didn't drink and drive.

When asked when Simon would be available for questioning, she shook her head. 'It will be a long time before he can make a statement. That's if he ever can,' she added, and went on to explain Simon's memory problems. 'I want him to get his memory back, but I hope he never remembers the details you just told me.'

Natalie is with Simon again now as Ruby continues to sleep. She mentioned that she would like to take Ruby to see him soon. I'm glad because I'm starting to feel the need to see him. I know Natalie wants to keep him calm and seeing Ruby or me might upset his apple-cart more than we'd like, but I want to see what Natalie has to cope with.

Ruby must be missing her daddy too as he played with her a lot, especially in the evenings before bed. He is a hands-on daddy, so of course that could be another reason she's so unsettled at night.

I'm going to do some yoga this morning. I ache all over, and I'm sure it's down to the lumpy mattress and poor springs on the sofa bed. I need to stretch out the kinks before my old bones seize up altogether.

DAY 12 Thursday 10th July

I'm writing this on Thursday morning as Ruby sleeps. Yesterday was such a long day and so much happened. I didn't get the chance to write and so this bit might be jumbled as I try to remember and put things in the right sequence.

Simon had his lunch yesterday and then dozed for a minute. When the nurse said she was going for her lunch, Simon asked, 'What about mine?' He couldn't remember eating it a few moments before. This constant forgetfulness is making Natalie anxious. We keep thinking we're seeing improvements, but this proved there was none.

He didn't have the memory assessment tests in the morning as he was in too much pain when they came, so they left the testing for that day. He wouldn't have scored a great deal anyway. His progress seems to have come to a halt.

Natalie was told he would have to stay in ICU for a while longer, because of his temperature and heart rate problems. He also has another complication; one of his foot wounds is weeping, and could be infected. They took swabs and sent them to the lab. Meanwhile, he's still taking wide spectrum antibiotics until they find out if he needs treating with something more specific.

Just as Natalie was preparing to leave him, he tried to get out of bed.

'You can't get out of bed, darling.' She tried to stop him. 'You have two broken legs.'

He continued to struggle, sliding his legs through the metal safety bars on the side of his bed.

'That's gonna hurt like hell, Simon. You have two broken legs!' She was raising her voice, trying to get through to him.

Simon blew his top. 'I fucking know!' he yelled, at a volume fit to burst eardrums. 'Broken legs! Fucking leave me alone!'

The nurses came running.

'Was that shouting coming from in here?' One of them asked, sounding surprised.

They hadn't heard Simon in a temper before. I had, and knew his voice would have been LOUD!

The nurses settled him, eased him back against the pillows and made him comfortable.

'Where did that temper come from?' They asked him.

Natalie smiled at them. 'That's okay. I don't mind the temper. That's the Simon I know.'

She was pleased. It seemed to her that Simon, the real Simon, was coming back. His temper outburst signified a huge leap forward in Natalie's eyes.

While Natalie visited Simon in the morning, I took Ruby to the park. She seemed bright enough, so I thought I might be wrong about her becoming ill. We met Natalie back at the apartment for a late lunch, and had a visit from two ladies that she had befriended in the ICU. Pam's husband had a triple heart bypass operation the previous day, and we spent time comparing notes and swapping encouraging words. They didn't stay long, but told us of another supermarket they'd found closer to the hospital. It was some useful information to share with fellow out-of-towners. They were here from Lismore, a small town close to Bangalow, and staying one floor down from us in the same apartment block.

When our new friends left, Natalie and I set out together in the same direction. I took Ruby to the supermarket our friends had suggested, and Natalie went to the hospital. I bought more food and took a call from Natalie on my way back, to say that Simon was awake, and it would be a good time to bring Ruby to see her daddy. I was outside the hospital entrance when I got the call, so I told her I'd join her in a few minutes. I planned to hand Ruby to Natalie and stay outside the room to give them time together, but when we arrived at the door Natalie beckoned me in.

What I saw in that room will haunt me for goodness knows how long. The sight that greeted me was beyond any fears for Simon that I might have imagined. The last time I saw him, he'd still been in the coma and looked so calm and peaceful. What I was looking at today was the face of a terrified animal.

I tried to keep the shock from my face for Natalie's sake, but it was so hard. I was stunned speechless by the sight of Simon on the bed. He looked terrible. He was awake and was sitting up in bed with his eyes wide open, but his eyes held an expression of wild fear and were skittering in one direction then another, moving quickly around the room, scanning and rescanning his surroundings.

His eyes reminded me of a petrified animal, caught in a trap, searching for a way out. His wet mouth hung open, in that slack dribbling kind of way that you associate with a severely brain damaged person, and he looked confused. He had the glassy-eyed look of the mentally sub-normal, and I almost choked trying to keep my emotions in check. He was a pitiable sight.

Natalie lifted Ruby from her pram and took her to say hello to her daddy. Ruby squirmed away from this stranger, and I couldn't blame her one bit, but Simon knew who she was. He started to play peekaboo with her as she hid against her mummy's shoulder, but

Simon's head movements and words were exaggerated and seemed grotesque.

Ruby didn't like what she saw and cuddled closer to her mum, sucking on her thumb for extra comfort. Then Simon started cracking his teeth and lips together vigorously. He'd taught Ruby how to make fishy noises a few days before the accident, softly patting his lips together, mimicking a fish. She had quickly copied him, just as she had when he'd taught her to moo like a cow, hiss like a snake and meow like a cat.

This new exaggerated version of a fishy noise was nothing like the gentle patting of lips that she knew, and it scared her. She squirmed more and struggled to get down and away from the scary man in the bed.

Simon became aware of me standing by the door, and he looked at Natalie questioningly and said, 'Huh?'

Natalie explained that I'd come to help look after Ruby while he was here in the hospital. She began to remind him about the crash, the broken legs, the bump on the head, etc. He didn't react. It seemed as if he didn't understand.

I smiled at him and asked him, 'How you doing, Simon?'

He answered automatically, without thinking, in a fast, deep tone, 'I'm all right.'

I felt my presence had scared him somehow. He looked even more afraid, and his eyes reminded me again of a panicked, frightened animal. I was moved to tears, but held them in check. I felt so sorry for him.

Thankfully, Natalie realised quickly that this visit should be a short one for Ruby. I took my little angel from Natalie without argument when she asked me to take her back to the apartment. I placed her in the pram eagerly. I couldn't wait to get out of there.

I was so upset by what I'd witnessed that I just wanted to get away and have some space to think, but I didn't have time to dwell on it too much. Ruby was sick again on the way back to the apartment. I cleaned her and unpacked the shopping. Ruby played quietly while I made her dinner. Se wasn't interested in eating it. Ruby refusing food indicated she wasn't well. She was very quiet.

Katy rang as I was clearing the dishes away. I'm afraid I dumped all my emotions on her shoulders. She rang me at the wrong time, and I couldn't keep my feelings inside.

I told her about my visit to Simon, explaining to her how bad he looked. I told her I didn't know how Natalie could stay so positive when she had to see him like that every day.

Katy tried her best to reassure me, telling me of people she had heard of with similar injuries to Simon, who suffered similar problems to his in the early days. 'They are holding down jobs and living normal lives now, Mum.'

I took some deep breaths to steady myself, and remembered some stories we'd heard about too. I told her of the nurse who cracked her head during an epileptic fit, had the same memory loss as Simon, but now worked in ICU. We exchanged more words of encouragement, and agreed that Simon might still have a long way to go, but he would get there.

When Natalie came home, she looked exhausted. Her shoulders drooped and dark circles ringed her eyes. I told her about Ruby being unwell, and we decided that an early night was the best thing for our little angel.

We bathed her and gave her a drink. She even refused her favourite supper-time yogurt, so we knew she was feeling unwell.

After our dinner, Emma rang, and Natalie told her of Simon's lack of progress. She sounded despondent as she talked with Emma, but her thoughtful sister-in-law soon had her smiling. Emma seemed to know just what to say to cheer Natalie and make her see the lighter side of this desperate situation.

They discussed his long-term prognosis and Natalie said, 'If he doesn't get better, I won't be able to have him at home. He'll go walkabout down the paddocks and won't remember how to get back to the house!'

Paul phoned me while Natalie was talking with Emma. We had a good chat, but I wasn't able to tell him of my feelings about Simon as Natalie was there. Instead, we talked of mundane things. He's arranged to have my prescription filled out, and just needs to find out how to get it shipped to me. He's wondering what to do with my garden. I have a large veggie patch, and he's overrun with beans, peas, courgettes and rhubarb. I told him to give the surplus to our neighbours.

He's missing me and feels lonely, but he's coping. I told him I miss him too, but didn't add that I'm too tired to notice he's not there most of the time.

One of Simon's nephews called. His father-in-law is a doctor, and he is coming to Sydney on business. He's offered to visit Simon to see if he can help in any way. Natalie is expecting him to phone and then to visit with Simon tomorrow.

Carol called to plead for her mum to be allowed to come and see Simon. Carina is going out of her mind with worry, and desperately wants to see her son. Natalie was insistent, and stressed that the shock of seeing her son might be still be too much for the elderly Carina. After what I witnessed today, I can only agree with her. I'm still reeling from the shock.

Then Natalie suggested that as David was arriving next Friday, maybe he should make the decision for his elderly mum. If David thought she could come, after he'd seen Simon for himself, then Natalie wouldn't stand in her way.

Carol agreed, and the burden of keeping his mum from seeing Simon, and thus causing her distress, was now taken from Natalie. His family would decide.

We had another early night after the round of phone calls. The emotional strain of the day has caught up with us, and we are both exhausted.

DAY 13 Friday 11h July

Ruby was sick every two hours during the night. She went as limp as a rag doll and was so pale. We gave her sips of water to keep her hydrated and thought we may have to take her to the medical centre this morning. We didn't get any sleep as Natalie dealt with Ruby when she was awake while I helped with changing her bedding and we both lay awake, worrying about her while she slept. This morning she ate a little breakfast and seemed much better. Thankfully it seems to have been a short-lived tummy bug, and we don't need to take her to see a doctor. I'll be keeping a close eye on her today to make sure she is over the sickness, but I think she'll be okay.

We have a mountain of laundry to do, with all the sheets and clothes that she puked on, and we're both like walking zombies we're so tired. Hopefully we'll be able to sleep this afternoon, when Ruby has her nap.

Natalie came back from the hospital at 11am this morning, while Ruby was still asleep. She'd called at the office downstairs, and the manageress told her we could stay where we were until Wednesday, but may have to move after that. So again we were under threat of having to disrupt our lives. Poor Ruby, she will be so confused if we have to relocate.

Natalie had some good news about Simon. They say he's well enough to move to a ward, so that's been a fast turn around from a couple of days ago when they were worried about all the little things going on with him. His heart rate and temperature problems and the threat of infection have now faded into the background.

He'll need a nurse in attendance twenty-four-hours a day because of his confusion, but the neuro ward will provide that for him. He now has to wait for a bed to be available. They said it could be a couple of days.

The plastic surgeons have reviewed his facial damage and decided to leave things for now. His sinus breaks are clean, and his nose isn't crooked, so they will heal and shouldn't cause him any problems. His lip has healed nicely, but if he wants it tidied up, they can do that at a later stage. So he won't have to endure more operations just yet.

One of the nurses told Natalie that she played noughts and crosses with Simon last night and Simon repeatedly won the games! This proves that his logical thinking is fine. Natalie and Simon play games like this frequently. They play cards, hangman, and board games instead of watching the television all night, so these games could be a natural way to unlock his brain, by using the familiar pathways to get things activated again.

This morning Simon asked Natalie if she had fed the fish. They don't keep fish, but after we had discussed this, Natalie and I began to think he was probably remembering the fishy sounds he'd made to Ruby the previous day. It was a fragile connection, but could mean he remembered something from the previous day. We knew it was a long shot, but even if it was a tenuous connection and very mixed up, we were convinced it was a small step in the right direction for Simon.

When Ruby eventually woke after a long morning sleep, she seemed much livelier. She ate some scrambled egg and crackers with no sign of sickness. Babies are so quick to bounce back. I wish Simon would bounce back as quickly. Natalie has gone back to him after being reassured that Ruby was safe in my care.

I called Paul this afternoon. I needed to hear his voice, and I needed him to know the real situation with Simon. I couldn't tell him when he phoned before as Natalie was in the same room and I don't want to upset her by talking about Simon in anything other than optimistic terms. Natalie had been so positive each time she spoke to me, and to everyone else that rang her, including her dad. Her words had given us hope and so we had all been thinking positively too.

I don't know whether Natalie was trying to ease the burden on everyone else, or whether she genuinely could not see the same Simon that I saw. In my eyes, it was no good telling us that Simon is, "a bit confused", and, "his short-term memory is shot to hell". People don't equate that watered down; simplified version of the truth, with what Simon is actually like at the moment.

His wild-eyed stare, his exaggerated movements and expressions, make him look like a caricature of himself. It's as if all the little nuances and gentleness of his humanity have been stripped from him.

Whatever Natalie's reasons, some people, including Paul, were being misled. Simon's condition was dire, and showed little evidence that it would improve in the short term. I will continue to support Natalie in her positive attitude, and I do believe Simon will make a good recovery, but it will take a long time. I had no idea exactly how long until I saw him for myself. When I witnessed Simon's condition yesterday, I was scared. I can see long months of difficult work ahead, physical and mental work for both Natalie and Simon.

I might have to stay longer than my planned departure date at the end of September, and I needed to warn Paul. It was a difficult conversation, and I know he was upset, but I don't want him to have false hopes that I'll be home in a few weeks, and life for Natalie and Simon will continue as it had before. I know that will not happen, and Paul needed to know it too. At least he knows that I'll be here for the long haul, no matter how long it takes. I'm not making any plans. We'll take it one day at a time. It's all we can do.

Natalie helped the staff to take Simon outside for some fresh air this afternoon. They hoped to give him a sense of place, so he could realise where he was and to try to orientate him in these strange surroundings. All he's seen so far is the room he is in at the ICU.

They wheeled him out into the car park, the only accessible outside space for his large reclining chair on wheels. Simon saw a motorbike at the far end of the car park, pointed to it and named the make and model. He's always been a keen fan of motorbikes, and his brain holds a huge amount of knowledge about them. Natalie was cheered that he'd been able to recognise the bike, but then he turned to her and asked, 'What am I on? Is it a Kawasaki?'

Natalie sighed and answered him with, 'I don't know, honey, but I guess you might be on something!'

The nurse giggled with Natalie as Simon smiled benignly.

Then Natalie blushed bright pink when she told me that he then turned to her with a strange, mischievous look on his face and said, in a very coy voice, 'I've seen you naked!'

'Have you really?' Natalie managed to splutter. 'Then I guess you remember who I am, then?'

The nurses burst out laughing, but Natalie was embarrassed. The image he had in his mind was a revelation to him. His thoughts were transparent to anyone watching him. He had a picture of his wife in an intimate moment in his head, and it was obviously a memory that he was enjoying remembering. The nurses were in fits of giggles and Natalie was trying to hide her embarrassment and her blushes

These two small incidents gave us hope and raised our spirits. Taking Simon outside had been a good move.

The father-in-law of Simon's nephew came to see

Natalie in the afternoon, but she was disappointed by his visit. She said he didn't seem interested in Simon and spent the whole time talking with the nurses about his own past cases. Natalie thinks he came for a nosey around, just because he could. She was not impressed.

We came to bed early again after being awake for nearly all the previous night with Ruby. Our evening was interrupted by a few phone calls for Natalie, but she kept them short as there wasn't much news to tell people.

DAY 14 Saturday 12th July

This morning, Ruby is bright as a button and back to robust health, though she still woke us at 5.30am. It's still dark as pitch outside, so goodness knows what wakes her so early. We didn't fight it and gave in gracefully to get up and feed her breakfast. I just stepped in the shower when I got a call from Paul's sister, Eileen, in UK. Natalie talked with her while I quickly got dried.

Paul had called her after I finished talking with him yesterday. He was upset by what I had to tell him and needed someone to turn to. I was able to reassure Eileen that Simon was starting to make improvements. I had to emphasise the positive, as Eileen tends to worry too much and Natalie was listening to the conversation. I enjoyed talking with her, though. She was another link from home that I was missing.

I also got a text message from my sister, Denise, to tell us she was thinking of us. The small messages filled with kindness help to keep me connected. I'm starting to feel isolated over here. Natalie spends so much time away from us and all I have for company is my little angel. She's a doll and so easy to look after, but she can't hold a conversation and can't begin to understand what's going on around her, thank goodness.

I'm alone at the moment. Natalie is with Simon and Ruby is sleeping. I'll do yoga while Ruby naps. It helps to ease the strain, emotionally as well as physically. We're going to the Broadway shopping centre this afternoon to get Simon some clothes to wear. He has nothing with him, and will need to wear something more than a hospital gown when they transfer him to the ward.

SAME DAY next entry, pm.
Natalie had some worrying news this afternoon. The doctors said that Simon's memory problems are definitely due to the brain injury and not to residual swelling or drugs. He's been assessed, and they say he also has some language problems as he can't seem to string words together properly and can't find the right words to communicate so uses words he can find, even if they are the wrong ones. That's why most of his conversation is gobbledegook. For instance, when asked, 'What day is it today, Simon?' his reply was, 'It's penguin shooting day.'

He couldn't remember Natalie's name today. He seemed to know who she was, apparently, but he couldn't bring his wife's name to his lips.

It's so hard to listen to Natalie when she tells me these things. I watch dark shadows flit across her eyes. She looks gray and sad. I long to hold her close as I did when she was a baby, like I hold Ruby when she's upset, but I can't. Sometimes she puts up a barrier that I can barely cross with words.

She went on to tell me that the neurosurgeon wants to send Simon to a brain injury rehabilitation place. They're now looking for one that is closer to their home. The closest will be at the Gold Coast, or maybe Brisbane, so they won't be on the doorstep, but will be much closer to Natalie's place than Sydney.

As the evening wore on, Natalie got lots of calls from Simon's family. The doctor who came to visit yesterday has told his son-in-law, Simon's nephew, that Simon was okay and doing fine, so of course, they all want to know what the big fuss is about.

Natalie wasted no time in telling them, one by one, repeating the same disturbing words to various family members. This time she didn't hide the truth behind her optimistic statements. She told them straight that the man in the bed has Simon's body, he even looks like Simon, but the real Simon, their brother and her husband, is not here yet.

It was so hard to hear her admitting to them what she barely admits to herself. She talked with Carol for the longest time and told her the medical details of his present state.

'He's still in PTA, you know? The post-traumatic-amnesia stage, and until he comes out of that we won't know what he'll be like. We don't know what, if anything, of the old Simon will be left.'

Carol would know what PTA meant as she is a retired nurse, but I had to have it explained. I had picked up leaflets at the hospital and Natalie told me more from what the doctors had told her. Post-traumatic amnesia happens after any brain injury, whether the patient loses consciousness or not at the time of injury. While in this state, the patient seems to be aware of things around them but is confused and disorientated. They can't remember everyday things or conversations and often do or say bizarre things. It can last from a few seconds, to hours, days or weeks. In some cases, it lasts forever.

Simon is asked twelve questions each day to assess the PTA. When he answers all twelve correctly for three days in a row, he will be considered to be out of the PTA stage. The length of time it takes to come out of PTA can indicate the severity of the injury and can give an idea of how far reaching the permanent damage to the brain might be.

It depends on where you look for answers, but some leaflets I read at the hospital suggest that up to one day spent in PTA will mean mild brain damage and one week would mean severe brain injury. It is two weeks tomorrow since the accident, and Simon is still not scoring well on the twelve questions they ask him.

These are basic questions. Any sane person would be able to answer them with no problem at all. They are, if I can remember them all; his name; his age, and his date of birth.

Today's date; day of the week, and what year is it?

What kind of place is he in? (A hospital.)

What is this hospital called? (The Royal Prince Alfred, or RPA for short.)

What is the name of his questioner? She tells him more than once every day, and it is the same person who asks him.

Then he is shown three pictures. These are simple

line drawings of everyday objects. I think they are of a fork; a house, and a tree. He is shown the same three pictures every day, and to make it even more-simple, he is asked to point them out from a selection of pictures, so if he can't think of the correct name for the object due to his language problems, he can get the question right by pointing.

The most he has scored so far is six out of twelve.

At the end of her conversation with Carol, Natalie promised to ring Carina, Simon's mum, to prepare her for what she might see if she comes to see him. She promised to advise her to bring one of her daughters as she will need some support and she needed to know that we'll be too busy with Simon and Ruby to help look after her.

We talked of other things for a while before Natalie could pluck up the courage to phone Simon's mum. I could sense that my daughter needed time to collect her thoughts before making the call to Carina. She'd done a round of calls that were harrowing for me to listen to and it had taken its toll on her emotional strength. So I talked to her of my day with Ruby.

I told her of the little things that Ruby had done that amused me, and of normal things that happened outside the hospital environment. It seemed to help to calm Natalie until she felt strong enough to make the call to Simon's mum.

We also discussed our immediate future. We wished we could have a plan to work to, some idea of what we were doing, where we were going and when, but we're in limbo, waiting for decisions to be made that we have no part of and no control over. We are full of questions, but no one can give us answers. When will Simon be moved? Where to? What hope of a total recovery can they give us? What quality of life can we expect for him, for his family, and what help might be available for them? All the answers to these questions will be down the road we're walking on, but we can't see them yet.

Natalie steeled herself and made the call to Carina. She loved and respected her mother-in-law very much, and I knew this call would be difficult. I listened to her speaking with a voice full of compassion, trying to prepare his mum for the visit. She tried to explain, in gentle terms, that her son is very damaged. 'You won't be able to hold a proper conversation with him, Carina,' she told her. 'Don't expect him to be able to talk with you in words and sentences that you can understand.'

This would have been difficult for Carina to hear. I know Natalie felt she was being cruel, but Simon's mum had to know the stark truth so she wouldn't be as shocked as I'd been, on my last visit to see him.

Simon and Carina have that special bond that only seems to occur in large families where the youngest child is a surprise; arriving late in life as a blessing and as a gift of love. I'm sure that's how Carina saw Simon. Giving birth to her youngest child when she was forty-four-years-old was not easy for her, especially as he was the youngest of seven.

She speaks to her son every week, sometimes for hours at a time. Distance might separate them, but emotionally they are very close. So to hear that she might not be able to hold a conversation with him would have been a bitter blow. She would have to face the fact that the Simon she talks with on the phone has gone, and won't be back for some time, if ever. *If ever.* Those words are so hard to look at as I write them down. I don't want to look down that path. It's unthinkable.

After the phone call, Natalie was visibly shaken. I poured us a glass of wine, and we snuggled under my duvet to talk. We dared to look into the future with half-closed eyes, and we faced some demons together. We have similar outlooks on life. I'm agnostic, a fence sitter where religion is concerned. Natalie is an atheist. She doesn't believe in God, but does believe things happen for a reason. She calls it fate for want of a better word. She believes that this has happened to Simon for a reason. What that reason is, is still unclear, but she's determined that whatever the outcome is, this experience that they are living through will make them stronger.

'I have a picture in my head,' she told me. 'It's of me and Simon and Ruby walking on the beach with the dogs. I keep telling Simon to think of this picture and use it as his goal. Positive thinking leads to positive things happening, Mum.'

'How do you stay so positive, Natalie?' I asked her as I often wondered where she found the strength for optimism when she faced the horror of how Simon is now.

'I don't know any other way to be,' she said simply. 'If you think negative thoughts, and you draw negative energies to you. So I stay focussed and think positive thoughts. Positivity is good energy, and positive thinking makes the positive energies flow and they help to fix the things that need fixing.'

It's Penguin Shooting Day

She has a simple philosophy, and I agreed with her
that it was better than believing in nothing. I held her
hand as we talked, sharing our strength, and combining
our energies for the fight ahead.

WEEK THREE: Delusions & laughter

DAY 15, Sunday 13th July

Yesterday was very hard on Natalie. She was emotionally exhausted, so she decided not to go into the hospital this morning. She would allow the nurses take care of Simon, so she could spend time playing with Ruby.

I took them to the park I'd found around the corner, and we played with Ruby happily for an hour, teaching her to climb the steps, sit down and go down the slide. Ruby loved every minute, and I couldn't resist taking out my camera and snapping her as she struggled to climb the steps, and then giggled all the way down the chute.

She is a daredevil and seems to take after her daddy. She likes nothing better than to slip and lose her balance and stagger to regain it. She collapses in fits of giggles when she falls over.

When she got tired, we bundled her into the pram and went shopping. Natalie wanted to buy some vitamin supplements for Simon. She has a Batchelor of Science degree, and she specialised in nutrition. Even though her studies were on animals, her BSc covered general nutrition too, so she knew what Simon's body would need to help it heal.

The doctors have already given their consent, and they will let her give him anything she wants to if she tells them about it first. So we shopped for Vitamin D3, to help build his marrow and muscle function; Vitamin E to help his heart and cardiovascular system, and it's also an antioxidant to fight all those free radicals to help in general healing.

He also needs a pre-biotic pill as he has a history of intestinal problems especially when taking painkillers, so he is probably having some bad tummy trouble at the moment, which would be masked by the painkillers. He's had a couple of bouts of bad diarrhoea already.

I took my digital camera to the photography booth at the supermarket. I'd taken some shots of Ruby and Natalie that would be suitable for Simon to put on his wall. It only cost me a few dollars to get them printed. We're hoping they will help to remind him of his family, give him a sense of his loved ones and maybe help him to remember what their names are.

We bought some picture books for Ruby and after walking home, spent the next few hours showing her the books. She loves the colourful illustrations, and we made up games to teach her the names of the animals in the books and told her what each of them says.

'What does a sheep say, Ruby?' I point to the fluffy white picture.

'Baa,' she replies, and giggles.

She is a ray of sunshine for us. She's our silver lining on the darkest of our dark clouds. I know I'm writing clichés, but she really does help to keep us sane.

Natalie went back to the hospital later this afternoon to see Simon. I'm hoping he will be well enough for a visit from Ruby. She needs to see her daddy, and I need to be in touch with the Simon that Natalie has to face every day. I need to stay grounded in her reality so I can see the best way to help her. I feel so useless sometimes. I can't find the right words, so I rattle on about anything, or stay silent and allow her to have some inner space. It's so hard. So very hard.

SAME DAY pm entry

Wow, what a difference! Natalie sent me a text to say it would be a good time to visit Simon with Ruby. I took her right there as she had just woken from her afternoon nap. I could see the change in him immediately. He was much more relaxed. His eyes were calm, and his whole demeanour was gentler. Softer. He was much more like the Simon I knew, and it was so good to see him like this.

He interacted with Ruby, making gentle cow noises with her, mimicking her when she moaned, copying her by slapping his face when she slapped hers in frustration at not being allowed to get down from Natalie's arms. He talked with her calmly, though his words were a little mixed up.

When he saw me standing by the door, he smiled at me. 'I feel as old as you today.' He grinned.

'Cheeky!' I told him, but I could understand where he was coming from.

He seems to have a grasp on his situation. He knows he's hurt, and he's in hospital and that he has memory problems. For him to acknowledge all this is a gigantic leap forwards.

Natalie had started the visit by showing him the photographs we'd had developed of Ruby. 'Do you know who that is?' she asked him.

'Haven't got a clue,' he said, innocently, and then he'd grinned like a Cheshire cat. 'Course I know who it is, it's Ruby, you daft bugger.'

Natalie had asked him if he wanted to see his little girl.

'Oh, yeah, I miss her so much,' he'd said.

She told me he then turned to her with tears in his

eyes and said, 'I just want to be a good daddy to her and run around with her.' So he was talking in sentences and thinking of his future. Amazing!

Natalie asked if he could remember that Ruby had been in to see him a few days ago.

'I know she's been, but I can't remember it.'

It's unbelievable that he could change so much in such a short time. Natalie is very pleased. Her whole face is brighter, and she has a spring in her step again. We're being realistic, we know there will be more bad days, but for now we are happy to celebrate the best day so far.

He scored eight out of twelve on the PTA tests today too. Can this day get any better? Natalie said she asked him the same questions at the start of her visit and he only scored six, but officially he got an eight today, so we're not worried. His consistency will improve.

When he saw me today, he didn't freak like last time. He seemed to know I had been before and knew why I was there in Sydney with them.

'Dreams,' he told me, shaking his head. 'Mixed up dreams.'

'Are you having nightmares about your mother-in-law, Simon?' I asked, laughing gently with him.

'Don't know what's real.'

I knew what he meant, it was obvious. He was sleeping so much that his reality was getting mixed up with his dreams; of course, he was finding it difficult to tell the difference.

His conversational skills are improving, though he tired very quickly. Our visit lasted ten minutes at most, but it was enough to cheer me and I'm sure Ruby appreciated seeing her daddy, though she was unsure at first. If we keep repeating the visits, it can only be good for all of them.

I brought her back to the apartment, and turned on the television. She watched some children's programmes, and I made her dinner. She loves the Teletubbies and Bananas in Pyjamas, but Shaun the Sheep is her favourite. She stands in front of the screen saying 'Baa,' and pointing at all the sheep.

Simon had a quiet afternoon after Ruby and I left. He was sleeping lots and started talking gobbledegook again when he woke, so Natalie came home early to see Ruby and played with her before bedtime.

Simon's brother, Joseph, called to discuss arrangements for Carina to visit, with him and David on Friday. They don't know whether they'll bring her with them, but David and Joseph will definitely be coming.

SAME DAY late entry

We'd been in bed an hour when the phone rang. Natalie dived for it, expecting bad news. It was the hospital.

Simon wouldn't settle and wanted to talk to Natalie. He was very upset. He was crying. He was confused, and didn't know where he was.

He thought he'd lost all his money and couldn't find his phone or wallet. He asked Natalie if she knew where he was. Did she know he was in the hospital? Did she know how to get there?

Natalie got dressed and went to comfort him. At least during the phone call it sounded as though he were making sense. He was talking coherently, even though he was confused about his situation. He had the memory problem again. He can't remember what's happened or where he is. Poor Simon, it must be awful for him to go through this disorientation every time he wakes.

Now I'm worried about Natalie. She's out in the dark. It's late. She's walking on her own on the streets of Sydney, and the area we are in is not the most salubrious! I'll worry until she gets home. I put the television on for some company because there's no way I'll be able to sleep until she gets back.

When Natalie came back hours later, her news was mixed. Simon was very upset, and it took her a long time to convince him that he was safe, and he could relax. The good news was that he had been talking in sentences, making conversation and making sense, even though he was still using the wrong word in the wrong context here and there.

He thought he'd been mugged because he didn't have his phone and wallet and watch. He said he needed to call everyone to let them know where he was. He couldn't understand how all these strangers, (the hospital staff), knew everything about him, or why they kept asking him to tell them his details.

He is obviously remembering the PTA questioning, and we took that as a good sign that his short-term memory is improving.

He knew he was in Sydney, which is the first time he'd been aware of this fact without being reminded of it.

'You've been in a car accident, Simon.' Natalie gently reminded him.

'Yeah, I know. But that was ages ago!' he insisted.

'Yes, it was, honey,' she reassured him soothingly, 'but you are pretty broken up and had a big bump on your head. So you can't remember things properly. But you are getting better.'

He was extremely upset and wanted to come home with Natalie. 'Why do I have to stay here?'

'They're going to fix you up here.' She looked at the night nurse on duty by Simon's side. 'Remember Raphael? He's helping you. He's looking after you, and you have to do as he says, okay?'

'He's a good bloke, Raphael. He's the one who phoned you.'

Raphael nodded. 'I'm sorry, Natalie. I didn't want to freak you out, but he wanted to hear your voice. I thought that would be enough, just a call, you know?'

'That's okay. Anytime he needs me, ring me. He's my husband. I love him. Course I'm going to come to help to calm him.'

Throughout their long conversation, Simon referred to Raphael by name. He hadn't remembered the name of any member of staff before. He could remember being questioned, and when Natalie talked about our earlier visit with Ruby, he could remember us being there, but couldn't remember any details about it.

She was eventually able to calm him and left him sleeping soundly. She arrived home at 11.30pm. Not late by normal standards, but we were in the habit of going to bed around 8.30pm because Ruby woke so early and we had exhausting days.

We briefly discussed the implications of this new development. Is he emerging from PTA at last? Were we beginning to see the Simon that we know? He was really trying to remember things, forcing his brain to recall what Natalie was telling him.

'It's so hard,' he told her as he struggled to remember.

'I know darling,' Natalie said, 'you are getting better now, but you're going to be confused for a while until your head starts to mend. Please just try to stay calm and do what the doctors and nurses tell you. I'm just around the corner if you need me, and I come to see you every day.'

We talked for a little while but we were both eager to get back to sleep. Even though Simon had been distressed; we took it as a positive turn of events. While realising that we still had a long way to go, for now, at long last, it looked as if Simon was on the right road.

DAY 16 Monday 14th July

This morning, Ruby has a runny nose and glassy eyes. Her head is warm too. I'm staying at the apartment, keeping her inside and warm. Our plan was to take her to see Simon every day, but we can't risk giving him an infection, so for now Ruby is confined to home.

I got a text through from one of my girlfriends. We are a group of eight ladies who all went to school together, and although we weren't close as youngsters, a school reunion in our forties gave us the opportunity to get to know each other in middle age. We now meet regularly and have holidays and weekends away. We have celebrated major milestones together. We have shared the proud joy of our children's graduations, engagements, weddings, and our grandchildren's births. We've also shared grief at family bereavements and illnesses. We support each other through good times and bad, but generally we just have a ball when we meet.

I miss them already, and I've only been away for two weeks. I was in the middle of trying to book us an autumn break when I was called away, so I left them in the lurch, with nothing confirmed. The text asked when I would be back so they could arrange something for my return. I would have to let them know that I might be away for months and tell them to go ahead without me. I'll have to try to get on the Internet and let them all know the situation. I can't put much detail on a text, and I think my last one, *'Simon ok, but has a long way to go,'* doesn't really explain the last two weeks very well.

I'm starting to miss home. I miss Paul, my family and friends. I miss my garden, my work, and all my normal daily routines that make up my life. But all those things will be waiting for me when I get back home. When Natalie can cope without me. When Simon gets back to his home and wants to have his wife and child to himself. When I become a useless spare part and no longer needed. When? I have no idea when that might be.

Natalie came home at lunchtime with no news of Simon's move to the ward. It could be today, but we have to wait for a bed. He had a different psychological test today and did quite well. He was shown some pictures and asked to describe what he was looking at. One showed a woman standing at a kitchen sink with a huge pile of dirty dishes overflowing the counters. A child was behind her, balancing precariously on a stool while reaching for a biscuit tin on the top shelf. Various other chaotic images were in the same picture. Simon inspected the picture closely and said at last, 'Looks like one disorganised housewife to me!'

Natalie had talked with Simon the previous day about the current season of Formula One racing, which had been showing on television. She kept him informed of his hero's progress and told him how well Mark Webber and Brendon Hartley, the Australians, were doing. This morning, he must have mixed that information into his own reality as he was talking about doing the qualifying races and stressing that he would need to go faster if he wanted to keep up with Hamilton.

Natalie was giggling at the things he was saying. He thought he'd been talking with Schumacher and Mark Webber had told Simon not to worry, that he would come good. Natalie showed him a picture of a racing helmet in a magazine she had bought for him. 'That's a good helmet, isn't it?' she asked him.

'Yeah,' he agreed, 'but I don't need to buy anything like that. My sponsors will provide all that kit for me.'

Natalie laughed even more, enjoying his delusion. The doctors had warned us that delusions can be part of PTA and not to be alarmed if he had them. They also advised us to humour him as far as possible.

When the therapist arrived to ask the daily round of twelve questions, Simon asked her, 'Does Brendon Hartley have to answer these questions too?'

The therapist humoured his fantasy, 'No, Simon, just you.'

'Oh, well,' he sighed. 'I guess the Australian public need to know what's going on.'

Natalie had to stifle a laugh. He was having a delusion of being a famous Formula One driver, something he had always fantasised about in private, but he was making his fantasy very public, and it was a welcome light relief for us to laugh at his confused perception of reality. On a serious note, the delusion was providing Simon with a topic of conversation, and he was talking lucidly, fluidly, in full sentences, and he was making very few mistakes.

Over lunch at the apartment, we giggled together as Natalie told me what Simon had talked about. She thinks the delusion has come from the magazines she bought him and the motor races that have been in the news on the television. He knows about this subject because he is a huge fan so it's easy to understand how his dream in real life could become his reality in this PTA stage.

Our spirits were lighter, and we went to King Street to buy wine for tonight. It helps us unwind at the end of the day and is a great aid to a restful night.

Ruby still has a sniffle and still feels warm, so we bought some baby Panadol just in case she gets worse through the night.

While we walked, Natalie told me that she was getting confused by all the conflicting reports and advice she was given at the hospital. Some doctors mentioned that Simon will need immediate neuro-rehab, while others said they may have to wait until he's mobile, before starting brain therapy. Some mentioned moving him closer to home so he can recuperate physically and then move him to a neuro place when he can walk. Others want to keep him here in Sydney.

It seems to us that he has so many teams looking after various bits of him and none of them talk to each other, so Natalie is being given mixed messages. She needs to know what the long-term plans are for Simon. We need to make some plans of our own, but until we know what their plans are, we're stuck. Will they move him back to Byron District until his legs heal? If so, what will that mean for his brain injury care? Will he have to wait for the necessary treatment? Will they know how to look after him in Byron? Will they be able to provide the twenty-four-hour nursing he needs? He still forgets he has broken legs and still tries to get out of bed if there's no one there to remind him. He still wakes confused, not knowing where he is or why he's there.

After our shopping trip, Natalie went back to the hospital, to see if she could find some answers, and I took Ruby back to the apartment for her nap. I'm using the time to write this diary, but I've had enough for now. I'm going to take a nap too.

SAME DAY next entry

Natalie phoned from the hospital, to say they were moving Simon to a ward and because she wanted to be there to help him through this, she would be late getting back to us. I was happy to feed and bathe Ruby and get her ready for bed. We had some cuddle time, reading her new books and making animal sounds to each other.

She loves the penguin and the giraffe noises I taught her. I'm not sure what noises they make, but Ruby was happy with my yip-yip-yip for a penguin, and my slurps as I pulled my tongue out to mimic a giraffe's long tongue.

She was soon copying me, and we were both in fits of giggles at her slurpy giraffe tongue noises.

Natalie and I had plenty to talk about over dinner when she finally made it back, long after Ruby went to bed. Simon has passed his first major milestone by being transferred from the high dependency unit to a normal ward, though his transfer raised a few smiles.

A group of nurses gathered to lift him on the trolley-bed. One of them was a particularly large man.

'I bet you could lift me all by yourself.' Simon said to him. 'You're like seven of these other guys.'

The man laughed good-naturedly as the team transferred him to the trolley and started to push him from the room.

Simon was still playing the part of the famous motor racer, and as they wheeled his bed through the ward full of desperately ill patients, he waved and called out, 'Bye, I'm off now! Ta-ta. G'day.' He nodded condescendingly to all the staff and patients as he passed, treating them all to his royal wave.

Natalie thought he might be using his normal coping mechanism for dealing with stressful situations. Simon always used humour to mask his feelings of awkwardness or embarrassment. But thankfully, the delusion of being a Formula One driver was fading as they reached the ward and he quickly settled.

Natalie was disappointed to find he was in a single room. We had hoped for some company for him, thinking he might benefit from conversation with fellow patients, but it was not to be. However, he was still being lucid and speaking quite well.

He asked if he could have his phone as he was keen

to speak to his mum and Natalie thought it would be a good idea. She asked if she could speak to Carina first, and Simon agreed. She dialled the number and explained to Carina that Simon wanted to talk to her. She advised her to let him talk and not to ask him any questions as that would confuse him.

Carina was overjoyed to hear Simon's voice and Natalie said he did very well, only getting a few words mixed up or saying the odd thing in the wrong place. His mum seemed to take it in good part and played along with his limited conversation.

Then his dad came on the line, and he hadn't heard Natalie's warnings. The first thing he asked Simon was, 'How long are you going to be in Sydney?'

Simon was confused, and he turned to Natalie, 'Are we in Sydney?' he asked, surprised.

One of the nurses on the ward reassured Natalie that once patients came to the neuro ward they improved very quickly. This nurse had seen many patients come through these injuries and in his opinion, Simon was doing exceptionally well. We found his words comforting, especially as he deals with this kind of thing on a daily basis.

We are still concerned, though. Simon is very mixed up. He can't remember what he does for a living today, but he could remember that yesterday. It's strange how the brain works. Will we ever understand it fully? Natalie is also worried that Simon is losing weight. The hospital food isn't nearly as good as Natalie's home cooking, and the portions are small. We may go shopping tomorrow for some snacks and goodies to help build him up.

DAY 17 Tuesday 15th July

Ruby seems better today, so hopefully we can take her in to see her daddy later. I spent the morning with her in the apartment. She helped me sort the laundry, happily carrying socks, from the bedroom to the bathroom, where I was loading the washer. She's such a little darling and loves to help do the chores.

Natalie came back at lunchtime to say the neurosurgeon had been to see Simon and told her that he will be assessed, within the next twenty-four-hours, to see what kind of neuro-rehab he might need. Once they have a clear idea of his needs they will look for a place for him closer to home.

When the surgeon had gone, the nurse explained that Natalie shouldn't get her hopes up of an early move. They would want to keep him on the ward for at least a week as another move would be too confusing for him at this stage. He seemed to have slipped back in his progress, and the staff put it down to the transfer. He only scored five on the PTA test, but Natalie was quick to defend him.

'They tested him just after he'd taken his meds and they make him sleepy, so he wouldn't have been awake enough to answer properly.'

We took Ruby to the park for some fresh air. She seems much better, and her nose has dried since this morning. After she'd played for a little while, we decided to treat ourselves with lunch at a Thai restaurant near the hospital. There are hundreds of Thai takeaways and restaurants in our area. We are spoiled for choice, as long as the choice is Thai!

While waiting for our meal to arrive, David phoned. He told Natalie that Carina wouldn't be coming with them on Friday. He said they couldn't get a flight for her.

Natalie's mood changed instantly. She walked outside to take the rest of the call, out of earshot of Ruby, but I could see her pacing and shaking her head. She was not happy. I asked her what the problem was when she returned to the table.

'Carina is desperate to see Simon and I feel bad enough about keeping her away for so long, and now!' She paused and sighed. 'Well, I'm probably being too harsh on David, but I suspect he didn't try hard enough to get a flight as he doesn't want the responsibility of looking after his confused mum.'

'How frail is she?'

I'd last seen Carina at Natalie and Simon's wedding, and she seemed sprightly enough then. She was dancing with the teenagers until the early hours of the morning, as were most of the family. I couldn't equate the frail old lady with the Carina I remembered.

'She gets confused easily, and some of the family think she's on the verge of Alzheimer's, but it could just be old age catching up with her. She can't walk far and is wobbly on her feet. She's eighty-two, Mum, after all.'

'I hope I do as well as Carina at her age.' I tried to bring a smile to Natalie's face as she looked glum. 'But you can't plan things for Simon's family. They know their mum, and they'll organise her visit. She will come. If I were in Carina's place, I know what I would do. Don't worry about her, she'll find a way, and soon.'

Eventually, I managed to persuade Natalie that Carina wasn't her problem. She had enough to worry about without taking responsibility for her frail mum-in-law.

'You can't help Carina,' I told her. 'You have to let her family organise things.'

We went back to the apartment when Ruby was tired and moaning for her sleep. We settled on my bed, talking softly for a few minutes, but soon we were fast asleep too.

When Ruby woke us she was bright and happy, chattering and squealing to herself in her travel cot. We thought she was well enough to take in to see Simon, and we were sure any risk of infection was gone.

Our visit didn't last long as Ruby soon became bored in the hospital. The whole point of taking her there was to let her see her daddy and to let Simon spend time with her, but all Ruby wanted to do was to run up and down the wards. The last thing she wanted was to stay by Simon's bed.

We did manage to chat to Simon and listen to his ramblings. He half makes sense if you listen, though his terms of reference seem weird. For instance, at one point he was talking about getting a helmet for Ruby to keep her safe.

'Can't be too careful,' he warned.

Natalie asked him what he was talking about.

He told us, 'Accidents happen all the time, you need the hard hat, stop the connections.'

I realised what he meant. 'He's talking about his safety equipment, the kind he wears at work.' In Simon's line of work, he wears a hard hat all the time. 'He wants to keep Ruby safe.'

'That's right,' he nodded at me. 'Can't be too

careful. Accidents happen even if you do the job right.' Then he went on, 'Can't do roofs anymore, it'll kill me. I've killed too many people. They're all dead in here. I'm killing them all.'

I couldn't understand that statement, it sounded ominous, but Natalie explained that he was probably referring to his sense of humour. When he joked with the nurses their reply would have been something like, 'You're killing me!' It was the standard Australian response to a good joke. So he thought he was literally killing them all!

As Ruby was getting fractious, I took her for a walk around outside the ward. After she'd investigated every nook and cranny in the long corridor, poked her fingers into every potted plant and picked up every piece of fluff she could find, I steered her back to her daddy.

The sun had been streaming through the large window in his room, and Simon had become very warm. I watched Natalie close the blinds and begin sponging Simon's brow with cold water. She did these things instinctively for him. It came as natural as breathing to her, to give him comfort. These were the little touches that the nurses wouldn't think to do for him; indeed, I wouldn't have thought about it either, but Natalie did because she loved him. She anticipated his needs and saw to his comfort. The details of her care never fail to move me.

'Now where were we?' Natalie sat with him on the bed and I took a seat in the chair beside them with Ruby on my lap. She took hold of his hand and started talking about their wedding day, or at least Natalie was trying to remind Simon about it.

'Remember all the rain we had? Then when it cleared you went up the hill to wait for me. Remember how you felt? We were so nervous. You were petrified of getting it wrong. You were so sure you'd muck it up, but you didn't.'

I remembered that she'd been concerned that he couldn't remember their wedding day. He didn't remember they were married. She was trying to open the memories by referring to his feelings on the day.

We'd discussed how strange it was that even though his memories were mixed up or missing, his emotions and feelings were still there and still strong. She was tapping into his emotions, and trying to force some connections to work in his brain.

Simon was shaking his head. He obviously couldn't remember any of it.

Ruby moaned, interrupting the romantic moment, and Simon reached for her.

'I wish I could hold you, Ruby. I really want to hold you, but my arm hurts too much.'

I placed Ruby into Natalie's arms, and she held her closer to Simon. Ruby squirmed and didn't seem to know who the strange man in the bed was, but Simon made some baby noises at her and won her around. She gave him a small smile and accepted some of his grapes, but soon tired of him and wanted to go explore again. I decided to take her back to the apartment and let Natalie and Simon have more time to talk.

The manageress stopped me on my way through the foyer at the apartments. We have to move tomorrow to a smaller apartment with only one room. Our time of enjoying a luxury two-room apartment was over. She could see my disappointment and apologised, but insisted that there was nothing she could do. I told her not to worry, and that we would manage. We'd have to.

DAY 18 Wednesday 16th July

Natalie started with a cold overnight. Ruby got over hers quickly, so we hope Natalie will too.

We packed early this morning ready for the move to a smaller apartment, and then walked to the pharmacy to get cold medications. By the time we came back, the manageress was waiting for us with good news. She had juggled things again and managed to let us stay where we were for now. We thanked her profusely. I didn't mind unpacking everything again.

I put Ruby down for her morning nap, and Natalie left to see Simon, so I have time to catch up with this diary before my morning yoga session. I can't always remember to write everything as it happens and I don't always get time, so I'm going to put a few things down now that I might have missed before.

At one point during the last few days, Simon seemed to be talking about the accident. He sometimes initiated discussion by starting in the middle of a thread, as if he were continuing an inner conversation.

'They were telling me to keep still, and I wasn't moving!' he was insisting. 'They told me I was all right. That it was going to be okay.'

Natalie quickly asked him, 'Do you remember the accident, Simon? Is that what you can remember?'

'What accident?' he asked.

It was a short-lived moment and who knows if he'll remember it again.

He still thinks he's a motor racer. He says things like, 'David Coulthard is a better driver than me, but he has fear. Not like me. I have no fear.' Another time he said, 'Donnelly didn't have all this shit when he crashed!' He was referring to the continual questions and hospital routines. He also thinks his own accident happened on the racing circuit.

Yesterday he told Natalie, 'It's a good job this happened before we had kids.'

She was quick to point out, 'We do have a kid. What about Ruby?'

He shrugged, 'Yeah, but she's not really ours.'

Natalie was left to wonder what he meant by that as he drifted off to sleep. The complexities of Simon's broken brain are beyond our understanding, but we worry that his thinking might never be clear.

SAME DAY next entry

Today, Simon thinks he's in New Zealand. He only scored five out of twelve but had near misses on a couple of questions. He got the day right, Wednesday, but he thinks it's June 2006, (it's July 2008) and thought he might be forty two, (he's thirty-eight.)

The speech therapist was encouraging this morning. He explained that Simon is using the most familiar things in his brain to describe and communicate what he needs. So his references to work and car racing when he's talking are quite normal. He's forging pathways through familiar territory to translate the things he wants to say. It's a good sign that his cognitive processes are still working.

Natalie was tired after lunch. I think this cold is getting her down. So I left her to rest, and took Ruby to the park to let her run around in the fresh air. She chased the magpies again and climbed the slide when the birds got bored with her. I took her to the shops and I bought more wine for tonight, after briefly considering not to buy it. We might turn into alcoholics over this, but I'll worry about that later. For now alcohol is helping.

When we got back to the apartment, Natalie was asleep. I kept Ruby quiet in the main room, reading stories and cuddling to make her sleepy again. She was ready for her nap when Natalie got up, and we put Ruby in the travel cot to sleep. I made coffee, and we did a crossword together, taking our minds to other places to give ourselves a break from thinking about Simon. It only lasted half an hour. Natalie was eager to go back to him. It's now 3.40pm, and Ruby will wake soon.

We talked about maybe going to the zoo tomorrow. We had planned to go a few days ago, but then Ruby got ill, first with the sickness, then the sniffle. Then Simon moved to a ward and Natalie felt she needed to be there to help him settle. I told Natalie that I didn't mind missing the tourist sights of Sydney. We were here for Simon, not to sightsee.

I made her I understand that I knew how she felt and if she needed to be with him more, now he was awake, that was okay by me. When she said that Ruby would appreciate a trip out, I realised that probably Natalie did too, but she was looking for an excuse so she wouldn't have to feel guilty at leaving Simon's side for a few hours.

Perhaps we'll go to the zoo tomorrow and leave

Simon to the care of the nurses, but I'm not making plans. We'll see what tomorrow brings first.

There's been no change in Simon, or news about what's going to happen to him. They have moved him to a four-bed ward, so we hope that might help to stimulate him if he has other patients to talk with.

In our chat, last night, Natalie explained that the romantic wedding talk I had interrupted yesterday had started with Simon proposing to her.

'I'll have to marry you,' he'd said.

'You already did, honey.' She'd laughed.

'Well, I'll have to do it again!' he said, adamantly.

Then she had begun to explain their wedding day to him.

I remember that wonderful day so vividly, and hope someday Simon will remember it too. They held the ceremony at the top of the hill on their property. The celebrant talked us through the ceremony, and Simon and Natalie exchanged the formal vows to ensure their union was legal and then they read their own vows. Their hands shook, and their voices wavered with emotion, but their words still stay in my mind and remind me how much they love each other. This love they share is so precious and rare but so obvious to any who see them together.

Simon went first, and he had to take some deep breaths before he could speak as he was so nervous. He looked into her eyes and told her, 'Natalie, I have no words to describe the way I feel about you.' He then said something like, 'You have given me fresh direction in my life. You have enriched my life by becoming such a big part of it.'

I can't remember word for word, but he used words like, 'I will work hard to make your dreams come true,' and he also mentioned that they would have good and bad times ahead. 'We can't expect it all to be easy.'

I remember him mentioning the qualities he loved about her. 'I love your intelligence and your positive attitude,' and he finished with something like, 'I love you because you love me enough to have chosen me to spend your life with.'

I remember Natalie's opening words clearly too. She looked at Simon and told him, 'I can't express how much I love you, or how happy I am to be marrying you today.' She faltered as emotion choked her, but her voice was strong when she started speaking again. 'Though we've known each other for almost four years, it seems like only a few days, and I knew from the beginning that you were my soul mate.'

She also mentioned hard times. 'There will be both joy and pain in our future, and we will face some tough times.' Then she said something like, 'I look forward to growing old with you and to us sharing life's most special moments.' One line I particularly remember is, 'You are all the riches I will ever need, and as long as we're together we will need nothing else.'

She ended her vows by saying, 'Most of all I love the way you love me and I feel privileged to be the one you have chosen to be your wife.'

Tissues were handed out among the guests, and I was proud to be standing by their side with Paul and Katy and the best man, Richard. The words were said with such depth of feeling. They spoke of things not always being easy and knew that they would have tough times ahead. Those words sound very prophetic with hindsight, though I'm sure when they were spoken, neither of them suspected they would have to live through times as tough as these.

Their wedding day was filled with laughter and love, and I will remember it forever. I hope Simon will remember it soon. What if he can never remember that important day? He will have the photographs and the amateur video I made for them, but it won't be the same as the memory he should have in his heart.

Natalie told me that the talk of their wedding day was interrupted again, this time by the medical staff. They wanted to catheterise Simon as he hadn't passed water for some time and they were concerned.

Natalie asked if it was really necessary and explained to them that he would probably drag the catheter out and do more damage to himself.

When they told her how long it had been since he'd peed, she agreed that it was necessary, but asked them to explain what they were about to do, to Simon.

The chap in charge was happy to explain things to Simon and began by saying, 'We need to insert this catheter through your urethra into your bladder and extract the—'

Natalie shook her head in disbelief. She knew that Simon wouldn't have understood a word of the medical jargon in his confused state. She interrupted the nurse.

'Let me talk to him.' Natalie asked and turned to Simon. 'Honey? Listen, these people want to stick that tube up your willy, but they won't have to do that if you can do a wee. Do you think you can do a wee for them?'

Natalie said that Simon got the message loud and clear. His face was a picture of shock and surprise, but he nodded vigorously.

'I think I could do a wee,' he said.

'Will you get me a bottle?' Natalie asked one of the nurses.

They got him one and left him alone. He performed perfectly, and a portable ultrasound of his bladder confirmed he had emptied it completely.

Due to little incidences like this, regarding Simon's welfare and comfort, Natalie feels she needs to spend more time at the hospital with him. She needs to be his carer, to protect him from harm and to help him in the only way she knows how, with love and consideration for his care. To watch her devotion to him and his obvious love for her and Ruby is so rewarding. Today he called them his, 'beautiful girls' and said, 'What would I do without you two?'

'Good job you'll never have to find out, honey.' Natalie replied.

The downside for me to all this devotion is thinking how they'll get through the next few months when Simon is moved to somewhere like Brisbane. With a six-hour round trip backwards and forwards daily, Natalie will struggle to take care of him as she would like to and if he's left to the care of others he might not respond so well. Then after that, when he can finally come home, what will it be like for them? How much of the real Simon can we realistically expect to come home at the end of this?

DAY 19 Thursday 17th July

Natalie is ill this morning. She has a headache and chills. She should stay away from Simon because of the risk of passing the virus on to him, but I think it will take more than a cold to keep her from his side.

Ruby woke us at her usual 5.30am, so we're all pretty tired again. It's cold in Sydney today. The weather forecast predicted a high of ten degrees, so it's not a good day to go to the zoo. However, we do need to go shopping. Ruby needs more nappies and the fridge and cupboards are bare.

We daren't buy too much at a time as we never know from one day to the next where we might be. The staff at the hospital can't seem to make their minds up when or where Simon will be moved and it's so frustrating not knowing. We think it's a safe bet that he won't be moved until after the weekend now, so we can shop for supplies for a few days at least.

Last night we treated ourselves to a Thai takeaway and had it delivered to the door after Ruby went to bed. We discussed the latest disappointments while we ate.

Simon is still in his delusional world of car racing. He's been talking of sponsorship deals and qualifying times. Natalie tried to steer him back to reality by talking about his workmates. 'Greg and Sam rang today to see how you're doing. Do you remember them?'

'Yeah,' he said.

'How do you know them?' Natalie pushed the point.

'I work with them.'

Natalie thought she was making progress and continued. 'Where do you work?'

He knew the right answer so Natalie felt she was

getting somewhere, but then he said, 'But, you know, Greg's a crap driver!'

He scored five out of twelve today, so that was another disappointment and when the therapist started asking him some other questions, he didn't do well on those either. He was asked to say as many animals as he could think of in thirty seconds.

He began well with, 'Elephant, octopus, err…' Then he came out with, 'artichoke.'

Natalie stifled a giggle as Simon struggled to find the names of animals in his fuddled brain.

'What about our animals?' She tried to give him some help. 'What pets do we have?'

'What pets?' He couldn't remember his beloved dogs today.

After the test was over, she talked to him about Max and Sasha and he seemed to remember them. 'And there's Puddy the cat, remember him?'

Simon nodded.

'Have we got any other animals?' she asked.

'No I don't think so.'

'How about the horses?'

'Oh yes,' he remembered them. 'Chico and Smoky.'

'That's right, but what about the big bay. What's he called?'

Simon seemed to really concentrate before he grinned and said, 'Wallace!'

'Well done!' Natalie praised him. 'What about the chucks?'

'Have we got chucks?'

Natalie nodded at him and watched his face light up as a memory came to him.

'I learned to weld when I made the chuck house.'

Natalie was so pleased he'd remembered this small detail. The chuck house was his latest project and he only finished it a few weeks before the accident. They got the chickens a few days before the accident, so it was good that he could remember building the henhouse.

At that point an elderly patient walked by. He was dressed in a hospital gown with his naked bum hanging out of the back. Natalie averted her eyes, but Simon called out to him, 'Did you have a car crash too, mate?' and added, 'Hey, we can see your bare arse!'

The funny side is wearing thin with Natalie now and she finds it difficult to keep humouring him. She just wants Simon back, the real Simon, so she can talk with him properly. So she can have a normal conversation with a husband who has compassion for others and would never have been so insensitive to point out a bare behind so loudly in public.

She's gone off to the hospital this morning with her shoulders hunched. She has that tired-eyed look about her. It's so hard to watch her suffering like this. As hard as it is for her to watch Simon, I suppose.

This morning she told me she'd dreamed about Simon. He was in hospital with his broken legs, but he had no brain injury. He was talking properly and they were making plans for the future. How awful it must have been for her to wake to the reality of this limbo world we're in.

She's feeling impotent, not in control and waiting endlessly for each little snippet of news, each tiny step of progress. It's so slow and frustrating to see him take a step forward then a step or two backward. It's heartbreaking for both of us.

Ruby is our saviour in these hard times. She's our ray of sunshine, even when she wakes us at 5am on a cold dark morning. She is full of smiles and giggles. She toddles eagerly to the windows and asks for the blinds to be pulled back. She pulls at them and turns to look at us to help her. She can't wait to start watching the aeroplanes coming in to land. The apartment is under the flight path to Sydney airport and planes of all sizes and shapes go over regularly in the morning and again in the afternoon. Ruby loves to watch them and waves to them all, shouting excitedly when she hears them; running to the window, reaching her arms out, asking to be picked up so she can see them better.

She had a long wait this morning. Sydney airport doesn't open until 6am.

I called my girlfriends this morning. We get together regularly and our monthly meeting in the local pub was scheduled for last night. As this morning *is* last night in UK, I knew they'd be in the pub when I called.

They put my call on speakerphone and it was so good to hear their voices. They seemed surprised that I was planning to be here until September, but I promised to give them details by e-mail soon. I didn't want to put a damper on their evening by telling them how bad things were for us here.

Paul phoned this morning too. He told me about the awful weather in UK. They are still having floods and record rainfalls, hailstones and thunderstorms. It sounds horrendous.

At least it's mainly sunny in Sydney, even if it is very cold.

Natalie chatted to her dad for a while, telling him of Simon's small progress, the disappointment and sadness clear in her voice. She told him we were hoping to find out something today, but we've been hoping all week for news of the impending move to goodness knows where, and still we don't know anything.

I talked with Paul about his plans for the weekend. He's working in Edinburgh for the next two days, so he's going to call in on some friends who live in Glasgow. I know they'll cheer him up.

I worry about him being lonely and I know he'll be struggling with running the house and organising paying the bills. We have drifted into a natural division of labour through the many years we've been together. He has the brains for computer and the brawn DIY. My brain is more comfortable with accounts, and my physical contribution to the teamwork is a little gardening and housework. We juggle things perfectly between us, but now he has to do it alone, with no help from me, as I'm too far away to do anything but offer advice.

It just occurred to me that we are a very similar couple to Natalie and Simon. Natalie does all their paperwork and Simon does the physical and practical work. Now Natalie will have to take over Simon's role, just as Paul has to take over mine. I know Paul will cope, he's a resourceful man, but he will be so lonely. Natalie will cope too, but the loneliness will be strange for her. Simon is still here, but he's not really with her yet.

Paul is planning to come over as soon as we know what's happening with Simon. He has to renew his passport as it runs out in October and he needs six months on it to come to Australia, so as soon as he gets the new one, he can make his travel plans.

We should know more about our situation by then too. I miss him so much, but only when I have time to think about it. Most of the time I'm too busy entertaining Ruby and keeping us all fed and clean. It's not much, I know, but it seems to fill my days.

Between cooking and washing, shopping and playing with Ruby, my days are exhausting, and my nights, well, I'm so tired I fall into a dreamless sleep when my head touches the pillow now. I am sleeping through the night at last and even when I wake in the small hours, I can usually go back to sleep pretty quickly. I have to really try hard to stop my disturbing thoughts from keeping me awake, but the last few nights I did really well.

I hope Natalie is sleeping as well as I am, but I suspect she's still having problems. She looks worn out most of the time and I wish I could help her more, but Natalie needs more than my help for her mental welfare, she's under such enormous strain.

SAME DAY next entry
I got a call from Natalie to take Ruby to see Simon. I packed strawberries and sultanas to help keep her at Simon's bedside; snack bribes always work with her.

I was surprised to find Simon out of bed, sitting upright in a chair, with his legs down. He had no bandages on his head and the scar was visible above his left ear. Apart from looking thin in the face, he looked fine.

He seemed more like the Simon I remembered and I think Ruby thought so too. He was so pleased to see her, but disappointed that he couldn't hold her. He tried a few times, but she was too wriggly and she squirmed to get down. He didn't have the strength to hold her. His right arm is still weak because of the broken shoulder blade.

Ruby wasn't too sure of this strange new daddy with funny looking hair. Half his head was shaved for the operation, and now he looks odd as his hair is lopsided.

Ruby is always unsure with strangers at first, what small child isn't? But with the right encouragement, I knew that Ruby would come round. I got out the strawberries and sultanas to tempt her and gave some to Simon so he could try to coax her to him. She took a couple from him, before toddling off down the ward.

I spent the rest of our visit chasing Ruby up and down the corridor, keeping her from harm and out of the way of the staff and patients. It was exhausting!

Simon soon tired and asked to get back into bed, but was told he had to try to stay sitting for a little longer. They wanted him to be upright so his insides would function better. Our lungs and digestive system are designed to work when in an upright position and when the body moves around they work best of all. Simon's insides were sluggish due to his extended prone position and his immobility, so they were trying to get him to help in his own recovery by forcing him to stay upright.

He didn't like it.

He complained and moaned that he was uncomfortable. He told them he had pain and still they made him sit upright. Natalie started to get angry on his behalf and thought they were being cruel, but when she went to ask if he could be put back into bed, she was informed that due to staff shortages there was no one available to move him. That really fired her up and she demanded, in the nicest possible way, that someone be made available quickly or she would move him herself!

Shortly after her visit to the desk, a social worker came to see Natalie. She had news for us. Natalie moved outside into the corridor to talk with her away from Simon. I could overhear snippets of the conversation while Simon tried to talk with Ruby.

It seemed they were looking to move Simon to a place six-hours drive from their home. She told Natalie it was an excellent rehabilitation centre.

'You might as well keep him here!' I could hear the desperation in Natalie's voice. She was close to tears with frustration. 'We can't go there, it's miles away. We'd have to relocate again to the middle of nowhere.'

Natalie explained the details of this conversation to me later. The social worker tried to clarify the problem they were having in finding him a suitable place to go. He still needs twenty-four-hour supervisory nursing care and some hospitals can't take him, as they don't have that facility. They looked at the Gold Coast and the Princess Alexander Hospital in Brisbane, but they won't take Simon until his physical injuries heal and he can walk again. Other places will take him in a wheelchair, but only when his PTA score improves. He's still only scoring between five and eight out of twelve. He needs to score twelve out of twelve for three consecutive days before he's considered well enough to have normal nursing care.

They talked in the corridor for ten minutes or so, discussing the options. I stayed with Simon, distracting him from Natalie's conversation by giving him more sultanas to feed to Ruby. He tried his best to coax her, but she wasn't going anywhere near this funny-looking fellow with bandages on his legs and lopsided hair.

I could see he was in pain. His face was pale and his eyes darkened as he winced.

'Are you uncomfortable, Simon?' I asked him.

'Yeah,' he said. 'I want to get back into bed.'

'I know. Maybe they'll let you get back to bed soon. Try to be patient a little longer.'

'I haven't been in bed since shower time,' then he added, 'haven't been showered since I got here.'

I wasn't sure if he meant he hadn't been showered since he got to the ward, or he hadn't been to bed since his shower. I didn't get chance to ask as Ruby ran off down the ward and I had to run after her.

I took Ruby home when Natalie came back to us, as she was getting irritable. She was bored and wanted the freedom to play without having me at her side to keep her from harm. I gave her some lunch and played with her before putting her to bed for her afternoon nap.

Natalie didn't get back for lunch until two hours later. It took them that long to get around to putting Simon back into bed. He was exhausted, but she had waited until he was fast asleep before leaving him.

She explained what the social worker had discussed with her.

'They might move him to Byron if they'll take him,

then on to the Princess Alexander at Brisbane when he's up on his feet.'

'Do they have the facilities in Byron for him?'

We'd already discussed this and decided that if they didn't have the specialist nursing care and therapies that he needed, he would be better off staying here in Sydney.

'They have neuro-rehab outpatients there and they reckon I can talk to the guy who runs it and he'll see Simon and me and we can all work something out while he's in Byron.'

'Let's hope they agree to take him.'

I thought it sounded a bit loose and disorganised, but I didn't understand how the Australian health service worked, so didn't say too much.

'He called his mum again today.'

'How did that go?'

'She told him she wants to come see him soon.'

'David and Joseph come tomorrow; do we know what time they arrive?'

'About 10am, I think. I asked Simon if he could remember who was coming to see him tomorrow and he said, "David and Katy, no David and..." I told him it was David and Joseph and he said, "Yeah, that's right. David and Joseph." He said it like he'd remembered!'

Natalie was happy that Simon was trying to remember and took each tiny step forward as a sign of his improvement. However, there was more information for us to digest and she told me what else had been discussed at the hospital.

Simon would be at risk of having an epileptic fit for the first six months after brain injury. He'd been on medication to prevent fits since the accident, but they had taken the decision to stop the medication to see how he goes without it. It seemed pointless to continue the meds if he didn't need it as the side effects aren't good. If he has no fits within the six months, that will be great, but if he does, they can work on getting the medication right for him. In the meantime, he won't be able to drive or operate machinery. He won't be able to go up in a cherry picker or climb scaffolding, so he won't be able to do his job. When he's well enough to return to work, he may have to do light duties, but that will not make Simon happy. Light duties drive him crazy!

They told Natalie that they tried him without a twenty-four-hour nurse last night, as he seemed so settled, but he got out of bed! Fortunately they had taken the precaution of lowering the bed almost to the floor and he didn't hurt himself, thank goodness. They found him on his hands and knees looking for the toilet. So the twenty-four-hour watch is back on.

We napped again this afternoon and Natalie decided she was too tired to go back to see Simon in the early evening. She phoned the hospital and spoke to him instead. He was fine about it and she explained how tired she was due to the nasty head cold she was suffering with. He was glad she had called, but said he would be okay if she didn't come until the morning.

'You go to sleep, honey,' she told him. 'That way the morning will come sooner.'

I was reminded of the times when she was little and I said similar things to her. On Christmas Eve and the night before holidays, when she was over excited, I'd tell her that the morning would come faster if she closed her eyes tightly and went to sleep. She was talking to Simon like a child and it had happened so naturally. I became suddenly aware of her subtly changing role. She was Simon's carer, more his mother than his wife. I hoped this state of affairs wouldn't last for long.

DAY 20 Friday 18th July

Natalie did some calling around today, to the insurance people, the tow-truck company and to Martin. Slowly, all the practical problems are getting sorted. The insurance people will visit the wrecker's yard and Martin can collect the personal items from the ute.

Martin also offered to take photos of the wreck for the family album. 'It might be interesting to show Simon,' Martin suggested.

Natalie agreed, 'Yeah, but I don't think I'll be showing him anytime soon.'

When she finished her calls we talked, and she told me more about the conversations she'd had with Simon yesterday. 'We talked about the accident and he asked what had happened.'

'Was I in the Rodeo?' (The utility vehicle.)

'Yeah, that's right.' She told him, relieved that he no longer thought he'd been on a racing circuit.

'Were there some bikes following me?'

She smiled and sighed. 'No, no bikes.'

'Who was following me?'

'No one followed you. You were following me, do you remember?' She said he was really concentrating and was trying to remember, so she encouraged him. 'We'd just been to the police station to pick up our gear that they found from the robbery.'

'Oh, yeah, the police station.' He seemed to remember that bit. 'So how did I end up crashing?'

Natalie began to tell him, 'You pulled out to overtake, then changed your mind and pulled back in. The back end slid out on you and you hit a tree.' She kept it simple. She didn't want to distress him too much and he was already starting to get upset about the little she *had* said.

He had a tear in his eye and he shook his head. 'I can't believe I did that.' He was accepting the facts, digesting what Natalie had told him and letting it sink in. 'How come I'm here?'

'In Sydney?' Natalie made sure she knew what he was asking.

'Yeah, how come?'

'You got smashed up pretty bad. We had to fly you down here to get fixed.'

'To the RPA?' He remembered the name of the hospital.

'Yeah, the one they do the television programme from sometimes.'

'What about the ute?'

'It's a write-off. Nothing left. You were very lucky to get out alive. The insurance will cover it. We can get another one,' she reassured him.

Natalie felt happy about this conversation. Simon was trying to remember and he was talking about the facts without getting them mixed up with his dreams. It seems as if he's made some kind of breakthrough and we had our fingers crossed very tightly that breakthroughs like this would continue.

The neurosurgeons had talked with Natalie and

explained that the delusions he's been having might be caused by the medication he was taking, but could also be due to the brain injury and the fact that he hadn't come out of PTA yet. They are changing his meds to see if that helps.

It's early morning, but Natalie is already at the hospital while Ruby sleeps and I'm writing my journal. Waking at 5am makes for a very long day. I'm tired, but that's a normal state for me these days. I know Natalie feels the same. We have no energy and feel drained all the time. My yoga helps. I feel energised after a workout, but I do it mainly to combat the effects of sleeping on the most uncomfortable bed I've ever been in.

Simon's phone just rang. I have control of it to take the heat off Natalie. At first I took calls from people who didn't know what happened and now I take calls to let them know how he's going. The latest call was from one of his workmates, asking if the blokes could do anything to help. He offered to mow lawns and chop wood at the property so everything would be tidied when we get home. I thanked him and said it was a good idea and asked him to do whatever he thought best.

People are so kind and thoughtful. One of the girls from Natalie's mother's group rang to see how she was doing. She told Natalie to let her know when we were coming home, as the girls wanted to fill her freezer with ready-made home cooked meals.

The house-sitter asked Natalie whether she would mind if she did some cleaning for her. She offered to do the onerous jobs like the kitchen cupboards, the oven, etc. Natalie was touched. 'Go for it, Shelley. And thanks,' she told her.

The generosity of friends and neighbours is amazing us. Where would we be without them?

SAME DAY next entry

It's 11am and I've just arrived back from seeing Simon with Ruby. We had to wait ages as they were assessing him for a move to another hospital here in Sydney. This is the first we'd heard abut a brain injury rehabilitation centre close by. At last things are starting to happen.

Simon has to start some physiotherapy exercises on his arm today as they found a blood clot there. They think it was caused by one of the many lines they had to put in while he was in ICU and now he's on more drugs to deal with that and prevent other clots from forming. It's another thing to worry about as the clot could move to his lungs or his heart and cause major problems.

I haven't had the chance to speak with Natalie yet about all these developments. We could only exchange a few words between the distractions of Simon and Ruby. I had to bring Ruby home for another nap. She tired us both out by running around the corridors and now I'm exhausted again.

SAME DAY next entry

David and Joseph came back with Natalie for lunch. They went directly to the hospital from the airport to see him this morning, arriving just after I left. Simon was lucid, so they were very pleased to see him so well. Joseph thoughtfully brought some photographs of his family and of Natalie and Simon's wedding. Simon was blown away and couldn't believe the photos. He still can't remember getting married.

We chatted for a short while over lunch before Natalie left with Simon's brothers to get them settled into the apartment we had booked on their behalf in our apartment block. She planned to go back to the hospital and they would join her there when they were unpacked.

They are like a breath of fresh air. They have very different personalities. Joseph is an artist and is caring and sensitive. He asked how we were coping and if we needed anything.

David is younger, closer to Simon in age and he does everything at speed, even talking. I can't listen fast enough and miss half the things he says. But he couldn't wait to see Ruby, his niece. He has three children of his own and clearly dotes on them.

Simon's brothers brought a different perspective to our lives and I could see the change in Natalie as she spoke to them. She was enjoying the conversation, talking about Simon's family and normal mundane day-to-day topics. Of course, we also talked of Simon and his progress and Natalie had news from the hospital to share with me. They found a place for Simon at the rehab centre in Sydney. That's what all the assessments were about this morning.

This place also provides accommodation for families, at a price, so we're looking at moving there when Simon gets a place. This was a relocation we wouldn't object to. We just have to wait for confirmation from the doctors then we can go ahead.

We will have to stay in Sydney for another two

months, as that's how long they say he'll need to be in rehab. So Natalie will have to fly home for a day or two to collect some things and organise paying some bills, but she can do that while I stay here with Ruby.

Natalie brought a brochure of the place for me to look at. It seems ideal on paper. Set in acres of grounds in the quieter suburb of Ryde, The Royal Rehabilitation Centre looks impressive. It boasts of teams of specialists that can deal with all his problems from his physical injuries, his brain damage, to dietary and psychiatric needs if he needs them.

Simon will have intensive, daily one-to-one therapy and rehab treatments to help get him get back on track as soon as possible.

Natalie has already made an appointment for us to meet the coordinator there on Monday morning so we can assess the place for ourselves.

SAME DAY next entry

This afternoon Simon was delusional again and when Natalie came home she couldn't stop giggling. He must have been watching some television coverage of the new book release and current film of Harry Potter. Simon has seen some of the previous Harry Potter films, so knows the story and the characters quite well.

Today, he has somehow mixed the story of the famous wizard into his reality and now believes he is a wizard in training. He was deadly serious about it too and Natalie has had a hard time trying to keep a straight face with him.

He told Natalie, 'See that man over there?' He pointed to the next bed. 'He's called Dumbledore. Watch

154

closely because he's going to disappear in a puff of smoke any minute.'

Natalie glanced at the sleeping man and smiled. 'Poor fella,' she said.

'How old are you?' Simon asked Natalie.

'I'm eight years younger than you.'

'Well, in one more year you'll be rid of me. I'll be gone. I'll be a fully qualified wizard.'

Natalie couldn't help laughing at him.

'It's clear you're a first year!' he said, pompously. 'You know nothing!' He got quite cross with her for laughing at him. 'You'll make a crap wizard if you don't listen.'

During the bizarre conversation, Simon complained that his feet were cold and Natalie offered to get him a blanket.

'No need. I'll cast a spell. I just need to remember it. Hang on...'

Natalie watched in amazement as Simon raised his hands theatrically and chanted, 'Feet be warm, feet be warm and never be cold again!'

Natalie doubled over with laughter and when she was able to sit up and face him, she asked if he still wanted a blanket.

'No need, I fixed it. They're warm now.'

She laughed even harder and couldn't hide her amusement from Simon. She said she had tears streaming down her face she was laughing so much.

'You don't understand anything,' he told her crossly. 'It's quite clear to me that you'll never make a good wizard.'

'If you're going to be mean to me, I'm going,' she threatened him.

'Oh, okay. I'll be nice then.' His mood changed instantly.

His conversation was erratic after that and when David and Joseph turned up; she explained the current delusion and warned them to humour him. She left them with the parting words, 'Have fun at Hogwarts!'

Natalie is now making the usual round of calls to let everyone know that we now have a plan.

We need to make some arrangements for the on-going care of the house and animals back home, but we can manage all that. Our main priority is Simon. We need to make sure he gets the greatest opportunity of getting the finest care available to make sure he has the best chance of finding his way back to us. This place at Ryde sounds like an answer to our hopes and dreams.

DAY 21 Saturday 19th July

Simon has some very mixed up ideas. This morning Joseph and David called round to our apartment while Natalie was at the hospital and we discussed their visit with Simon.

Simon thought that he was Natalie's brother and when Joseph put him right on that score, he then thought that Paul was Natalie's stepfather and believed she had some brothers. Joseph didn't know much about Natalie's family background and wanted to make sure Simon had things right. I sadly told him that no, Simon was wrong on all counts. Paul is Natalie's real dad and she has only got one sister, Katy. We thought he might be getting Natalie mixed up with an ex-girlfriend from years ago.

The Harry Potter phase didn't last long, fortunately, and he was talking normally to his brothers in the early evening after Natalie left them last night. He was mixed up about the ordinary things in his life, but his conversation skills were improving.

When Ruby woke from her morning nap, we went to join Natalie at the hospital. We talked and joked on the way to see Simon.

'I wonder if he had a good night, or if he's been racing his McLaren all night?' Joseph asked, smiling.

'He could have been on his broomstick playing Quidditch!' I grinned back at him. 'It's so good to see the funny side of all this.'

Joseph agreed and talked of our ordeal.

'It can't be easy for you,' he said. 'You've done an amazing thing. Come all this way and now you have to cope with all this.'

We talked of Natalie's incredible control, her focus and determination.

'She's an amazing girl.' Joseph told me.

'No, she's an amazing woman!' I told him. 'Sometimes I forget she's thirty-years-old, but this has brought it home to me just how self-sufficient and resilient she is. I'm so proud of her.'

'But it's great that you came to help her. That has to make things easier for her.'

'I'm here to help with Ruby, to free Natalie to care for Simon and organise things for him. That's all I can do. I can't help her deal with the emotional side of this. I feel useless most of the time because I'm rubbish at that kind of thing.'

'I'm sure she appreciates everything you do,' he said, kindly.

We talked of family, of loyalties and love, and agreed that Natalie and Simon were lucky to have us all supporting them. When we arrived at the hospital Simon was sitting out in the communal area. Large comfortable sofas are arranged to face a huge picture window overlooking North Sydney. There's a drinks and snack machine along one wall and an Internet connected computer terminal and phone. Almost like a home from home for the patients and visitors.

Ruby played and ran around the huge space while Simon's brothers talked to him and Natalie took care of his comfort. She raised the back of his chair when he asked, gave him her sunglasses, lowered the back of his chair, moved him out of the sun, tucked in his blankets, raised the back of his chair, raised his feet, lowered his feet. It was exhausting to watch her and Simon was unrelenting with his requests.

He wasn't happy. He was uncomfortable. His eyes were hurting. He couldn't see properly. The sun was blinding him.

David and Joseph helped to distract him and Natalie took Ruby for a walk while I settled at the Internet machine in the corner and had time to send a few e-mails. I informed everyone on my contact list about our plans to move to the new place in Sydney, but I couldn't tell them when this might happen. I wish I knew myself.

I brought Ruby home for her lunch and a nap and Natalie wasn't too far behind me. Simon was tired out after having so many visitors and needed to sleep. Natalie was tired too.

Natalie's having a nap now. I think Simon tired her out with all his demands. I'm going to try to read for a while as sleep evaded me last night for a few hours. If I can stay awake through today, hopefully I'll sleep much better tonight.

David and Joseph came back to our apartment later in the afternoon for a cup of tea and a catch up. They seemed pretty happy with how Simon was and agreed that their mum should see him soon.

We all left together and I walked with them for a little way. Natalie went on to the hospital, with Simon's brothers, but without me. I took Ruby in a different direction. We went to the park. She'd seen her daddy once today and wouldn't be happy to be cooped up in the hospital again.

WEEK FOUR: Hopes & uncertainties

DAY 22 Sunday 20th July

It's three weeks now since the accident. We're starting week four, and Simon is still in PTA. This is extremely worrying as it could indicate that the long-term outcome of the brain damage could be very severe. However, Simon scored ten yesterday on the PTA test, his highest score so far. We were overjoyed, but because he'd had so much stimulation from his brother's visit, he became confused very quickly. In his conversations with David and Joseph, Natalie had to keep interrupting to set him right and correct him as his memories were so mixed up.

He thought he'd been working in Western Australia before the accident, but it's more than ten years since he worked there. He insisted, and mentioned people he'd worked with, such as his boss; and he named the company he worked for. He was convinced that he'd been there only a few weeks ago.

At the end of the visit as Natalie was preparing to leave he asked her, 'Where's Natalie?'

'I'm here. I'm Natalie.'

'No, you don't understand,' he insisted. 'I mean the girl I live with. My Natalie!'

'I live with you, honey. I'm Natalie.'

'No!' He shook his head and became quite agitated. 'I mean the lady who carried Ruby!'

'That was me!' Natalie kissed him. 'You're just confused because you're so tired.' She looked into his eyes and saw panic, so she tried to reassure him. 'I have to go now, honey, and you need to sleep. I promise you'll feel better when you wake up.'

'I love you, honey,' he said, accepting her for who she said she was.

It has to be hard for Natalie to cope with him when he can't remember who she is.

David and Joseph left the hospital and went to the airport for their flight and Natalie came home alone. Tonight when we were eating dinner, she told me how much she appreciates my being here. She's said it before, but today I think it hit home, how difficult it would be for her if I weren't here. As if I'd be anywhere else! I suspect that Joseph has been singing my praises and told her what a huge thing he thought I'd done for her. I reassured her that I didn't think it was such a big deal. I had my health and financial security to be able to help her, so it was easy to come and do what any mother would want to do in the circumstances. I told her that I wasn't going anywhere and would be staying as long as she needed me and not to worry about leaving Ruby with me so much, as looking after my grandchild was a bonus for me, not a chore.

She seemed happy with my explanation. I don't want her to think she's burdening me unnecessarily. She has enough to fill her mind, without worrying about her mum.

Tomorrow will be a busy day. We have to check out the rehab place and see what kind of accommodation they can offer us. I need to ring the Australian Immigration department and find out how I can extend my tourist visa. We learned that Simon will be booked into the rehab unit until the first of October. This is a reviewable date and could move forwards or back, depending on his progress, so it's not set in stone.

We have everything riding on this place and the sooner we get him there, the sooner we can all get home. My leaving date is the twenty-fifth of September, so even if he makes excellent progress, Natalie will need help with Ruby for a little while longer after they get home. I won't outstay my welcome, but I will stay for as long as they need me. That's if I can manage to extend my visa.

DAY 23 Monday 21st July

I started with a bad cold last night, and took some of the cold and flu pills that Natalie had got from the pharmacy. My cold seems different to Natalie's virus though as this one has gone to my chest. I have a high temperature, chills, a cough and aching bones. Thank goodness the pills knocked me out for the night. Hopefully, I will be able to function today.

Simon may have had problems sleeping last night. They moved another patient into the ward who is much more badly brain damaged than Simon, and he makes a lot of noise. When Natalie came home last night and told me about this, I remembered I had earplugs with me, (I always take them on long-haul flights, and they were still in my bag.) She went back to the hospital with them, to give him the best chance of a good night's sleep. I hope they helped.

Simon scored nine on the PTA test yesterday, but he was tired, so we took that as a good sign that he might do better after a good night's sleep. We hope his score will increase today. Natalie will be leaving him early this morning as we have a taxi booked to take us to Ryde.

Last night, over our glass of wine, we talked of our hopes and expectations. We hoped the team at the brain injury unit might be able to help us to help Simon more.

I admitted that I felt lost and totally out of my depth with him. I don't know how to talk to him. Do I pander to his delusions, his wrong thinking? Or do I try to reinforce the facts? He is so confused sometimes that it feels cruel to keep correcting him, especially when he is so sure he's right. Which approach is the best one to take? Which will do him most good? How can we best help him?

Natalie said that she tries to reinforce reality, especially when he's lucid. If he's delusional, she's just as lost as I am, but still tries to bring him back to the real world.

I was talking with him yesterday about the rehab place and telling him that Natalie and I are going to check it out and make sure it's right for him. He said he thought it would be good to go there, but he thinks he'll only be there for a few days. I skimmed over that by telling him that no matter how long it turns out to be, Natalie and Ruby and I will there too, real close by, to help him.

'Yeah, well, that'll be good too,' he agreed.

I told Natalie about this conversation later.

'I talked to him about the rehab place too,' she told me. 'I waited until he was in a clear frame of mind and made sure he could understand me.'

I was interested to know how she had dealt with Simon, and how she had prepared him for the move.

'I told him that it will be a long hard road, and he'll have to be strong. I told him that he'd have to work hard and push through the pain and focus on getting better. I didn't want to make it sound rosy for him. I know he'll have to be prepared for this, and it isn't going to be an easy ride, Mum.'

I thought that she was harsh with him, but I kept my thoughts to myself and listened while she went on.

'He had a tear in his eye when I'd finished. He said he didn't think he was strong enough. He said, "I have to get my head right". He seems to know there is something wrong with the way he's thinking, so that has to be another step forward. I mean, if he's acknowledging his problem, that has to mean something, doesn't it?'

'I wonder how he knows there's a problem. It's so strange how the brain works, isn't it?' I couldn't begin to imagine how Simon's brain was trying to function around the injury or what his jumbled thoughts and memories must feel like to him.

'He explained about the other night, when he was asking for me, and I was right there beside him. He said, "I knew who you were, I knew you were Natalie, but there was something I wanted to say and the words were coming out wrong".' Natalie looked hopeful. 'So even the fact that he knows there's a problem will surely make a difference in how he can cope with trying to solve it.'

She was looking to me for confirmation of her theory, and I nodded. 'It sounds as if he's had another breakthrough. His thought processes are certainly coming on in leaps and bounds now, aren't they?'

'Yeah, seems like it.' Her smile was short-lived. 'But he knows that depression will be a big hurdle for him. He got depressed after the last accident, with the bike. He had all this pain and all the frustration of being immobile and he was so scared of becoming a burden on me. He's expecting to get all those feelings again, and he worries that this time it might be worse.

'I tried to tell him that there would be a lot of people at this rehabilitation place who can help him with all of this. I explained about all the various therapists and specialists who are trained to deal with every aspect of his progress, including the depression.'

'The sooner we get him there, the better.' I couldn't wait to get him into the next stage of his recovery and all our hopes are hanging on the promises given by the rehabilitation place.

SAME DAY next entry

Disappointment! The place seems good and looks as though it has everything that Simon will need, but they only have two units, each with four places. The first unit is for patients still in PTA, like Simon, but there are no places available in there and won't be for another three weeks at least. The second unit is for patients who have emerged from PTA. This unit is for patients who have scored twelve in the PTA test on three consecutive days. There is one available place in this unit, and if Simon can attain the scores he needs before someone else takes the place, he can move in. Our hopes of him achieving those scores soon enough are very slim.

Our journey back from Ryde was tense. Natalie was angry that they had dangled the carrot and snatched it away without giving him a chance.

'Why didn't they make it clear when they came to assess him that there were no places yet?'

'Maybe they thought he would improve more quickly, and the place they have would be suitable for him?' I tried to see it from their point of view.

'They know how long he's been in PTA, they know his scores! He's not going to make a miraculous recovery overnight, is he?'

'We don't know that, Natalie. Maybe he will. Maybe that's how this works. What do we know about it anyway? He could start scoring twelve today, who knows?'

'Oh, come on, Mum! We both know that's a long shot.'

So we're waiting again. We're in limbo and still not getting Simon the best care he needs. He really has to get out of the hospital soon. The place is starting to depress him. The food isn't good; he can't sleep and can't get comfortable. He isn't getting any kind of therapy, for his brain injury or for anything else.

Natalie went shopping for him yesterday and bought him shirts and shorts, sweaters and socks so he can feel more normal. She'll take them in for him this afternoon, but I can see from the set of her shoulders that she's not looking forward to breaking the news about the rehab place having no room for him yet.

Natalie plans to see a social worker this afternoon to see what can be arranged for our accommodation. This apartment we're in won't be available after Wednesday of this week, and if we don't have a place over at Ryde, we'll have to move into a one-room apartment here, unless we can find something else.

It's unsettling for us, not knowing where we're going to be from one day to the next. We have to shop day by day for supplies as we don't know how long we'll be here. Paul can't post my pills as he doesn't have a permanent address to post them to. Martin can't post Natalie's bills from home for the same reason. This limbo is causing us all kinds of practical problems and a host of mental ones that we keep shelving. It's enough to have to cope with Simons problems, without our own inconveniences adding to our anxieties.

I have to ring the Immigration Authority today to see what I need to do to extend my tourist visa. I was hoping to do that once Simon was settled in the rehab place, but I can't wait for that now, it might take weeks, and I need to set things in motion because I have no idea how long the process will take. So I'm waiting for Ruby to get tired so I can put her down for her nap.

At the moment, she's playing with the plastic laundry basket. She loves to fill it with her toys and books then climb in with them. She sits in there for ages. Not doing anything, just sitting with her toys in the security of the plastic basket, occasionally throwing a toy out or reaching to put another beside her. She's so funny. She's so cute. I could watch her for hours.

SAME DAY next entry

I've just waited on the phone, listening to piped music, for more than half an hour. It cost me a fortune on the mobile, but it was a call I had to make. Eventually, a helpful lady answered, and I got all the information I needed to enable me to extend my Australian visa. I have to get a copy of Simon's medical certificate and write a letter of support to go with it, giving reasons for the extension. Then I complete a form that I can download from the Internet and send it, with a not very small fee of over two hundred dollars, and then I should be okay to stay in Australia for a further three months. It would be cheaper and easier to fly to New Zealand for a night and come back into Australia for another three months. My tourist visa would allow for this.

Realistically, the form filling is the way to go, so now I have to work out how I can get all the paperwork I need to begin the process.

DAY 24 Tuesday July 22nd

I've been here for over three weeks now, and it still feels as if we're camping out in Sydney. We're still waiting for decisions to be made on our behalf. We still have no control over our future plans, and we're still waiting for Simon to improve so we can move on.

It can't have been easy for Natalie to break the news to Simon about the situation at the rehab place. She said she approached it in a positive way, (how else would my girl have done it?) She told him what a good place it was and how he should get there as soon as he could. Then she explained about the PTA questions and how they have an impact on his future.

'So you see, honey, they're not just silly questions with no purpose. They measure how good your brain is getting. If you can score the full twelve out of twelve for three days in a row, we can get you into the rehab place right away, but you have to do the work.'

No pressure on Simon then!

Natalie will reinforce the issue again this morning and hope he can cope with the pressure. She knows her husband, and she obviously thinks he'll respond to some forceful encouragement. He scored a magnificent eleven yesterday, so he's very close to hitting the target.

Natalie tried to go through some of his memories with him last night. She told him about the wedding again. He still can't remember any of it. He thinks they live in a small apartment and Natalie thinks he's remembering the tiny three-room place they shared in Melbourne, but it could be somewhere totally different and he could even have been sharing it with some other girl for all we know.

Natalie told him about their home, the large property they bought together a few years ago. 'Remember you got the job with the construction firm because my company wanted me to move north to work on a new sales area?'

Simon hadn't got a clue.

'We rented a small place and looked around until we found the house in the countryside near Bangalow.'

'Bangalow! Where the hell is that?'

'It's a small town in northern New South Wales,' she told him. 'We looked at lots of places before we found the right one for us.

'It's close enough to the beach to get there in a short drive. You go surfing there with Martin all the time.' She tried to reassure him. 'We have a lovely place, Simon. I wish you could remember it.'

She showed him some wedding photographs that Joseph had brought for him, pointing out the view from the top of the hill, showing him their house below.

'We have a four bedroom house with acres of paddocks and gardens and a pool.'

'How do we afford the rent on that?' Simon was shocked.

'We don't rent it, we have a mortgage. We own it.' She told him, proudly.

'Wow!' Simon shook his head in disbelief.

'Do you remember Martin and Sally? They live next door across the paddocks.'

Simon said he did remember them.

'What about Samantha and Josh who have the cattle farm on the other side?'

Simon remembered all the neighbours and his friend Richard. He recalled some work colleagues and more friends, but he could not remember anything about their home.

'Don't worry, honey. It will come.'

Natalie had started making plans to go home for a few days to pay some bills and check on things. One more reason would be so she could bring more photos for Simon, she really wanted him to remember their home and the wedding.

I'd arranged for a friend to video the wedding ceremony and I edited the whole thing, added some music and put it on DVD for them. It's an amateur production, but it captures the day. Surely, if he can watch this, it will force the connections in his brain and help him to remember. Natalie also has DVD footage of Ruby's first day at home, of the dogs, the pool and so many bits of Ruby's infancy. We hope they will all help Simon to piece together his fragmented mind.

Natalie didn't get to see the social worker yesterday, so she'll try again today. She did approach the nurses to ask whether the new noisy patient can be moved. She explained how distressed Simon had been due to his lack of sleep. She argued that he was a patient too and needed to be kept calm and stress free. They agreed to move the noisy patient, so hopefully Simon will have had a better night last night.

This morning Ruby woke us at 6am and at 7am, the hospital rang. Simon wanted to talk to Natalie. He was very upset. He'd just woken and couldn't remember where he was. I listened to the one-sided conversation. Natalie told him again about his broken legs, his bump on the head, the car crash. He was asking Natalie if she knew where he was. Did she have a car here? Did she know how to get to him? He was very distressed and disorientated.

We'd been here before. Each time he wakes he can't remember the details of his situation and has to be reminded. He doesn't trust strangers, so he doesn't believe the hospital staff when they tell him what's happened. He insists on speaking to Natalie. She's the only person he trusts.

Natalie talked to him gently and calmed him. She had left her watch with him yesterday so he could check the time for himself. 'Can you remember that I came to see you yesterday?' she asked him. 'Do you remember that I left my watch with you?'

He seemed to remember, now that he had the watch on his wrist to focus on.

'What time is it now, honey?'

He told her it was just after 7am.

'I'll be with you in about one hour. Will that be okay, honey?'

He seemed to agree that it would be.

'I'll be with you real soon. Try not to worry, darling. Try to go back to sleep for a little while. Will you do that for me?'

She was so gentle and persuasive. I was very proud of her and the way she was handling things. She was dead tired, very concerned and troubled at Simon's repeated distress, but she stayed calm and talked to him in reassuring tones, even though I knew she was so far past the simple state of being distraught herself. She was close to the edge of reason but was holding it together for his sake.

Natalie left as soon as she was ready. She needed to see him and reassure him that everything was going to be all right. She'll help him to shower and shave, and she'll dress him. She'll talk to him and calm him and prepare him for the PTA tests by going over the questions with him. I'm not sure if this would count as cheating the test, but Natalie sees it as helping Simon.

The only question he got wrong yesterday was the day of the week. Natalie had asked him previously, and he'd answered, 'Tuesday', with confidence until Natalie gave him a disappointed look and then he quickly changed his mind and said, 'Tomorrow is Tuesday.' He grinned, knowing that he was right, but it didn't count. The first answer was the wrong answer. He later got it wrong on the official test too, but it was the only question he got wrong. Hopefully he'll reach the elusive score of twelve today.

Richard, his friend from home, who was their best man at the wedding, is visiting family in Sydney and is coming to see Simon today. We're hoping he will help him to set his memory cogs whirring. He is also bringing Simon a few home comforts, like Simon's own sunglasses and some clothes.

Talking with Richard about familiar things should really help Simon. He'll be able to discuss their shared interests, men-stuff that mates do together that Natalie has no part of. We're hoping he'll be able to help open up different pathways in Simon's brain.

Linda, Simon's closest sibling in age, called last night. She's bringing Carina on Saturday, and they plan to stay for two nights. Carina will be able to spend some quality time with her son at last. Simon will benefit from seeing his mum too. He will have something to look forward to if he can remember from one day to the next that she's coming, and it will break the monotony for Natalie and me.

Our days are endless and each one is the same as the day before, revolving around the hospital visits, Simon's needs and Ruby's naps and feed times. We live with the constant underlying tension that uncertainty brings. Will Simon continue to improve? How soon can we get him moved? Where will we stay next? What else do we have to organise? Who else could we speak to, to get some answers about Simon? Where do we go from here? These are questions we face daily, but we never seem able to answer them.

It's a difficult time for us, and the strain is beginning to show in Natalie's face. She smiles, but her eyes are sad. Her shoulders droop, and she drags her feet when she walks. Her constant haunted expression is heartbreaking. I'm not much use. I can never find the right words to say to her. I can't find the magic solution to lift her spirits the way she can lift Simon's.

She's so patient and strong. Nothing is too much trouble for her if it concerns Simon's welfare or Ruby's. When Simon is cold, she'll give him an extra blanket and tuck it around him. If, in the next minute he's too hot, she'll take it off with grace and patience. She'll do this thirty times in as many minutes if he asks her to, each time with gentleness.

Her compassion and her caring are endless, but I feel she is wearing herself out. She needs a break.

I'm hoping we can get into the rehab place soon because at least, once he's there, Natalie won't be able to visit him at all hours of the day. Visiting is strictly controlled there, and no visitors are allowed before 3pm as the patients are busy doing therapy sessions until then.

Natalie will at last be able to take time away from him to recharge her batteries. The rehab place should, in theory, be good for us all.

SAME DAY next entry
After Ruby's nap, I put her in her pram and we went to King Street. I went to the Internet cafe, and while Ruby ate biscuits to keep her quiet and happy, I downloaded the forms I needed to extend my visa.

I got Simon's medical certificate photocopied, and I sent a few e-mails. Ruby was getting bored by then, so I gathered my papers, paid at the desk, and went back to tackle the next item on my list of things to do.

I went back to the apartment block and spoke with the manageress. I told her of our predicament and explained that not knowing where we were going to be from one day to the next was adding to the strain and it would really help if she could give us some assurance. She sympathised and checked her books.

'I can do some juggling and maybe keep you in the same place for another week, how would that be?'

'Excellent, that's great news. Now for the other thing I need to ask you. Simon's mum and sister are arriving on Saturday and will need a small apartment for two nights. Do you have one available?'

She said she may have one, but advised me to check later in the week. Again, nothing was certain!

I went back up to our apartment. I don't like to take Ruby to the hospital before Simon is ready as it means we hang around waiting, and she soon gets bored. So I made coffee and let her play with her toys. When I say toys, I use the term loosely. She has three rattles of various designs that I threw into my suitcase because they were small and easy to carry. I also packed a small cuddly cow that I found at the side of Natalie's bed and a small soft zebra that I'd seen Ruby playing with.

Since we've been here, Ruby has taken to playing with anything she finds and now her toy collection includes plastic serving spoons, spatulas, potato mashers, my shoes, empty cereal boxes, the laundry basket, an empty nappy box and her favourite toy, some stacking eggcups.

While she played, I read through the forms I'd downloaded and printed and found that I don't have to apply for the extension to my visa until the beginning of

September as it only takes a couple of weeks to process. That is a relief as it's one less thing to worry about for the time being.

Natalie called eventually, and I took Ruby to see her daddy. He was washed and dressed, shaved and fresh and was sitting in a regular wheelchair for the first time. He looked like his old self, and it was clear that Ruby recognised her daddy this time.

We chatted about the rehab place and had quite a normal conversation with him. He did say a few off-the-wall things about motor racers being better off than bike riders, like poor Casey Stoner who died. I tried to remind Simon that Casey Stoner was not dead. He is still riding Moto GP, but my comments might as well have been addressed to the wall. He simply didn't listen to me.

I witnessed more of his fanatical behaviour today. Apparently this is a classic symptom of brain injury.

We were sitting in the communal area, and the sun was streaming through the huge picture window. The bright light was bothering Simon, and he asked to be moved about six times in five minutes, each time he only wanted to be moved a fraction of a turn to satisfy him. Natalie suggested they walk to the other end of the corridor and sit by the back window. So we moved to the shady side of the building.

Still Simon complained that he wasn't in the right spot, and he couldn't see properly. The light wasn't right, and she had to move him again, and again, and again. He was getting quite annoyed with Natalie for not understanding his needs and his language turned loud and blue. I felt so sorry for her.

It's hard to watch this behaviour and so difficult to stand by uselessly while Natalie takes the verbal abuse with supreme grace and patience.

When the nurse came to check his blood pressure, temperature and heart rate, she asked him a few questions to prepare him for the PTA test. He got some of them wrong, and he tried to explain to us *why* he'd got them wrong.

'You're pushing me. No! You're putting the pump on me.'

I asked him, 'Do you mean were putting too much pressure on you, Simon?'

'Yeah, you're all putting pressure on me. I can't have my lunch if I don't get them right.'

If only it was just his lunch at stake.

I brought Ruby home for her lunch and a nap and almost collapsed from exhaustion.

My cough and cold symptoms are getting me down, and now Ruby seems to have started with the same kind of cough.

Sydney viruses are getting us all and being cooped up together doesn't help. I thought we might be picking up these bugs at the hospital, and we know we should stay away from Simon while we're ill to stop the spread of infection, but Natalie can't stay away, and I'm too tired to argue when she asks me to bring Ruby. I do my best to protect Simon. I don't get too close, and I walk away from him to cough, into a tissue, to reduce the chance of passing it to him.

When Natalie came back from the hospital, she was exhausted too. She was totally worn out both physically and emotionally. She explained some details about the reason for the early-morning phone call she'd taken from the hospital. The hospital phoned because somehow Simon had managed to get out of bed and was packing his stuff to leave. He was determined to go home, even though he didn't know where home was. Who knows what damage he might have done to his feet by standing up? Goodness knows what had happened to make him so determined to leave.

It looks as though we are entering a less desirable stage of his recovery. He's angry and stubborn, impatient and has no tolerance. I hope this stage doesn't last long, I don't think we could cope.

Natalie made some calls after lunch. One call was to the insurance company to discuss some details about the wrecked ute. Another call was to Shelley, the lady who was kindly house-sitting for Natalie. She was leaving, after staying for three weeks. She'd been a great help and was still being thoughtful. She'd filled the freezer and pantry with food for when we got back and even remembered to stock up on animal food too. People like Shelley are pure gold. Natalie was so grateful for her kindness.

Another call was to the airline company to check out flights at the weekend. Natalie was planning to go home for a night to see the animals and sort out some paperwork and pay some bills. She needs to see the neighbours, make sure the horses and dogs are okay and check through her pile of post. She's using the visit from Linda and Carina to her advantage. They can visit Simon and take over for a couple of days, so he won't miss her so much when she's away.

I want her to stay up at home for two nights. She needs a break from Simon, he is wearing her out, but she won't hear of it.

'I need to come back for him. I can't leave him for so long.'

Her love for him is so strong. A lesser love would be crumbling already, and I worry how this love of theirs will survive. They have such a long way to go. I sometimes worry that Simon won't return to us, but Natalie never loses sight of the real Simon waiting for her at the end of this journey. She's so sure, so optimistic that she will get her husband back.

I'm not so sure, though I try to be optimistic for Natalie's sake, my words don't match my thoughts. I can't bear to think what kind of life she will have in the future if his personality changes drastically. How will that affect their relationship? Will she be strong enough to cope with that? Maybe I'm being too pessimistic after seeing him this morning in such an agitated state. He's probably having a bad day, and this will pass.

This evening, we chatted again while getting Ruby ready for bed. The afternoon visit from Richard seemed to go well. His conversation had jogged a few things into place for Simon regarding their home and mutual friends. When Natalie got back to the hospital, Richard had already left, so she missed seeing him, but Simon could remember the visit from his friend and talked with Natalie quite normally about seeing Richard and remembered some things they had talked about.

When Simon asked about the dogs, Sasha and Max, and asked about Martin and Sally, Natalie decided to ring Martin from the hospital and let Simon talk with him, hoping to help Simon slot another piece of jigsaw into place in his mind.

The call was a bit strange, and Simon said a few odd things, but he did know who he was talking to. Martin, on the other hand, must have been left wondering, especially when Simon answered a question about how soon he might be back on his feet, with, 'I don't have much wrong with my legs.'

Thankfully, Natalie was happier when she came home. She'd booked her flights to go home for the weekend. She was leaving us on Sunday morning and returning on Monday evening. She would get two full days at home and should have time to organise most of the things she needed to do.

She spent nearly the whole evening on the phone after putting Ruby to bed. So many people called her. Family, friends and neighbours, were all eager for news. As she talked, while I cleared away our dinner things, I got to hear more snippets of information that she hadn't had a chance to discuss with me yet.

She's still stressing the positive, explaining that she thinks Simon will make a full recovery, but is now admitting that it will take a long time. Some of her friends in Bangalow are planning to visit her while she's at home at the weekend. I hope they don't tire her, she has a lot to do, but it will be good for her to talk with friends and see familiar faces.

One of her friends had a baby on the same night that Simon had his crash. She was in labour when Simon was fighting for his life in the same hospital, though Natalie didn't know it at the time. She wants to bring the baby to see Natalie while she's home. I know that visit will cheer her. They have become close since Natalie moved to Bangalow.

She called to reassure Martin that Simon did indeed have two badly broken feet and wouldn't be expected to walk for at least a couple of months. They discussed his earlier phone call with Simon. Martin had been shocked by a conversation that had seemed odd and surreal.

Simon had diverted to other topics mid-sentence and referred to unrelated events and people that bore no relevance to the discussion. At least Martin will now know just how serious Simon's brain problems are. Martin had plans to pick Natalie up from the airport. He didn't need to be asked to do this; he just took it for granted that he would. He is such a caring man and has a lovely caring family.

We had an early night when we thought the phone had stopped ringing. We called the day over at 9.15pm as I still felt ill with my virus, and Natalie was exhausted from all the emotion of the day, and talking about Simon all evening.

DAY 25 Wednesday 23rd July

We didn't have a good night. Ruby has caught my virus and has been awake most of the night with a fever and a cough. She has a runny nose and couldn't suck her thumb because she couldn't breathe at the same time as suck, so she became quite distressed. Fortunately we had the baby medicine to help bring her high temperature down and lots of cuddles helped with the rest. However, Natalie only managed an hour of sleep and that brief hour was filled with nightmares, so she hasn't rested properly at all.

At 5am, the phone rang. Natalie hurried to my room, to take the call, and huddled on the sofa next to my bed in the darkness. As expected, it was the hospital. Simon was very upset. He couldn't remember anything. He thought the staff in the hospital were telling him stories and trying to make him sign things over to them.

Natalie patiently explained his situation, reinforcing the facts of his injuries and the accident.

'You've been in hospital for three weeks now, darling. You had a really big car crash.'

Simon said something to her.

She answered him, 'Yes it *is* something to do with you, honey. It was *you* who had the crash.'

Her calm tone and gentle words were enough to get through to him eventually, and he agreed to try to go back to sleep until it was time for her to go see him.

'No I can't see you now, honey. It's 5am, and I've been up all night with Ruby, she's sick.'

Simon was asking her to go now.

'No, honey, we're not allowed to come in until visiting time, remember?'

Simon argued that he wanted to come to her.

'No, honey, you can't come to us, you're hurt. You have two broken legs, and the bump on your head is quite bad. That's why you can't remember. You're confused, that's why you have to stay in hospital so they can take care of you.'

Simon continued to argue and plead, and Natalie tried to talk him round.

'Listen to me, honey. The doctors and nurses are very good. I've met them all. I come to see you every day, but you can't remember. You've just woken up, and that's why you're so confused.'

Finally, she asked him, 'Do you trust me?'

She listened to his reply, which must have been, 'Yes.'

'Then will you do something for me?'

He must have agreed.

'When you put the phone down, I want you to close your eyes and try to sleep. Try not to worry. Try not to panic. The doctors and nurses are there to help you. Sleep now, honey. I'll come to see you soon, okay?'

Natalie returned to her own bed, and we waited for Ruby to wake up. After her unsettled night, she slept until 7am, but we didn't.

I stared into the darkness, my mind a mixture of fear and regret. I was so tired and ill that my head felt as though it were being crushed. My cough was annoying, and I was aching in every bone. Natalie wasn't ill, but her sleeplessness was guaranteed. She was impatient to go back to the hospital to see Simon, but she was bone weary after being awake all night with Ruby.

When we eventually got up, Paul phoned. He's concerned about our accommodation problems and wanted reassurance that we were settled in one place. He was relieved when I told him that we were okay for now. He's desperate to come over and help in some way. He even looked into doing a work exchange with the Australian branch of the company he works for, but it couldn't be arranged for months.

I was touched that he'd thought along those lines and tried to work out a way to join me, but it was proving impossible. We'll wait until we're settled at the rehab unit and maybe he can come and stay with us there for a few weeks.

Ruby's cough is bad this morning. She's going to be a handful today and will need lots of cuddles and tender care. Wish I was feeling up to the task, I'm so ill!

SAME DAY next entry

Ruby is a darling, even when she's not well. She makes my illness fade into the background. I coaxed her to play, and we giggled and chased each other around. She loves rough play. Being thrown around and bounced on the bed is her favourite game. I'm sure I'm not as rough as her daddy when he plays these games with her, but I think I'm a good substitute.

She watched with interest while I did some yoga and thought it was a good idea to tickle my tummy in the middle of a stretch! So I abandoned my therapy to chase her again.

Natalie came home with the news that Simon's caseworker has been to see her. There is a chance the place at the Gold Coast will take Simon for rehabilitation. They needed his PTA score to be around nine or ten, which it wasn't when they were first asked, but it is now. There's a chance they may have a place for him, and we have our fingers tightly crossed.

It would be ideal for Natalie. It's a one-hour drive from their property, so she could be based at home. She could look after the animals and the house. She could think about returning to work and getting on with her life. I know I'm getting my hopes up and I shouldn't. We've been disappointed so often, we're bound to be let down again. Natalie said that she's trying not to think about it too much for the same reason.

The rehab unit in Brisbane is holding a case conference tomorrow too, so they might come to a different decision based on Simon's current situation and may offer him a place. There's also still a place at Tamworth, a six-hour drive from home, but Natalie's already turned that one down. We'd just as well stay here in Sydney as to relocate to Tamworth.

After one visit from the caseworker, we're thrown into a spin again. I'm beginning to get used to this roller-coaster ride in limbo. We have no control. We're waiting for someone else to make the decisions that will affect our immediate future. These decision makers seem like demented jugglers who throw all the balls in the air at once then wait to see which falls into their hands first.

Natalie spoke to one of the neurosurgeons this morning, who tried to explain to her in simple terms, what had happened in Simon's head. I listened with mounting dread as she told me what he'd said.

He described memory as being like a filing cabinet, with everything neat and filed in sequence, with a labelling system so we can find memories easily when we look for them. The accident had tipped up the filing cabinet, broken all the drawers, spilling lots of the memories over the floor, wiping out any semblance of order and destroying all the labels. Anything left inside the cabinet had been shaken about so much that possibly none of the memories would be in the right sequence and some of them would have labels missing.

'No wonder he has trouble remembering anything!' I was astounded. 'How can anyone start to fix that?'

Natalie shook her head. 'He also explained that Simon will probably have permanent problems with short-term memory. He'll have trouble retaining new information, so won't be able to learn new skills. He'll make a new memory and try to file it away, but because the drawer is broken, it will slip through and disappear.'

'But how will Simon be able to manage if he can't remember anything?'

'That's not all, Mum,' she went on, 'the neurosurgeon said that in all honesty, Simon probably won't get much of that missing memory back.'

'How much memory are we talking about?' I asked.

'They won't know for sure until he comes out of PTA. This chap said that Simon could pick out the odd memory file and slot it close to where it should have been in the cabinet, but his memory will never be the same as it was before the accident.'

She went quiet, and I couldn't think of anything to say. How many years? Gone! All of their shared history was inside the last few years.

'But he remembers the dogs! He knows who you are, and Ruby.' I was trying to remember my conversations with Simon. 'Even me. He knows who I am.' I'm grasping at the evidence that proved the specialist was wrong. 'I don't understand.'

'Well, obviously he hasn't lost every single memory of the last few years, but when I think about it, I guess most of it is gone. He still can't remember marrying me. He can't remember when we met. Can't even remember Ruby being born, and that was one of the most emotional days of his life!'

'He does remember bits, though. Maybe he will remember more with time.' I tried to be encouraging.

'I'm not so sure, Mum. The neurosurgeon said not to hope for too much. We know he has trouble finding the right word when he's talking, and this bloke said this probably won't improve much as it was the language processing part of his brain that was damaged most.'

'You mean he will always have trouble with conversations?' I was shocked.

'That's what this chap said.' Natalie couldn't look me in the eye. 'He said I might never have a proper conversation with him again.'

'You will!' I insisted. 'He's improving all the time and what about when he was delusional? He was talking quite well then, wasn't he?'

I was so angry that this person had shattered Natalie's hopes in one short conversation. What did he know anyway? How could he predict what Simon's future was going to be like? How could he tread so carelessly on Natalie's dreams of normality for her and Simon?

'But mum, he also said that he was optimistic that Simon will emerge from PTA quite soon, but when he does, because of the damage, he might think that his yesterday was many years ago.'

I stopped arguing then. I felt I'd been punched in the stomach.

'Phew, that's gonna be difficult to explain to him.'

I'm getting lethargic here in Sydney. I wonder whether I'll ever be able to return to normal after all this. My typical week at home is three days of working nine to five in an office, but I don't know if I will still have a job to go back to. My part-time work left me four days to enjoy my hobbies and interests of, sewing, writing, and gardening. How did I fit it all in? These lazy days in Sydney are spoiling me. Ha!

The weather here is warming up at last. We just went for a walk to the shops to buy aspirins, cough sweets, tissues and wine. (Can't forget the essentials.) We enjoyed some sunshine, peeling off layers of coats and sweaters as we walked.

Earlier, Paul had told me of the massive flooding still happening in England. We saw some pictures of it here in Australia on the television news, and it was upsetting. The news gives us another topic of conversation, but only briefly. No matter how terrible the world news is nothing can overshadow our constant focus on Simon's recovery. The sooner we can get him into rehab, the faster he'll improve, and the better off we'll all be.

This evening, Ruby didn't settle at all. She reached screaming pitch at 8pm. We managed to eat dinner while she was in the moaning stage. After we had eaten, Natalie brought her to join us, to try to settle her down. Each time she put her back to bed she cried again, louder and with more conviction. I think she was feeling ill and hadn't seen her mum for most of the day and was telling us, in the only way she knew that she wasn't at all happy!

Right at her loudest screaming session, the hospital rang. Simon was agitated and wanted to talk to Natalie.

She left me with Ruby in the bedroom, and went

into the main room to talk with him, but Ruby screamed even louder when her mum left.

I tried my best to comfort her, but she'd had enough of her mum abandoning her and yelled all the more. I couldn't hear what Natalie was saying to Simon, but I imagined it would be a repeat of the same conversation she had with him each time the hospital had to phone her. How wrong I was!

Natalie stormed back into the bedroom and held the phone out, and I knew that Simon was getting the full blast of Ruby's ear-splitting screams of frustration. She stormed out again and finished her conversation rather quickly. When she came back to take Ruby into her arms, I asked her how he was.

'I told him to grow up and stop being so stupid!'

We couldn't talk much until Ruby was settled, but I could see that Natalie had reached the end of her rope.

Eventually, when Ruby was asleep, we poured some wine and Natalie told me about her conversation with Simon. He was upset and angry.

'I have to get out of here. I can't sleep. This place is crap!' he told her.

'How can you get out of there with two broken legs?' she'd asked him. 'You can't even remember what day of the week it is, so how are you going to find your way home?'

'I can't sleep,' he insisted.

That's when she stormed into the room and let him hear Ruby screaming. 'So you think you're having trouble sleeping? Listen to this!' She'd yelled into the phone.

When she went back into the other room, she told

him, 'You're going to have to grow up, Simon, and realise you have to stay in the hospital until we can find you another place. You can't come home until you're all fixed up. Now go to sleep!'

'You bring my wallet and phone tomorrow so I can get out of here!' he demanded.

'I'll talk to you tomorrow,' she told him flatly and hung up on him. She too, had had enough.

When Ruby finally went to sleep, we talked more about Simon's other problems. The orthopaedic surgeons had taken x-rays of his feet. One foot has an unusual lump on it, and this has turned out to be the wire scaffolding holding his small bones in place while they heal. Now that the swelling has gone down, this wire is too prominent and needs to be removed, but can't be taken out until the bones have healed. So there's a danger that the wire could poke up through the skin and could become a potential infection risk.

Today he will have his plaster casts removed and replaced by fibreglass ones. They will leave a window over the lump of wire to keep an eye on it. If it does pierce the skin, it can be dealt with. The surgeon told Natalie that it will only be a thirty-second job to take it out under anaesthetic, but this can't be done for another three or four weeks.

He has some problem with his left eye. It hurts for him to look at a bright light and when he reads, his eyes focus at different points. His left eye seems to be focusing on a slant. The neurosurgeon said this should settle, given time, but if it doesn't he may need to look into it more. That would explain his agitation when we sat outside the ward in the brightly lit communal area a few days ago. Poor Natalie was run ragged by attending to Simon's every whim when he asked to be moved a hundred times to be out of the sunlight.

Natalie told me she met a man yesterday who had heard about Simon. He came to introduce himself as his wife was in the female ward of the neuro unit down the corridor. Natalie told me his harrowing story.

He thought his wife had the flu, and it was so bad that he brought her to the A&E department. They sent her home. His wife got worse, and so he took her back to the hospital. It wasn't flu it was meningitis, and because she didn't get the treatment in time, it damaged her brain. Now she has no memories at all. She can't remember who she is, where she lives or anything about her life. She can't remember her husband, her children, her family or friends. She can't hold any new information in her memory and has to be told every few minutes who she is and what her name is. This poor girl has no hope of any improvement. Even rehab won't help.

This place holds so many stories. I told Natalie of another lady on the ward that I'd met. She had a large scar on her forehead. She told me that she'd been having dinner with her husband and suddenly went blind. By the time she got the words out to tell her husband, she'd gone deaf and then she lost all sense of feeling. Fortunately, she made it to hospital in time to stop the haemorrhage in her brain that had caused these symptoms. She came into the ICU at the same time as Simon and went home yesterday, fully recovered and functioning normally. Talk about life being a lottery!

Then there are Pam and her friend staying two floors below us here in the apartment block. We keep bumping into them on our journeys to and from the hospital. It has been touch-and-go since her husband's triple heart bypass. He's still in ICU and has all kinds of problems, but he's still hanging in there.

'He's one tough fella,' I told Pam last time I bumped into her in the lift.

'I know,' she said, smiling sadly at me.

It was good to see her smile, she'd looked so sad and forlorn the last time I spoke to her.

All our new acquaintances are from various backgrounds. Some, like me, are from different countries, but we've all been thrown together in this place and it feels as if we're reaching out to snatch brief comfort from each other every time we pass in the streets and corridors.

DAY 26 Thursday 24th July

We had a peaceful start to our day for a change. Ruby slept until 7am after her disturbed night, and we didn't get an upsetting early-morning call from Simon. Maybe the short sharp shock last night did him good, who knows, but he didn't ring back and he didn't ring this morning. Hopefully, Natalie managed to get through to some part of his brain that could respond to straight talking. I hope so.

When Natalie got back from the hospital this morning, she told me that Simon had new casts on his legs. He scored the magic twelve on the PTA test, so Natalie was very pleased with him. If he can repeat the result over the next two days, we'll have a chance of the place at Ryde. However, the RPA (Royal Princess Alexandra), in Brisbane are revising their cases today, and we could get a decision from them later. The facilities there are better than the Gold Coast hospital. The Gold Coast rehab unit is ward based and would be no different to where he is now. We're told that the one in Brisbane is a special unit attached to the main hospital, so it will be more like what we saw at Ryde.

The juggler's balls are in the air again. We're still waiting to hear from all of them.

Natalie suggested a shopping trip this afternoon, but Ruby slept longer than usual, so Natalie went on her own while I stayed with Ruby. She woke only fifteen minutes after Natalie left, but she's happy to play with her grandma. I love playing with my little angel. I am so going to miss her when I eventually have to go home.

When Natalie got back from the hospital this evening she was in a very positive mood. Simon had had a good day. He was lucid and remembered a few things, though he said they were hazy.

He told her the caseworker had been to see him and told him that Brisbane had offered him a place. He didn't know any details, and Natalie wanted to know whether they will take him now, or will they want to wait until his legs are fixed? The caseworker had already left, and there was nobody else who knew about the news, so we'll have to wait. Maybe she'll find out tomorrow.

I've taken a sleeping pill. I can't cope with this sleep deprivation any longer, and I'm still so ill with my chest cold. I told Natalie, so she knows I won't be able to help in the night if Ruby starts playing up.

'That's okay, Mum.' She smiled at me. 'You have a good sleep. I might take a pill myself tomorrow.'

DAY 27 Friday 25th July

I did get a good night's sleep at last. I woke a few times with my cough and again with Ruby crying, but each time I went right back to sleep. I could escape from the tossing and turning and give my mind a rest from whirling into the future in horrible permutations of what might be ahead.

It was pure bliss to sleep. However, Natalie was up from 3am with Ruby, so I'll need to return the favour later and let Natalie have a nap.

Ruby had other ideas about afternoon naps today. She woke early from hers, just as we'd got our heads down, so we gave up ideas of sleeping and went to the park instead. Ruby wasn't happy and moaned a lot, she was still tired, and so we came home after a short time. She's a cheeky little imp when she's smiling and happy, but can be a real grumpy-pants when she's tired, like all of us I suppose! We put her back to bed, and after only ten minutes she awoke and was as bright as a button. Oh, what it must be like to be a child again and have the delights of uncomplicated rest.

We got a chance to chat more this afternoon and Natalie told me about her morning at the hospital. She was informed that Brisbane did want to take Simon, but didn't have a bed for him yet. The Royal Rehab Centre at Ryde has been ringing to check his PTA scores every day this week. They desperately want to take him because due to his youth and his typical brain injury, he should be easy to help and would only need to stay with them for a couple of months.

Natalie intends to search the Internet to see if she can find a brain injury rehab centre closer to home. We know it will be easier for us to have Natalie's home as a base instead of living in these strange places. Sydney is supposed to be a great city, but I'm going stir crazy in my little part of it.

I suppose Simon is feeling much worse. He's desperate to get out of the hospital and hates waking to see strangers looming over him. The other patients can wander around freely because they don't have broken legs. Some of them stray into his personal space, which Simon hates. They have neuro problems too and don't seem to have any sense of privacy, or respect for the privacy of others. He says it's like being in a lunatic asylum. So poor Simon doesn't sleep well at all.

Today, Natalie told me, he was very tired, but he did remember bits and pieces about their wedding and their home, so the missing memories seem to be slowly coming back.

He scored ten on the PTA test today. We knew it would be too much to hope he would score twelve three times in a row. So it looks as though we'll be here at least until Tuesday as Natalie isn't back until late on Monday evening. She leaves on Sunday morning, and I can't wait for her to go home. She needs some space to herself and can't get it here.

Carina and Linda arrive tomorrow. I'm looking forward to their arrival, and now that Simon is improving, the visit should go well for Carina too.

Natalie rang Simon after we put Ruby to bed, to check how he was. She was really concerned about leaving him. She had tried to prepare him for her short absence, and it hadn't gone well. Simon didn't want her to go. She was on the phone for more than an hour.

He was insisting that he couldn't take it anymore and wanted to get out of the horrible ward.

Natalie spoke to him kindly, calmly and with the utmost patience. She explained that there were things she needed to do at home. She explained again why he had to stay in the hospital, why he had to wait for a bed in rehab and even had to explain why he *needed* rehab. It was so difficult as most of the time, Simon thinks there's nothing much wrong with him.

She had to go over and over why he couldn't come home; telling him that she didn't have the facilities for him, there was no hoist to get him out of bed, no toilet facilities for a wheelchair, etc, etc. She must have had this conversation with him a hundred times already, and each time when Simon became more upset she became more patient with him. This time, Simon was really distressed. He didn't want her to go and told Natalie he felt she was abandoning him in that awful place that he hated. He was acting like a child and pleading for his mummy not to leave him.

Natalie told him about the possibility of moving to a nicer ward, with patients of his own age whom he could talk to. She'd discussed this earlier with the staff on the ward, and they had agreed to do something about it for him. The ward is pretty bad, because the other patients have far more problems than Simon. We could understand why he felt as he did.

The nurses who do the twenty-four-hour watches are not fully trained nurses. They don't do anything other than call for backup when things get out of hand. Most of them don't try to have a conversation with patients, and to be fair, most of the patients can't hold a proper conversation.

So these nurses read magazines and ignore the patients. We could empathise with Simon, but it was so very hard to watch him suffer.

Natalie ended the conversation by promising to go see him first thing in the morning, but when she came off the phone she was so sad and depressed.

'I'll have to cancel the flights. I can't possibly leave him like this, can I?'

I wanted to agree with her, but I couldn't. I knew Simon was suffering and would miss her tender care of him, but it would only be for two days and one night. Natalie needed a break, but I didn't tell her that. She couldn't see past Simon and his needs, and she was blocking out her own needs. I was concerned about my daughter. She was reaching breaking point. She didn't seem to be getting much support from the hospital now that Simon was on a normal ward, and Simon was very demanding of her time. Ruby wasn't sleeping, so Natalie hadn't slept either. She had to find a way to pay the household bills and organise things at home.

We looked at her options, and we discussed putting the flights off for a week, or suspending them to re-book them later. I suggested that I could fly up and try to do what needs to be done and take Ruby with me, but Natalie said I'd never find all the papers that needed to be dealt with and she'd spend more time on the phone trying to tell me what to do. She couldn't re-organise anything tonight as it was too late to call the airline company, so we decided to sleep on it.

DAY 28 Saturday 26th July

This morning I phoned Paul and told him of my feelings. I explained how difficult it was for me to watch Natalie wrestle with all this and he said that Simon should grow up and see sense, (exactly what Natalie had said to him when she lost her temper with him the other night), but we both agreed that, with a brain injury, that wasn't going to happen overnight.

I explained, as best I could, about the rehab situation and Paul found it difficult to understand why Simon couldn't get a place if he needed one so badly. So I asked him that if *he* found it hard to understand, how he thought Simon was coping as he couldn't get his poor damaged head around it either.

Paul worried that Natalie might become Simon's nurse rather than his wife, pampering to his every whim at all hours of the day or night. I've worried about this too many times. Will she end up with two children to look after instead of one child and a husband she can rely on to support her? It breaks my heart to see her now. She's coping and still holding it together, but she won't be able to for much longer if she doesn't take a break.

Paul shares my concerns, though I warn him not to voice them to Natalie. She doesn't want to hear it anyway and would rise to Simon's defence every time. So I keep quiet and ask for Paul to do the same. All I can do is watch and wait for the meltdown. I know it will happen if she can't get away for some respite.

Natalie phoned the airline company this morning and found she couldn't change her flights without losing a lot of money.

She can change her return flight to an earlier time, so she might look at doing that if she decides to go at all. I hope she goes. She really needs to.

She's at the hospital now, trying to explain to Simon, again, how much she needs to go home. The hospital will have to manage Simon. That's what they are there for. She should let them do their job! I get so frustrated. I can't interfere. Natalie knows her husband best, but sometimes I think she's wrong to put him so high on his pedestal. She's wrong to pander to his every whim. She's wrong to be so patient with his demanding behaviour. It seems the more patient she is, the more demanding he becomes and the more he leans on her emotionally. If she took the prop away, maybe he'd learn to survive on his own. He will have to eventually when he goes to rehab. They won't allow her to be there most of the time. But for now she is his primary carer, spending every minute possible at his bedside or taking him to other places in the hospital in the wheelchair to get away from the pressures of the ward for a while.

I also worry that Natalie isn't spending enough time with Ruby. She often doesn't get home from the hospital until it's time to put Ruby to bed, so Ruby doesn't get to play with her mum. I have a feeling this is the reason for Ruby's unsettled nights. When she's awake at night, she gets to spend time with her mum. I'm sure Ruby doesn't reason it out the same way I can, but my theory makes some kind of sense to me.

Oh well, I knew this trip wasn't going to be an easy one, but it's turning out to be a lot harder than I thought it was going to be.

I know that Natalie is getting frazzled at her edges. I'm just about holding it together inside, but I think one day soon we'll both unravel, and it won't be a pretty sight.

When Natalie came back from seeing Simon she was very stressed. She was upset that nothing was going right. This waiting for a place in rehab is endless. The hospital staff are very unhelpful and don't seem to recognise that Simon's distress is a problem they should solve by moving him to a different ward.

On top of all that, there is no apartment available for Linda and Carina, and they'll have to share with us. This is less than ideal. Carina is a very confused lady and is inclined to wander around at night. As she won't know where she is, she'll bump into things, or get lost. So it looks as though we might be in for a few more sleepless nights.

Natalie knows she's being pulled in too many directions at once, and I'm sure she realises that she's near breaking point. I told her to try to take a break when she goes home, but she says she's going to feel so guilty about leaving Simon. She said she's worried that he'll do something stupid, and the hospital would be forced to tie him down again. Nothing I say will help, so I stay quiet and let her rant and spew it all out of her system.

I think the final straw for Natalie, was when the accommodation for Carina and Linda fell through.

The lady who was supposed be vacating that room had to stay here longer than anticipated. Her husband was at the hospital, but instead of taking him home as planned, he'd taken a turn for the worse and is now in a bad way.

'But we booked the room. The manageress should have told her to get out!' Natalie yelled.

I reasoned with her, 'How do you think she could do that, when the lady's husband is so ill? Come on, Natalie. See sense. We'll manage.'

'I know.' Natalie's shoulders slumped. 'I'm sorry. I know it can't be helped, and I really don't want that lady to move out. How could she? It's just that everything seems to be going wrong for us.'

Something has to start going right soon. It just has to. We can't take much more!

WEEK FIVE: Visitors & fixations

DAY 29 Sunday 27th July

Carina and Linda arrived last night. Their flight was delayed, so we went to bed later than usual. The manageress had given us extra mattresses and clean bedding for our guests, and I made a bed on the floor of Natalie's room and gave Carina and Linda my sofa bed to share. We were all tired. Carina and Linda didn't mind retiring at 9.30pm, especially when we told them how early Ruby would wake.

Ruby was unsettled, but thankfully only woke a few times during the night and didn't wake in the morning until 6.30am. What a blessing to sleep in! I don't think Linda and Carina thought it was much of a lie-in, though.

Ruby was quite excited about our guests, and Linda and Carina were happy to see her. Linda had brought a battery operated toy for Ruby and busied herself showing Ruby how it worked. Ruby was fascinated, and while Linda kept her occupied, Natalie finished her packing and called Simon.

She had made the agonising decision to go home, and I was very thankful. I didn't hear the details of the call, but I guess she made him understand that she would be gone for only one night, and cheered him up by reminding him that his mum and Linda were coming to see him in a couple of hours.

Natalie left me quite a few instructions on what to do for Simon. I hope I can remember them all and live up to her expectations of me.

She told me how to prepare him for the PTA test; to make sure he got some quality time out of bed; to make sure we take him to the cafeteria for more stimulation; get him some of his favourite drinks; collect his laundry; take him clean boxers.

I reassured her that we would manage and told her to stop worrying, but my words went unheard. She didn't want to leave him and simply couldn't let go.

Natalie put Ruby to bed for her morning nap before she left us and was still giving instructions on her way out of the door. I was glad when she finally left, but I still couldn't relax. Ruby wouldn't settle as Carina and Linda needed to use the bathroom and shower, and the door to the bathroom is a shared door to the bedroom that Ruby was trying to sleep in. So I brought her through to the main room and played with her for a while. Finally, Linda and Carina left to visit Simon at 10am, and I could settle Ruby for her morning nap.

The peace is blissful! Linda is like a whirlwind. She talks endlessly and never sits still. She's very entertaining, and I love to hear her chat. She is like a breath of clear mountain air, and in normal circumstances I would have thoroughly enjoyed her company, but in my little stress-bubble here in Sydney, she wore me out. Carina is so sweet, and her quiet nature is a complete contrast to her youngest daughter.

I hope Natalie will be able to relax a little on her trip home. She was so wound up about leaving Simon. She hates to hand control to anyone else, but I'm glad she saw that she really had to go on this short trip. I don't mind taking responsibility for Simon for a few days. Linda and Carina will help too because I still have to look after Ruby and her needs.

Natalie wants me to make sure Simon has been moved to a better room. She made them promise to move him today to a room with people of his own age. I can manage to do everything else she asked me to do, but if the hospital fails to keep their promise, I don't know what I'll be able to do about that.

I have to give Simon some money and take him to buy some drinks and whatever else he might need. I have clean clothes to take for him, and I have to collect the worn ones to bring them back to launder for him. I have everything ready for when Ruby wakes. Linda and I exchanged mobile phone numbers too, so we can contact each other when we need to meet up.

Ruby only slept for half an hour. I think she'd been over stimulated and couldn't get into a proper sleep. So I took her to the hospital to see her daddy and to meet with her auntie and Grandma Carina. We met on the balcony of the cafeteria and enjoyed some fresh air in the sunshine. Simon chatted quite animatedly to his mum and Linda while Ruby ran around chasing the pigeons.

I think Linda and Carina soon became aware of how mixed up Simon was, though. He was still confused about time lines, about where he worked and lived.

Linda took the same line as Natalie and kept correcting him, but that only made him more confused, so I steered the conversation to a topic that he would be able to talk about, which was looking for a new car to replace the ute when he got home.

He knew they would have to replace the wrecked ute and like most men, he could talk for ages about the merits or demerits of various models of car. It was a safe topic for Simon to discuss.

Then Linda talked to him of mutual friends back home in Geelong while Carina was happy to sit with her son and hear him speak. We stayed until lunchtime, when Linda took Simon back to the ward to eat. She planned to take Carina to the cafe while I took Ruby back to the apartment for her lunch and a much-needed nap. My poor little angel was very tired. We arranged to meet back at the hospital later.

When I got in, I rang Natalie to let her know that although Simon hadn't been moved, another guy had been moved into his ward and this young man could speak quite normally. He and Simon had already been talking together. She was pleased to hear this news.

Our conversation was short as she'd just arrived at the house and let the dogs off the leashes. They were busy mauling her and fussing over her. I knew they would have missed her, and I could hear the joy in Natalie's voice as she was talking to them. I could hear them yipping and growling happily at her.

Simon was expecting her to call when she got home, so I guess she'll be calling him now.

She gave him his mobile phone yesterday so he could call her at any time he needed to. This was a risk as he could call anyone at any time and talk gibberish, but Natalie trusted him to be okay with it and it helped him cope and accept her absence.

I took Ruby back to the hospital later this afternoon and met with Carina and Linda at Simon's bedside.

Simon said he was frustrated at all the questions he was being asked.

'They tell me I have to score ten out of ten, but when I do, they change the questions! What's all that about? I don't understand it.'

I asked him what had changed.

'Three questions aren't the same anymore!' He yelled, loud enough for the whole hospital to hear. He was very angry about this, but he looked panicked and scared.

'Is it the pictures?' I asked, knowing that they could be the only thing they would have changed, but I didn't know why they would have done this.

'Yeah, they changed the damn pictures! How am I supposed to get ten out of ten if they changed the answers?'

I went to ask what was going on, but nobody knew anything about it. I went back to Simon and tried to explain about the questions. I told him they were designed to measure his progress, so perhaps if he answered all the questions correctly, they were trying to make it harder to see if he could get even better. I tried to do what Natalie would have done and talked to him calmly, reassuringly, and tried to accentuate the positive angle for him. It seemed to work, and he accepted my explanation, but was still upset that they hadn't told him about the changes beforehand.

Linda and Carina were concerned about his angry outburst and Linda went to see whether she would have more luck than I, in finding anything out.

Meanwhile, I tried distracting Simon by helping him coax Ruby with some sultanas. She sat on my lap and was quite happy for a little while to take her treats from daddy and Simon enjoyed interacting with his little girl.

Linda did manage to track down someone who knew about the PTA tests and they explained to her how the PTA test worked. Linda then tried to explain this to Simon.

'So once you answer all twelve questions, the pictures have to change to make sure you really can remember new information from one day to the next.'

'Sure I can remember, but how can I when they change the answers?'

He still wasn't getting it.

'Simon,' I began, my brain was running out of explanations, so I tried to keep it simple. 'Up until now you have been shown the same three pictures every day, is that right?'

'Yeah, I guess.'

'So you've been getting them right, remembering them from one day to the next?'

'Yeah.'

'Well, now they want to see if you can remember three different pictures from yesterday until today. Do you think you can do that?'

'Yeah, I guess.'

'What did they show you yesterday?' Linda asked. 'What were your pictures?'

'They were the new ones.'

He couldn't tell us what the pictures were.

We didn't know what to make of this and couldn't do anything to help him. However, when the lady came to do the test, we were asked to leave, so we waited in the corridor with fingers crossed. She emerged from the ward and told us that he had scored twelve, and we were amazed. We quickly went back to congratulate him, but Simon was far from pleased. He was not happy.

'She forgot to change the pictures!' he said, glumly.

We didn't understand what he meant and thought he was confused, but Simon was adamant that they got the test wrong. He was so upset and agitated that Linda went to find the person who tested him, to ask what it was all about. When Linda came back, she was very angry too.

The test he had today wouldn't count, as the staff member who tested him yesterday, didn't make a note of the new pictures that had been shown to Simon, and so there was no way of knowing whether he got them right or wrong. Today he was asked to remember the previous pictures that he'd been given since day one, so as not to demoralise him altogether. But this meant that he would have to start again tomorrow to score his three twelve's, in a row, to be considered to be out of the PTA stage.

I was so cross for Simon and knew that Natalie would be livid about this. We had so much depending on the outcome of these tests and one more day of delay could mean the difference of getting a place in rehab or losing it to someone else on the waiting list.

I asked Linda to look after Ruby while I went in search of some answers. I found the therapist who did Simon's test and asked her if she realised how important the outcome of these tests were for Simon. She said she understood but stressed that one more day wouldn't make much difference. She also pointed out, quite arrogantly, that there was no guarantee Simon would have scored top marks today even if he *had* been shown the correct pictures. Bloody hospitals!

I came home early and left Linda and Carina to spend more time with Simon. Ruby needed a nappy change, and it was close to her dinner time. When I left, Linda was quizzing Simon about the new pictures he had to remember for the test tomorrow.

'Try to make up a story in your head to remember them. A bird, you could think of being as free as a bird...'

Linda and Carina didn't return until after 8pm, and we ordered a Thai takeaway for dinner. By the time it came, Carina wasn't hungry anymore, and she didn't like the Thai food, so I made her some toast and tea. I came to bed, leaving them watching television as I am dead on my feet.

DAY 30 Monday 28th July

Ruby had quite a good night. She was awake for about half an hour between 3am and 3.30am but then slept until 6.30am. Linda offered to take her out for a walk while Carina and I had breakfast and showered. I was more than glad to take her up on the offer, and I went to take my shower while Carina spent a little longer in bed. When Linda got back an hour later, Carina was still in bed, and Ruby was tired and crying for her sleep.

However, Simon rang at 9.30am and asked when someone was coming to visit him. Natalie was usually with him by 8.30am every morning. As Linda still hadn't eaten and needed to shower, and Carina still wasn't out of bed, I decided to go to the hospital and hoped Ruby could sleep in the pram.

Thankfully, Simon was dressed when I got there, and I arranged for him to be put into a wheelchair. After making sure he could push himself along using the wheels, I managed to get him outside into the small garden where we could enjoy some morning sunshine. Ruby was still moaning, so I put the back of the pram on its lowest setting and moved her into the shade. She did finally go off to sleep, but it wasn't ideal for her. I know she would have preferred her bed.

Simon's phone rang while we were chatting and I listened to his conversation, curious about whom the caller might be. It wasn't obvious from the conversation, but it sounded as though someone was offering to do some house-sitting for them.

Simon started to explain the accident, but in his confusion he was referring to the motorbike accident he'd had a few years ago. He then started ranting about the woman who knocked him off his Yamaha. He complained that she got her license back right away, which wasn't fair as he wasn't getting his licence back for another six months and he had insurance, but that didn't count because he hadn't done anything wrong.

His whole conversation was skewed and unreal, and I felt so sorry for the person who had called.

The facts of this previous accident are that a woman did knock Simon off his motorbike, and she didn't have a license and was driving illegally. Consequently, she also had no insurance. Simon was totally mixed up about the two accidents and what happened, but the poor caller wouldn't have my knowledge of these events to help them make sense of Simon's one-sided conversation.

Later in the same call, Simon did recall the details of his present situation and told the caller what he had been told had happened. However, he still thought it was the insurance people who were insisting he couldn't have his driving license until he'd been through rehab and been signed off as fit to drive or fit to work.

He can't seem to grasp that he needs rehab for his brain injury. He can't see that there's anything wrong with his head, but I'm sure that by the end of the call, the person who rang him would have no doubts at all about that fact.

When Linda and Carina arrived, our conversation turned to ordinary topics. We discussed the house, the property and the dogs. Simon still thinks he's been working in Western Australia and doesn't get home often, so doesn't see Ruby very much. We reminded him again about how he works close to home and has done for four years. He gets home every night and sees Ruby every day.

'It doesn't seem like that to me,' he told us. 'I can't remember seeing Ruby as much as that.'

We talked to him of the last few years, or as much as we knew about it. Carina told him of the first time Simon had introduced her to Natalie.

'We went for a meal and then to the casino in Melbourne, remember? Natalie wasn't impressed with all that gambling was she?'

Simon couldn't remember anything about it.

I talked of his home and their move to Bangalow, but he couldn't take it in. He started to complain that he felt dizzy and tired, and his eyes weren't focusing properly. I think we had tired him out by trying to stir up his memories, and he couldn't cope with all the stimulation we were giving him.

Ruby was awake by now and was very cranky, so I took her home for lunch, leaving Carina and Linda to take Simon back to the ward. Linda is a hairdresser and had brought her shears so she could cut Simon's hair today. Half his head was shaved at the site of the injury, but now that his hair had grown longer everywhere else, he was looking lopsided. I'm sure that's why Ruby didn't recognise him. His funny hair made him look odd.

Ruby didn't want lunch and was very unsettled. She wouldn't go back to sleep either, so I took her to the shops. We needed more nappies, and I bought a bottle of wine for when Natalie got back tonight. I thought she might appreciate a little relaxation aid.

Linda and Carina arrived back at the apartment just as I got in, and I was amazed when Linda told me that she had taken Simon out to the shops. I thought he wasn't allowed to leave the hospital grounds, but she had taken him as far as King Street. She'd taken him into some shops to get him a scarf and some socks and a book for Ruby.

Linda gave the book to Ruby, and although she spent a few minutes looking at the pictures, she was overtired and cried to go to bed. I took her into the bedroom and cuddled her until she relaxed enough to go into the cot.

When I went back into the main room, Carina was in bed and fast asleep too. Linda and I had some coffee and chatted until our two sleepyheads woke. Carina had already rested on a chair by Simon's bed while Linda stole him away for his illicit walk to the shops. I guess his mum was finding the visit very tiring.

We all went back to the hospital, taking Linda and Carina's small amount of luggage with us. They planned to get a taxi to go directly to the airport later.

Simon was happy to see us, but Ruby was very fractious. She hadn't had a good nap all day, and I'm sure she was missing her mum. Simon looked better now he had a proper haircut, but Ruby was still not convinced about the man in the bed. Linda tried repeatedly to win her around, but her attempts only had the opposite result, and when Ruby became more upset, she came running to me for comfort. I was reassured that she trusted me to take care of her, but I could see she didn't want to be troubled by these new ladies any longer.

Simon was a little better this afternoon and seemed to have some of his memories back in the right order.

Linda questioned him about the company he worked for, and he knew he worked for them, but thought they were based in Western Australia, not in New South Wales.

At every chance, Simon steered the conversation back to his fixation with the PTA tests and kept complaining about how they got the pictures wrong. He was upset at the unfairness of it and wouldn't let it go. When the therapist came to test him, I took Ruby away so she wouldn't distract him, but Linda and Carina stayed to watch.

He scored a perfect twelve again but complained to the therapist about the previous day's mistake. He was not happy and felt he had been treated shockingly. Linda went to speak to the therapist, who was a different lady to the one who questioned him the day before. I followed Linda with Ruby in my arms, leaving Carina with her son.

The lady apologised about the mix-up and explained that the staff member responsible had been reprimanded, but I pointed out that no amount of reprimands would help Simon's situation. I explained again about the place at Ryde that was dependant on Simon attaining the necessary scores quickly. She didn't seem to understand the urgency and insisted that it only amounted to one extra day in hospital if he continued to get twelve for another two days running. I told her that one day to us wouldn't be so bad, but to Simon, each extra day he spends here is pure hell. She reiterated that Simon can be out of here by Wednesday if he continues to score the twelve he needs to, but then added ominously, 'That's if Ryde still have a place for him.'

Eggs-bloody-zactly! I spluttered inside my head, but kept my lips firmly squeezed together.

Linda and Carina left, at 4.30pm, to get their flight back to Melbourne. I stayed with Simon and gave Ruby a sandwich and some fruit to keep her happy.

'It's been nice to see your mum and Linda, hasn't it?'

'Yeah, but it was scary. I can't believe the change in Mum. How did she get so old?'

I didn't know how to answer him, so I remained quiet.

'She seems so frail so suddenly.'

'Maybe you're remembering her from years ago, Simon. I last saw her at your wedding, and I can't see that she's changed much since then.'

He was clearly shocked by the change he noticed in his mum. I could see that he was very upset about her seeming so old to him.

'She is eighty-two, Simon.' I gently reminded him.

He shook his head, sighed deeply and turned to play with Ruby, reaching to tickle her tummy.

I had planned to stay as long as I could with Simon, so he wouldn't miss Natalie too much, but shortly, Ruby became very upset. She wouldn't sit still. She wanted to run around the corridors, and I had to chase her everywhere, so we weren't much company for Simon anyway.

Natalie rang me while I was at Simon's bedside, to say that her flight had been delayed by two hours. She wouldn't arrive in Sydney until after 9pm.

I told her I was still with Simon and passed the phone to him.

I could see he looked disappointed, but he told her it was okay, and he would wait to see her tomorrow morning, but he asked her to ring him when she got back. I knew she would want to go to see him, but I also knew that she would be exhausted after her time at home.

I had to leave Simon shortly after Natalie's call. Ruby was so tired she was screaming with frustration. I put her in the pram as I was too weary to keep chasing her around, but she didn't like being cooped up. I left him reluctantly, he looked so alone and sad, but even Simon could see why I had to go.

I bathed Ruby, gave her a snack and put her to bed. She was fast asleep by 6.30pm. Now I'm waiting for Natalie to get home. I know we won't get much chance to talk tonight. She'll phone Simon when she gets in and that conversation will last for ages, but that's okay, we'll have plenty of time to talk and catch up over the next few days and weeks.

As I've spent more time with Simon over the last two days, it has become clear to me just how badly twisted his thinking processors and memory problems are. I fear that Simon will take quite a while to return to normal, and I worry that he won't ever be quite the same as he was before. I hadn't wanted to believe the negative words of the neurosurgeon about the outcome for Simon, but now I think this person may be right in his pessimistic prognosis.

I don't know, though. Maybe this promised intensive rehab will be the miracle that we're hoping for, though goodness knows how they can put the memories back in the right order for him.

I'd like to see what they could do to improve his short-term memory enough to enable him to go home and function without needing constant supervision. If he can't return to work, then he will at least have to be able to look after Ruby so Natalie can work. Will he ever be able to manage that? I sincerely hope so, or Natalie will have such an enormous burden to bear.

I try to picture them in the future as a normal happy couple, but I can't help seeing the worst-case scenario. If Simon looks normal and sounds normal, but isn't truly functioning normally, then how can he be responsible for anything or anyone? I can't shake that picture from my mind. It's a living nightmare, and I glimpse it every time I look at Simon.

I think Carina has seen the same future for them. We were talking this morning when Linda took Ruby for a walk. She could see the great weight on Natalie's shoulders and she told me it was good that Natalie was strong. I know my daughter is no wimp. She certainly has the strength to see her through most things and the confidence and intelligence to fight many battles and hardships, but this situation will test every fibre of her being before it's over.

DAY 31 Tuesday 29th July

When Natalie finally arrived back, last night, she looked much better. She's obviously enjoyed her trip home, spending time with the dogs and her friends and neighbours. She had the sparkle back in her eyes and a renewed determination in her voice.

She told me she had already called the Brisbane rehab unit and found out some details about the place. It didn't sound quite as good as the facilities here in Sydney, so today she is going to push to try to get him into Ryde as soon as possible. If he scores his twelve today, there should be no reason we can't move there by the end of this week.

This morning, Natalie is making calls, seeing people at the hospital and checking things out. She seems to have fully charged batteries after her trip home, and her vigour has infected us all. Ruby is much better today. She's not quite as congested with her cold, and is much happier to have her mummy back. She's sleeping now, and I think I might try to get my head down too.

SAME DAY next entry

Just as Ruby was waking from her nap, there was a knock on the apartment door. We got so few visitors that this was unexpected. To my surprise, I opened the door to see Natalie with Simon in his wheelchair. She'd brought him round to see our apartment, and he looked so happy and well. He looked so incredibly good that I couldn't stop smiling at him.

We chatted about the same old things, the little problems that Simon has to deal with in his world. He focuses on them and fixates about the tiniest upsets, I suppose it's because he has nothing else to talk about.

The latest upset was about the all-night-nurse who has to keep watch by his bedside. This young chap was using his laptop and Simon couldn't sleep for the tap-tap-tapping of computer keys.

They also keep waking him to take his painkilling tablets. Natalie has told them repeatedly to leave them on his table when he's asleep, and he'll take them if he needs them when he wakes.

Then he talked about the questions again and got cross about the day they forgot to change the pictures.

Each of these little episodes is magnified out of all proportion as Simon fixates on them and refuses to talk about anything else. We tried to steer him to other topics, but he kept bringing these niggles back into the conversation. I left him with Natalie and went out to King Street. I thought they might enjoy some family time with Ruby. I wanted to send some e-mails and had some errands to do.

When I logged on to the computer in the Internet cafe, I had lots of messages from my friends. It was so good to hear from them. I could read of ordinary things and ordinary lives that were still going on outside my stress filled little piece of Sydney. I read of their general ups and downs, the weather, health problems, marital strife, weddings and babies. It was all there. All the gossip surrounding my home life over the last few weeks was condensed into a few e-mails, and I relished every word of normality.

I went in search of the photography shop. Natalie had brought a disc back with her, of photos that Martin had taken of the wrecked ute. I offered to get them printed as she thought Simon should see them. I think she felt he might better understand what had happened to him if he could see the evidence.

When I saw the photos on the screen in the shop, I was speechless with shock. The assistant was commenting on the wreck, asking if the driver were okay, but I just nodded my head and paid, holding my breath to stop the tears from flowing.

The car is so badly damaged. Simon is so lucky to have survived. The whole front of the car is crumpled into the space where the driver's seat should be. How did he get off so lightly?

I brought the prints back, and Natalie asked Simon if he wanted to see them. He said he did, but his face was impassive as he looked at them. Natalie pointed out the bloodstains and the damage to the driver's seat. She told Simon how lucky he'd been not to lose his legs.

I saw Simon going paler and interrupted her. 'Let's not go there? He didn't lose his legs, and they will be fine. Let's concentrate on how lucky we are that Simon is here with us, and we can move on from this.'

They both agreed. I put the disturbing photos away.

Ruby has warmed to her daddy. I think that seeing him in her own surroundings is good for her. I know Simon is much happier to see her for such a long time, and he got to play with her, which is something he can't do at the hospital.

When Simon got hungry, we went out to the cafe at the corner of our apartment block for lunch. Ruby shared an omelette with me, and I got a fruit frappe, which she loved.

Simon had a steak and salad sandwich, and he seemed to enjoy it very much, but ate with no inhibitions, like a child. He made lots of noise and mess and didn't seem to care about the sideways glances that he was attracting from other diners with his lack of table manners.

We talked about a new car, Simon's favourite topic after he got his moans out of the way, but Natalie mentioned that they wouldn't need a car for at least another six months as he wouldn't be able to drive until then and Simon got very upset. He hadn't realised it would be so long. He thought that after he'd been to rehab, he would be able to go back to work and drive a car and everything would be normal. Like us, he's been pinning all his hopes on rehab, and now he seemed shattered.

Natalie explained again, about the risk of epilepsy and how that was the reason he wouldn't be able to drive for a while, but stressed that he hadn't had any fits, so it wasn't too much of a worry.

She told him he should treat this time as a holiday as he would be getting full pay while he was off work. He took some convincing, but eventually he came around. We went back to the apartment for a short while, but as Simon was very tired, we decided to take him back to the hospital for a sleep.

We were getting into the lift when Simon asked, 'Where's my wife?'

'I'm here, honey. I'm Natalie. I'm your wife.'

'I think I had a kid with someone didn't I?' he said to her.

I was standing right next to him with his daughter, Ruby, in the pram. His confusion was due to his tiredness. He needed to sleep.

I went with Natalie, to keep her company on the walk back to the hospital, but we didn't stay long with Simon as he was very tired. We came back to the apartment after getting him settled into bed. We planned to have a nap too, but as soon as we got our heads down, the phone rang.

The first call was from Natalie's boss, asking how things were going. She spoke to him for a few minutes, and we tried again to sleep. The second caller was Simon. He'd had the PTA test and scored another twelve. He was given three more pictures to remember until the next day and he wanted to tell Natalie what they were before he forgot, so she could remind him later. I'm sure that wasn't in the rules of how these tests are supposed to work, but that didn't concern Natalie. She helped him all she could because she wanted to get him out of there as soon as possible.

Natalie gave up on sleep and went to see him. She wanted to speak to his caseworker to see what the situation was at Ryde. He should have a place now that he'd passed the test a third time, (not officially though, due to the hospital cock-up), but there's the possibility that this place has been given to someone else. That would be devastating news for Simon.

In our opinion, we think Simon will only need one month of the intensive therapies in rehab, for his memory problems. It's clear that he'll have ongoing issues, but the rehab is designed to help him cope with those, not to cure them as that will be impossible.

The way he's been improving over the last few days has been very encouraging. If we can get him home by the beginning of September, I could be going home to Paul by the end of September. I daren't get too excited about it, though. There's so much that's still unknown.

Natalie and I had previously discussed the other patients we'd seen at Ryde. Some of them are so severely damaged that they need help with eating. We were told that some of them need to relearn skills like bathing and shaving, getting dressed and making meals. Simon already has those skills. He can shower and shave, and he can get dressed, even with his two broken legs, he can manage, so he's halfway there. It shouldn't take him long to convince the specialists that he's ready to go home. We've got such high hopes for him. I hope he comes through for us.

When Natalie got back from the hospital this evening, the news was bad. The place at Ryde had already been taken. What was worse, the unit at Brisbane didn't even have him on the waiting list! There'd been a breakdown in communication between the two hospitals and Simon's referral hadn't been seen or considered. What next? What else can go wrong for Simon?

He is really disappointed but has taken it surprisingly well. Natalie was told that there is a chance of a place opening at Ryde next week. To give us an extra option, Simon's case manager is ringing Brisbane on Thursday to speak with the person she originally arranged Simon's place with. This person is on leave until Thursday, so we have to wait again!

Due to all this extra stress on Simon, Natalie has requested that he be moved to a private room tonight so at least he can have a good night's sleep. Surprisingly, her request was granted.

She's also asked if the special twenty-four-hour nurse can watch him from a distance, so Simon is not disturbed by the presence of someone being in his room.

DAY 32 Wednesday 30th July

Well, despite all of Natalie's well made plans, at 1am Natalie's phone rang. I leapt to answer it before the loud ringtone woke Ruby, and I heard Simon on the line.

He was quite upset as he'd woken to find someone by his bed going through his things. He asked me if he had his wallet with him as he couldn't find it and wanted to know what else he was supposed to have because he thought this person had been looking at all his stuff and he wasn't sure what he was supposed to have, or whether any of his things were missing.

I talked to him as I'd heard Natalie talk to him when he was in this state. I was quiet and calm and tried to reassure him that it was nothing to panic about. 'Do you know who it was?' I asked.

'Some guy. I told him to get out of my room. He'd no business in here.' Simon told her crossly.

'Has he gone now?'

'Yeah, but he'll be coming back. He left his backpack.'

'Do you have your call control? Do you know what button to press to call for help?'

'Yeah, it's here. It's one of these buttons.'

I could hear him fiddling with the call control.

'Nah, that just makes the light come on.'

'Try the other one.' I whispered.

I heard a nurse arrive and start to talk to Simon during our call. I heard her asking if she could explain something to him.

'Simon,' I got his attention and when I could hear that the nurse had stopped talking I went on, 'Put the phone down now and listen to what she has to say. If you're still not happy, ring back and I'll get Natalie to talk to you.'

'Okay, I'll do that, bye.'

By this time, Natalie was perched on the edge of my bed listening. I explained what had happened.

'I bet it was the special nurse going in his room to check on Simon and he disturbed him. When will those people learn to read the notes?'

Sure enough, that's what appeared to have happened, though we won't know for sure until Natalie asks some questions this morning.

Hopefully, if Simon gets the twelve score today, he may be able to move to a normal ward where he doesn't need to be watched constantly by morons who are used to dealing with very severe cases of brain damage, so don't care what they do while they are supposed to be looking after them. So far, these under qualified special nurses have done nothing but upset Simon by keeping him awake, moving his stuff, watching television while he wants to sleep, disturbing him at every opportunity and being totally insensitive.

Simon really needs to get out of there.

Today, Natalie intends to bring him back here again, so we can take him to the little park to watch Ruby play on the swings and slide. I'll do some shopping while they have some family time and I'll buy us all something nice for lunch.

Paul phoned this morning, he wanted to know if there's been any news about our move. He's just as frustrated as we are that nothing seems to be happening and can't understand all the delays.

'I'd be tearing my hair out and demanding that something was done by now if I were there.'

'Well, that won't get us very far if there are no places to be had.'

I then tried to stress the positive side of things, about how we thought that Simon probably wouldn't need to be in brain injury rehab for long because he's come so far in the last few days.

We know his feet will be reviewed in a week or two, so if the casts can come off and he can start to learn to walk again, he may be able to come home, and by then, his head will have improved more too.

SAME DAY next entry
When Natalie brought Simon back to the apartment, he was very happy. He'd scored his final twelve, and that meant no more tests! We now need to be patient while we wait for the first available place in rehab for him.

Simon was tired after his disturbed night. Natalie suggested that he took a nap, and I left them to go do some shopping.

I was away for an hour. When I came back, Simon was asleep on the sofa in the corner by the window.

When he woke, shortly after I got in, he started to talk and didn't stop for the rest of the afternoon. Natalie played with Ruby while Simon monopolised me with his monologue. I had already heard this conversation over and over again, but I realised that Simon had nothing else to talk about except the harassment he'd been receiving in the hospital. I distracted him the same way I distracted Ruby. With food.

We made lunch with some ready-cooked chicken and salad that I'd bought, and Ruby was happy to beg food from us as we ate. Simon wanted to sleep again after lunch, so I offered to take Ruby out to the park. All I wanted to do was sleep. We'd had a disturbed night too, but I could sleep later.

Ruby wasn't too interested in playing when we got to the park. I think she was tired too. So I put her back into the pram, and we went for a long walk through the backstreets to the Memorial park. After an hour or so, Ruby was still wide-awake, and I was dragging my feet, so I headed back to the apartment.

Simon was awake and continued with his monologue. He was fixating on the same things, covering the same ground repeatedly. He was still complaining about all the bad things that had happened to him at the hospital, about the staff not giving a damn, the man with the laptop, the questions being changed without telling him, and the intruder in the night.

It's Penguin Shooting Day

No matter how many times we tried to change the subject, Simon would interrupt with his fixations again, and it took a concentrated effort to distract him from them, especially when Natalie and I were so exhausted. Ruby needed to sleep, but couldn't settle in her bed while Simon was talking so loudly.

Eventually, Natalie took him back to the hospital. Ruby and I could enjoy the peace and have a little nap at last.

Natalie came back early. I think Simon's constant talking had worn her down. To distract him, she'd been playing UNO with him. A card game they played at home that she'd brought back from her trip. She proudly told me that Simon not only managed to play the game, but also won nearly every hand.

He's still in his single room for the night and shouldn't be disturbed as he is now out of PTA and doesn't need the twenty-four-hour watch over him.

The nurse who was in charge last night came to apologise to Natalie about Simon being upset the night before. The special nurse who disturbed Simon hadn't read the instructions to keep his distance and had been reprimanded. It had been the nurses own bag he was taking things out of, but as Simon was confused, which is normal for him on waking, he misunderstood the situation and believed the nurse was going through his things.

Allowing Simon to keep the single room was the hospital staff's way of trying to make up for the disturbances and Simon's lack of sleep. Let's hope he sleeps better tonight.

DAY 33 Thursday 31st July

We had a glorious, blissful and very rare, event-free night. Simon didn't ring until 7.45am, but we'd been up more than two hours by then. Ruby woke at 5.30am, but because we went to bed at 9pm and slept well, we were all full of life and ready to face the day.

Natalie is hoping to hear news from the hospital in Brisbane today. We're not hoping for miracles, just a small break in our run of bad luck!

If he gets a place at the unit in Brisbane, at least we can go back to Natalie's place and have a familiar home base. I can look after Ruby and the animals while Natalie visits Simon. I shouldn't make plans. I know it isn't going to happen, but if it weren't for bad luck we wouldn't be having any kind of luck at all.

SAME DAY next entry

Natalie brought Simon to the apartment again, and he seemed much better today. He wasn't obsessing so much about the little things that bugged him. He did tell us few times about the tea lady who disturbed him to ask if he wanted a drink when he hadn't asked for one!

Natalie and I exchanged a small smile, but we were both relieved when he dropped the subject.

We could have a normal conversation with him at last, with just the odd hiccup where his memory didn't gel with what he was trying to say. He seems worse when he's tired, getting his words wrong, saying things like paper when he means pillow, or bread when he means book, but when he's rested, he doesn't seem to have so much trouble.

Two neurosurgeons came to see him on the ward this morning. They are just as frustrated as we are about the slowness of getting Simon into rehab. They told Natalie they would ring the Gold Coast and see if they can get him in there.

They stressed that he really needs to be in intensive therapy now and is wasting valuable time by staying at the RPA. They don't seem to mind that he is spending so much time away from the hospital. I guess as far as they are concerned, he's one less patient to care about if he's not on the ward.

From our point of view, Simon does so much better when he comes to the apartment. He talks more and makes more sense. He plays with Ruby, and she seems much happier and more confident around her daddy. She even went to him voluntarily this morning to ask to sit on his lap for a cuddle. It was the first time she had approached him since the accident without being offered a bribe. She clearly knows that the man in the wheelchair is her daddy and was quite happy to sit on his lap while he read her a story. It was a touching sight. It was wonderful to watch Simon being a daddy and to watch him enjoying the company of his little girl.

The neurosurgeons noticed that Simons jaw is lopsided, so he's scheduled for some x-rays later this afternoon to check this out. Natalie has just left, with him, to keep the appointment.

Ruby is taking her afternoon nap, and I'm having some peace and quiet to write this journal. I hope Natalie comes home with good news. If the Gold Coast rehab unit has a place for Simon, it will be the best option for us. At only one hour drive from their home, it would be ideal. I just hope it will also be good for Simon.

SAME DAY next entry

Natalie came home with some new options to consider. Not that we have any control over the final decision, but the doctors are stressing how important it is that Simon moves into therapy as quickly as possible. Now that he's out of PTA, the options have opened for him. One possibility is to send him to Byron District hospital until his legs mend. He can have neuro rehab while he's there.

He certainly seems well enough for that now, but would he be swapping one unsatisfactory hospital environment for another one? It's out of our hands, and all we can do is hope that something happens soon.

DAY 34 Friday 1st August

Simon rang last night at 7pm to say goodnight to Natalie. I listened to a regular call from a loving husband who was missing his wife. There was no stress, no anger, and it was lovely to hear them talking normally. He didn't ring this morning, so he's definitely improving. We're hoping against hope that he gets a place in rehab soon. We're so desperate that I think Natalie will take the first one that's offered to her now, even if that place is on the moon.

Paul rang this morning, and we had a good long chat. He's pleased that Simon is doing so well, and we hope this might mean I will get home sooner than expected. I miss him very much and all this waiting around is so frustrating for us both.

I asked Paul to tell me about his life as I feel so cut off from everything at home. He told me that friends and family are rallying around to help stop him from feeling lonely. He has so many invites for dinner that he doesn't eat at home much. He told me he had a list of chores. He is working his way through them to make sure he keeps on top of things. He's serviced my car, plans to tidy the garden at the weekend; he's scrubbed the cooker, blitzed the bathroom and is considering decorating the bedroom.

I told him that maybe I'll stay here until he completes the list and works his way through the whole house!

'What do you have planned for today?' he asked.

'That's easy.' I told him, 'I'll be looking after Ruby. That means playing with her, feeding her, changing her and keeping her happy. I have to go to the shop to buy milk and matches for the cooker, oh, and I might get some money from the cash machine. I may go to the Internet cafe and send some e-mails. A very busy day, lots of stimulation!' I laughed.

'Well at least you're getting to spend time with Ruby. What's she like now?'

'She's a little angel. She's playing with a plastic potato masher right now. It's one of her favourite toys. She loves poking her fingers through the holes.'

'I wish I could see her.'

'I'm taking lots of photos, and I'm storing the memories of her cute little ways so I can share them with you when I get home.'

'I can't wait.'

'Neither can I, but it won't be much longer. Maybe another couple of months at the most.'

We ended our conversation on a wistful note, but it had been good to talk with him.

Natalie left soon after my conversation with her dad. She had been called in to see the head nurse and was expecting a telling off. Simon had told the ward staff yesterday of his outings to our apartment, and they were very angry about it. Natalie should have sought permission from the registrar to take him from the hospital grounds. It never occurred to her to ask permission as they seemed quite happy to let her take him from the ward and our apartment was only a few hundred yards from the hospital.

Natalie might be gone for a while this morning as she also wants to see the case manager to talk about having Simon reassessed to see if we can get him into the hospital at Byron. The assessment has to be current before they can do a referral.

If she doesn't return to the apartment by lunchtime, I'll have to take Ruby in to see her daddy. We need to keep up the daily contact for our little angel now that she's accepted him at last. They may not let him come here today, especially as it's raining heavily in Sydney.

Ruby cried this morning when her mum left. She doesn't usually cry these days and normally accepts her mum leaving without much fuss, but today I had to distract her. I took her to the window to watch the planes coming in to land. She loves to wave at them and watch them fly overhead. Today there weren't many, so we watched the birds instead.

It's Penguin Shooting Day

Our apartment overlooks the tops of houses and trees, and there are lots of birds to see. I pointed out some large black crows that were being chased by smaller Indian Mynah birds. We saw a small flock of bright-green and red rosellas, and another flock of white and grey galahs with bright pink bellies.

We had a colourful and tuneful display; an interesting distraction for my tired little angel. I opened the window, and we laughed and pointed at the birds as they chased and swooped through the trees. Ruby started pointing them out to me and was delighted each time I praised her cleverness when she spotted them.

She's back in bed now enjoying her morning nap, and I have space to write this journal. It's interesting for me to look back to the beginning. When I read the first pages I can see how far we've come, and it's so good to realise just how far that is in such a relatively short time. The ups and downs of our day-to-day existence and the steady progress of Simon's improvements are amazing, considering the state he was in when he arrived in Sydney.

I'm glad I thought to write it all down. This journal has helped me deal with my roller coaster emotions. I've been able to unload my anger and sadness, my helplessness and the hopelessness I felt at times. I've also recorded the small joys and funny episodes to remind me it hasn't all been bad.

Yesterday we told Simon about his delusional periods. He can't remember anything of the last five weeks. We'd been told he wouldn't recall much, but hadn't realised that he wouldn't remember most of what happened while he was in PTA.

He can only dredge up snippets of things. Most of what he does remember are the upsetting incidents. Everything else has been reduced to tiny fragments. So Natalie had a lot of fun telling him of his delusional stages. She couldn't help laughing when she told him of the Harry Potter stage when he was casting spells.

'You were chanting, just like in the films when the kids are learning how to cast spells. You were deadly serious!'

'Did they work?' he asked, laughing with her. 'Did my feet get warm?'

'You said they did!'

'Wow! They say the mind is a powerful thing!' He shook his head, smiling.

Natalie then told him of his time in the ICU when he thought he was a famous motor racer. 'You were on first name terms with Webber and Michael Schumacher was a big mate of yours.'

'I don't remember any of this.' He was amazed, but not upset by Natalie's revelations.

'They told us you wouldn't remember any of it,' I told him, 'but at that time you slept a lot and sometimes you couldn't tell what was real and what was a dream, so we guess that's why you got mixed up.'

'Yeah, you were convinced you had sponsors and the great Australian public needed to know how you were doing!' Natalie held her sides as she rocked with laughter, giving him impish sideways glances to check that he was laughing too.

'Oh, man!' Simon held his head in his hands. 'Unbelievable! How am I going to live this down?'

'You can't! Sorry, honey, but we already told everyone!' Natalie was shaking with mirth. 'It was the highlight of my day. You think I'm not going to share that with everyone who called?'

'There was so much bad news, Simon.' I jumped to Natalie's defence. 'We were glad to pass on some light relief to everyone, and you certainly provided us with that.' I was laughing too, and Simon joined in. It was so good to laugh together. It was pure heaven.

Simon has come so far, so fast, and he's been very lucky. Things can only get better from here.

SAME DAY next entry

Natalie and Simon came back at 11am, just after Ruby woke. The head nurse had listened when Natalie told her that Simon was doing better and improving more when he spent time with us in our home environment. She pointed out that because the hospital ward had already let him down on so many issues and as he had to wait so long to get into a rehabilitation place, it was only fair that they allow her to give him the stimulation and family therapy that he responded to so well. The nurse couldn't refuse Natalie after she put her argument over so eruditely.

No news yet on our move, but people from the Royal Rehab Centre at Ryde came to see him again this morning. When Natalie was telling me about the meeting with the people from Ryde, Simon became upset, and a bit manic about the questions they'd asked him. He kept interrupting Natalie to tell me he didn't need rehab.

'I'll manage on my legs once these casts are removed. I don't need them to show me how to walk!'

He doesn't realise how badly his feet have been damaged, and he's expecting to walk again right away with no help. He also thinks the only problem he has with his head are the missing memories. He can't see that his manic behaviour, his obsessions and his unclear thinking are problems that he has to deal with too.

'There are other things you have to fix, Simon.' Natalie tried to be gentle, but Simon wasn't in the mood for gentleness. He was full of anger and resentment.

Natalie turned to me, 'He thinks he'll be able to get into a car and drive with no trouble, but the lady who assessed him this morning told us it won't be as simple as that. Simon could be driving along quite happily but if something unusual happened it might throw him and he wouldn't know how to react because of the brain injury so he could have another crash. She then tried to explain to Simon that they have to make sure he can cope with many issues, not only with his driving, but also with other areas of his life.'

Poor Simon looked panicky and afraid, and it became obvious to me as the conversation progressed that he felt he had to defend himself. They had asked him if he could remember anything about the accident, and Simon got the impression that they were trying to pin the blame for the accident on him.

'I can't tell them what happened,' he shouted. 'They tell me I was overtaking on double white lines, but I've never!' He then yelled at the top of his voice, shaking the walls of our tiny apartment, 'Why would I? All my life! I just wouldn't do that!'

'But you don't remember anything, honey.' Natalie tried to soothe him in her quietest calming tone. 'You only know what various people have told you, and most of them don't know the facts anyway.'

'That's just it.' He yelled loudly. 'They all tell me different, so how am I supposed to know anything? They're trying to trick me into saying something when I don't know anything.'

'You just have to tell them what you know.' I said. 'And if you can't remember anything, then that's what you tell them. That you can't remember. No one is trying to trick you, Simon.' Amazingly, I managed to get his full attention, so I pressed my point, hoping to reassure him and calm him down. 'These people aren't interested in blame. They're not judging you.'

'Yes they are. They all are!' His voice grew even louder as he became more agitated. 'All these questions and tricks. They changed the pictures to trick me. Now they're asking all these questions again. I'm a chippy. Ask me! Ask me any question about my job and I'll tell you, but I'm not going to be any good at anything else. I don't know about books and tests.' He started rambling about not being good at school so how could he be good at any exams they wanted him to pass.

'The tests they want you to do are easy, Simon.' I interrupted him. 'You just have to trust them. They're there to help you.'

'No they're not! They don't care!' He yelled at the top of his voice.

Natalie glanced at me and shook her head.

Simon's shoulders dropped and he continued in a quieter voice. 'They're just interested in the next dollar.

Look at what they did so far. Making noises so I can't sleep. Waking me to take my pills after we told 'em not to. They don't even read the notes!'

On, and on, he rambled, bringing up every little incident that had upset him. He couldn't remember most of the last five weeks, but because these incidents had been so upsetting and he had fixated on each one so much, they were the only things he could remember with any clarity. We met so many good people at the hospital and so many positive things happened, but Simon didn't remember any of that and so saw the whole hospital experience as a bad one.

I read between the lines of what he was saying and began to realise what his problem was. He had no idea what all the questions were about and he was so afraid of getting them wrong and failing the tests. I begun to see that he thought they wouldn't let him go home until he passed the tests in rehab.

'You have to believe the doctors want to help you, honey.' Natalie interrupted his monologue. 'Some of the staff are just as you said, they don't care, and they need to shape up, but the doctors do care. You have to listen to them, Simon.'

'But I can't do what they're asking me! I'll never get out of rehab. The—'

'Simon!' I interrupted this time, and it was no easy thing to do. He was in full flow and very loud. 'They aren't going to ask you to do anything that you can't do. They won't be testing you on your Arithmetic or your English or anything difficult like that. It won't be like schoolwork.'

He was listening to me so I continued, 'I don't know what they *will* be asking of you, but I do know that they want to help you get home as soon as possible'

'I want to go home.' He sounded like a little boy, and my heart went out to him.

'Well, the quickest way for you to do that is to do everything they ask you to do. But remember, they won't be asking you to do anything that you don't know how to do.'

He went quiet for a while and seemed to be digesting what I'd said. He stopped rambling and became calmer, and we were able to talk of other things.

Natalie took the opportunity of this quiet phase to go out to do some shopping, leaving me with Simon and Ruby who we'd just put to bed for her nap. Goodness knows what our little one makes of all this yelling, but I guess it can't be good for her.

Simon was happy to talk about normal topics, and I spoke to him of his home, holding out the carrot of his goal for him to focus on. He could remember his home with more detail now, thank goodness, and we talked of playing darts on his veranda at Christmas, of throwing balls for Max to fetch. We talked of all the ordinary everyday things that he couldn't wait to get back to.

Natalie brought burgers back with her for lunch, and afterwards we lolled around and dozed while Ruby played quietly with her toys. We were roused by Natalie's phone, and as she listened to the caller, her face brightened. It was great news.

Simon was being transferred to the Royal Rehab Centre at Ryde on Monday. He had a confirmed place and all we had to do was accept it. Natalie did that right away and then rang the number she'd been given to book our accommodation.

We have a two-bedroom villa with a microwave to move into on Monday. It has no other cooking facilities, and the laundry is a shared room. It didn't sound as well-equipped as the apartment here, but we'd make do. A villa, no less! I couldn't wait to see it.

Natalie and Simon went back to the hospital shortly after the call. Simon had an appointment to see a dentist about his jaw and Natalie wanted to find out more details about the move.

Simon is still uncertain about rehab. He thinks he doesn't need any of it and just wants to go home. It's difficult to make him understand as he doesn't think there's much wrong with his brain. I hope they can help him and help him quickly. I can see the end in sight and like Simon; I want to go home too.

Natalie came home in time to give Ruby her bath, and we enjoyed a quiet evening. Carol phoned, and Natalie gave her the good news about Simon's move to rehab. She told his big sister that it would be good for Simon to be more independent.

I was relieved to hear my daughter admit that. I'd been thinking it myself, but couldn't bring my opinions into the open. Simon leans on Natalie a lot, and relies on her to sort all his problems. It seems he can't cope with even the tiniest upset without ringing her. Tonight he rang just as we were falling asleep to tell her that someone had woken him to take his blood pressure.

Natalie was very calm and reassuring as ever, but said to him, 'Well I can't do anything about it now. I'll see you in the morning.' He took some persuading, but eventually, Natalie put the phone down and went back to bed.

It's so hard for me to stand back and watch this behaviour and not say what I feel, but I know my daughter and she wouldn't thank me for interfering in the way she conducts her relationship with her husband. It was good to hear her talking about Simon gaining some independence from her because at last she can see what I've been witnessing for weeks. She will find it difficult to let go. Simon still sees Natalie as his protector and turns to her at every opportunity. It's hard on her. She needs someone to take care of her too, and though I can do that to some extent, who can she lean on when I go home? I can't stay forever, and I really hope Simon will recover enough to take responsibility for himself. I hate to think of Natalie being his carer for life, even if he only needs partial care.

This dependency is the most frightening. He might look like Simon and sound like Simon; he may be able to love Natalie like the old Simon loved her, but will he be able to fulfil her emotional needs as well? Will he be able to take some of the burden of responsibility from her shoulders? I hope so. With every atom of my being, I hope he will.

DAY 35 Saturday 2nd August

Natalie brought Simon back to the apartment again this morning, and I escaped to the Internet cafe to send some e-mails. I feel I'm abandoning Natalie when I leave her alone with him because it is very hard to communicate with Simon sometimes. On the other hand, I am giving them space to be a normal family unit without my interference. I did need to send some e-mails, though, so my excuse to get away was genuine.

I had a few messages in my in-box and once again I immersed myself in other people's lives. It gives me comfort to know that life is going on outside my little bit of the world. I sent a block e-mail to let friends and family know we will soon be on the move.

A tantalising aroma from the pie shop reminded me that Simon likes typical Australian pies, so I bought some for lunch and headed back. Simon was in a good mood, and he and Natalie were discussing his dissatisfaction with his sunglasses. He needs some new ones as the lenses in his favourite pair are scratched.

I busied myself with preparing lunch and putting the pies to warm and realised that Simon was again obsessing about a topic. The subject this time was his sunglasses. He wanted Natalie to go out and find a shop that sold the designer style he liked, but she'd already looked in all the shops nearby and told him so.

'Are you sure you looked for the designer sunglasses that I like? Are you sure you looked for Arnettes?' he asked her.

'Sure I'm sure. There are no Arnettes around here. We'll have to look on the Internet.'

'Have you got the Yellow Pages?'

Natalie and I looked at each other and shrugged.

'You have to have the Yellow Pages, have a look!' Simon insisted.

'What for?' Natalie asked. 'You won't find anything in there.'

'How do you know? Look for the Yellow Pages, will you!' Simon insisted.

By some miracle we found a Yellow Pages directory in a kitchen drawer, and gave it to Simon.

Within a very short time, it became apparent that Simon couldn't remember how to use the directory. He held it at an angle and was looking under 'A' for Arnettes. He was reading out all the entries from air conditioners to aquariums, to armoured cars.

'I don't understand this. I know I'm doing it wrong, but I can't work it out.' He was laughing at himself, which made a pleasant change from his angry outbursts.

'You won't find the name of the Italian designer of sunglasses in the Sydney Yellow Pages.' Natalie told him. 'It's an Italian company, and even if you did find them, you wouldn't be able to buy a pair of sunglasses from them over the phone.'

'What do I look for, then?'

'Try sunglasses.' I suggested.

He turned to the pages beginning with 'S' and began to read a list of entries.

'Security guards, silverware, spotlights, sunglasses!' He read the short list of sunglasses entries and started to get cross. 'There are no Arnettes on the list!'

'They won't be listed under Arnettes, Simon!' Natalie was losing patience with him, which was very unusual. 'Try sunglasses retailers, then I can phone some shops to see if they stock what you want.'

'So do I have to look at the 'R' pages for retailers now?' He looked so confused.

'Give it to me.' Natalie reached for the directory.

'No! I can do it. Just tell me what to look for!' Simon held tightly to the book. He seemed determined to do this for himself.

I took this a great sign, but Natalie was frustrated with him.

Eventually, Natalie left him to it and came to help me with lunch. After our meal, Simon was still obsessing about the sunglasses, so Natalie took the directory from him. She found and phoned a few retailers to try to appease him and discovered that the style Simon wanted was now obsolete so he would have to get some different ones anyway.

Simon wouldn't leave it at that, and he decided to phone the directory service. When he got through, he asked for the number for Arnettes and Natalie started laughing and shaking her head.

When Simon was told there was no number listed and was asked, did he have an address for Arnettes, he said, 'I don't know! Surely there's an Arnettes listed in Sydney!' He was astounded to find that there wasn't.

Fortunately, by this time, he was tired and when Ruby went to bed for her nap, Simon finally fell silent as he dozed on our sofa. Natalie and I took our cue from him and settled down for a snooze on my sofa bed. When Ruby woke us an hour or so later, Simon started talking about the sunglasses again right away as if there had been no sleep break at all. He was insistent that there had to be an, Arnettes, in Sydney and couldn't understand why there was no number listed.

'We'll look on the Internet when we get back to the hospital.' Natalie suggested.

They left soon after, and I wrapped Ruby warmly and let her play outside on our tiny balcony. She loves to be outside, and the small outside space is as good as anywhere when I'm too tired to take her to the park.

There's a little walled planted area and Ruby loves to dig out the mulch and scatter it over the floor-tiles. She pulls leaves from the shrubs and pokes her fingers into the dirt. She giggles and smiles and talks to herself and loves it when the birds swoop low over her. She can spot an aeroplane when it's just a dot in the sky and points and calls for me to look at it.

When it started to get dark we came inside, and I made her dinner. Just as she finished eating, the lights went out. I looked outside and saw that the whole of our part of Sydney was without lighting. It wasn't yet fully dark, and I could see well enough in the twilight to get Ruby ready for bed, though didn't risk putting her in the bath.

I rang Natalie to see if the hospital had been affected. She said they were operating on emergency generators. I asked her to come home early before it got completely dark, or to wait until the power came back on in the city. I didn't want her to walk home alone on streets with no lights. Fortunately the power was only off for an hour, and I could fix our dinner while Ruby played.

Natalie didn't get back until after 7pm and just had a quick cuddle with Ruby before putting her to bed. Ruby didn't seem to mind. We'd had a lovely time, playing and reading stories while we waited for her mum.

WEEK SIX: Move to rehabilitation

DAY 36 Sunday 3rd August

Five weeks have passed since the accident, and it feels as if we are a world away from where we started. On this first day of week six, we have blue skies in Sydney, and we plan to go to the park with Ruby when Simon comes back with Natalie.

Paul phoned again this morning. He was making sure we were happy with our move and the new apartment would be suitable. I told him what I knew, but stressed that we wouldn't know more until we got there. I reassured him that we'd manage whatever it was like.

He suggested that if I can come home earlier than expected, then perhaps we could have a holiday somewhere together instead of him travelling to Australia. He knows there won't be much point in him coming over here once Simon is back at home. Paul thought Simon wouldn't want his house full of in-laws and would prefer some peace and quiet to help him get back to normal as soon as possible.

I told him it sounded like a good plan, and it gave us something to look forward to at the end of this separation.

I can't wait for Simon to get home to Bangalow. It will be so good for Natalie to have him to herself without doctors and hospitals telling them what they can or can't do.

I'm hoping the rehab place can give us an indication of how long Simon will need to be there, but we won't know anything until Tuesday or Wednesday of next week after his initial assessments have been completed. Then he has an appointment on Monday 11th August for his feet to be assessed. We hope they'll be able to take his casts off so he can start physiotherapy.

SAME DAY next entry

Today went as planned, but with a minor problem. We went to the park, and I left Natalie to play with Ruby while Simon watched them from his wheelchair. I went to try to get some money from the cash machine. Paul had transferred some money from UK into Natalie and Simon's joint account, and Natalie had given me Simon's cash-card to draw some out. Simon gave me his pin number, and I was all set. However, the machine wouldn't accept the number. Simon had remembered it wrongly, or perhaps remembered an old number he'd used in the past. When I rejoined them in the park, I explained my problem.

'It has to be that number, I always use that number!'

'Maybe you changed it after your wallet got stolen when the car got broken into?' Natalie suggested.

'Maybe. But what's your mum want with my money anyway?'

'It's our money, honey. It's a joint account.'

'Since when?' Simon looked shocked.

'Since we got together. Since we bought the house together. Since we got married.'

'It's my money, actually, Simon.' I explained. I didn't want him to think I was sponging off them. 'Paul transferred a load of money into your joint account to help you out and to help me pay my way here.'

Simon nodded and then shook his head. He clearly found this information confusing.

'Let's go eat.' Natalie suggested and scooped Ruby up to put her in her pram.

Ruby didn't need to be persuaded; she'd heard the word eat and knew that she would soon be having lunch.

We ate at the cafe on the corner again and tried to enjoy some normal family conversation with our meal, but Simon was upset. The money situation with the joint account and me needing access to it had unsettled him, and now he was finding other things to stress about. He started to complain about the rehab place and the move that was planned for tomorrow.

He is worrying about all the tests he thinks they are going to give him. He thinks he'll be tested on his driving skills and his job. Even though we've told him so many times that the rehab has nothing to do with this, at least in these early stages, he won't believe us.

Simon thinks it is the insurance company that is insisting he go to rehab. He still thinks he has to go there to get his driving license back. No matter how much Natalie and I try to explain things to him, he just doesn't get it. He doesn't understand that his brain damage needs to be assessed and addressed. He doesn't think there's anything much wrong with his brain and can't see the point in wasting time with all this rehab.

I'm sure he's scared. He's like a frightened little boy inside, and the only way he can deal with these feelings is to get angry and upset. He's convinced that he'll be asked to do things that he won't know anything about. He feels out of his depth and afraid that if he doesn't pass the tests, he won't be able to go home.

His voice was getting louder as he became more upset, and other diners were beginning to stare. We finished our lunch in double quick time and decided to take Simon back to the apartment. He argued all the way and finally told us that if they didn't let him out of rehab he'd create such a ruckus that they'd have to send him home.

'You know I can make a fuss when I want to, Natalie.'

His tone was threatening, and I felt sympathy for my daughter. She would have to be his defender and his protector if he started to become difficult.

He's already told her he doesn't want to be on his own while they settle him into the new place. He wants her to be there with him so she can shield him from their questions and answer for him if he doesn't know what they want from him.

'They'll want to know all kinds of stuff, and I won't know anything. What can I tell them? How will I know if they're trying to trick me?'

He's becoming paranoid about being tricked into something. He thinks everyone is against him and trying to wrong-foot him at every turn. We'd been told that the paranoia is another symptom of the brain damage, and it's so hard to reassure him that he has nothing to worry about. We repeatedly try to restore his confidence and tell him that everyone is on his side, but it's no use. I hope this worrying symptom doesn't last too long.

DAY 37 Monday 4th August.
We made the move. We are now housed in a tiny two-bedroom villa at the Royal Rehabilitation Centre at Ryde.

The word villa evokes pretty images, doesn't it? This place couldn't be further from those mind pictures. The dingy, dark wood exterior gave us a brief clue to the old and shabby interior we found inside, but it's clean, and it will do.

Natalie rode in the ambulance with Simon early this morning, and I stayed at our apartment with Ruby to do some last minute packing. Natalie came back when Simon was partially settled to help me with all the baggage. She didn't like to leave him as he still had lots of initial assessments to complete, but time was getting on and she had to come back to help me. I could not have managed alone.

We had two large suitcases, the pram, four smaller bags, the baby bath, heater, travel cot and various boxes of toiletries and food. We had to make numerous trips in the tiny lift to get everything down to the ground floor and into the waiting taxi. Thank goodness it all fitted.

We called at the office and gave a thank you box of chocolates to the manageress of the apartments who had been so kind to us over the last few weeks. Her help in keeping us settled in one apartment had made such a difference to us.

By 2pm we were settled in the new place. Calling it a villa is a vast stretch of the imagination. The long terrace of wooden buildings is set at the top of a very steep hill. The dilapidated housing must have been built more than fifty years ago and has certainly seen better days.

The decor inside is a dingy grey, and when I saw there was a large balcony my heart lifted, but only until I saw the notice on the patio doors. *'Strictly no access.*

Balcony unsafe.' The doors were padlocked and when I looked out at the rotting timbers hanging over weed infested garden areas, I sighed with disappointment.

I was glad to find that the bedrooms were roomy, and the bedding was clean and fresh. The living room has a small television, and although the kitchen area is sparse, it is adequate.

Everything in the villa is geared towards wheelchair accessibility, so in the bathroom, the toilet is high and the basin is low. There is no bath, and the shower has a drain in the middle of the bathroom floor.

We have no dining table and nowhere to put things safely out of Ruby's reach. Added to this, there are emergency call-buttons in every room, just at Ruby's height! These red buttons fascinated my little angel, and of course she was drawn to them. I spent a long time trying to teach her that these red buttons were not to be touched. She got the message but still couldn't resist them. We discovered later that they weren't connected to anything, so it wouldn't matter if she pressed them.

Natalie helped me unpack, but she couldn't wait to go back down the hill to the Brain Injury unit to see how Simon was settling in.

Ruby took the move in her stride. She happily explored her new surroundings, running from one room to the next, opening drawers, pulling at dangling wires and showing me exactly where I needed to take action to make the villa child-safe.

When Natalie came back, she was not happy. Unlike Ruby, Simon had not taken well to his new surroundings and complained about every little thing. He hadn't liked being left alone when Natalie came to help me with the move. While she was gone, various people drifted in and out of his room, asking him questions. He felt they were putting him under pressure to answer when Natalie wasn't there to help him. He is feeling vulnerable and is beginning to get depressed about the situation. He's not happy about the things they told him he would be expected to do whilst he's there.

Natalie explained that he's been put in a four-man unit. Each patient has a private bedroom, and they share a communal living and kitchen area. All the patients are expected to cook and clean the unit, and a schedule has been drawn up to share the work evenly. As Simon isn't mobile yet, he'll get his meals delivered, but he has to do things like setting the table and pouring the drinks. Poor Simon finds all this demeaning.

In his words, 'It's crap! I never do any of that stuff at home! Why should I have to do it here?'

He actually does help with chores like this at home!

Simon also got upset because he couldn't remember what had been said to him in Natalie's absence and he thought someone had said that he needed to be there for at least a month. That news really made him upset, because he thought he'd be here for a few days at the most. Natalie told me that she'd tried to cheer him up by reminding him that the assessments hadn't been completed yet.

She told him that a decision will be taken about how long he needs to be here when they've done them all. When the assessments have finished, and the specialists have the results, they will call a family meeting to discuss a plan of action. Natalie had been told to expect this meeting to happen tomorrow.

Apparently, Simon has always been a glass half-empty kind of guy and would always see the negative side of any situation. That's why it's so hard to motivate him now, especially as he's feeling very low. I pointed out to Natalie that this place will try to make him more independent, so he doesn't have to rely so heavily on her, but she immediately defended him by saying that even in normal circumstances Simon relies on her.

She explained that, beneath his tough exterior, Simon is not good at communicating with other people. He's intolerant and opinionated, and relies on Natalie to soften his lack of social graces when they're in company, especially with strangers. She didn't tell me anything I didn't already know, but her words made me realise that Simon isn't going to change and become a nice amenable puppy, just because they want him to.

Natalie is so upset on Simon's behalf that she is regretting the move already. She thinks it may have been better for Simon to be transferred to the hospital at Byron so she could go home.

If Simon could have rehab as an outpatient, that would be brilliant for us all, but I don't think we can change things now. I think they'll want to keep him here for a while now that they've got him on the unit.

Ruby likes her new home. Right outside our front door, there are lots of open grassy areas for her to run around in, and she loves to explore. She picks dandelions and clover; she chases birds, pokes at insects and picks up twigs. She's most contented when she finds something interesting to carry around with her. If she can have a stick, a pebble or a leaf in each hand, she's happy, but when she finds another attractive item, she has to make a decision. It's so funny to watch her make a choice. Does she put the twig down in favour of the spiky seedpod she found? Or does she drop the pebble? Sometimes she tries to hold all her finds in her tiny hands and gets upset when she keeps dropping them.

This evening, my little angel went to bed with no fuss at all. She was tired out after our nature walk. I think she'll be happy here, even if her daddy is not.

DAY 38 Tuesday 5th August

Things are moving so slowly it's frustrating the hell out of us. Natalie went down to the Brain Injury unit at 8am to see when they'll need her for the family meeting. She was shocked to find there wasn't a meeting scheduled! The receptionist didn't know anything about it and said she'd get the social worker to ring Natalie later.

Simon is frustrated and bored. He keeps phoning Natalie, just for someone to talk to.

We had such high expectations of this place, but we are now feeling very disappointed. Poor Simon finds that he's sat alone for hours on end with nothing to do. The highlight of his long morning was a half-hour session of physiotherapy, but then he complained that a five-year-old could have done what he'd been asked to do. He had to turn a wheel a hundred times using his arms. He said that Ruby could have done it easily. He also complained that the physiotherapist spoke to him as if he were a child. She was patronising, and he's not happy at all with the attitude of this young woman towards him.

When the call from the social worker came, Natalie was given an appointment to meet her at 11.30am. We hung around the villa doing crosswords while we waited for the clock to tick around. Ruby had her nap, and we made coffee. We were killing time and knew that Simon would be doing the same. We are very frustrated.

I took Ruby for another nature walk while Natalie went to attend the meeting. Ruby picked clover flowers, and I found a four-leaf clover at my feet. I made a wish for us to get home quickly and put the lucky find in my purse.

Then Ruby picked some dandelion seed heads, and I showed her how to blow them. She giggled, watching the fluffy seeds floating off in the breeze. I was enjoying spending time with my grandchild, on this gloriously warm morning, but I knew this peaceful interlude wouldn't last. Natalie went to the meeting with many questions prepared, and if she doesn't get the answers she wants to hear, I know my daughter will not be pleased, and I know she won't let it lie until she does get some satisfactory answers.

We met back at the villa. The meeting had lasted about half-an-hour and Natalie was steaming with anger. She said she felt she'd been interrogated about Simon. She was asked what kind of person he was before the accident. What type of personality did he have? What was his family background and medical history?

She kept her cool and explained as much as she knew, but said that Simon could answer most of these questions far better than she could and explained that even though he had a brain injury, he wasn't totally mentally impaired and was quite capable of telling them what they needed to know.

She then asked some questions of her own. She asked about Simon's neuro rehab and enquired when it would start. She explained that he was going crazy with boredom, and as far as she could see, he had swapped one intolerable hospital environment for another.

The social-worker explained that the rehab team were currently busy and as Simon was still getting evaluated they couldn't start work with him until all the assessments were complete. She stressed that Simon would need a thorough review from the neuro-psychiatrist, which was to be scheduled either today or tomorrow. Then the whole team were planning to meet, on Thursday, to discuss Simon's case, and Natalie will probably get her family meeting on Friday.

The family meeting would allow the team to explain the goals that Simon will need to meet before he can go home and give Natalie and Simon the opportunity to ask further questions.

Natalie argued that as far as she and Simon were concerned, these delays in organising everything added to another wasted week. She explained that it wasn't just Simon they had to consider. The whole family, including her mum, had been displaced, and we had responsibilities at home to get back to. She pointed out that if Simon is doing nothing but sitting alone in a room waiting for the odd therapy session once a day, he could just as easily do this at home, and go to the local hospital at Byron as an outpatient.

The lady argued that Simon shouldn't be moved yet as he was under threat of having seizures and infections, at which point Natalie admitted to me that she almost lost her cool and exploded at the social worker, but she managed to express her opinion calmly albeit through gritted teeth.

'The seizure threat will still be there in six months time, so you're not telling me you plan to keep him here for that long! As for the risk of infection, that's hogwash. All his wounds are healed. I'm no dimwit. I have had some medical training. Don't try to fob me off with this rubbish. I want to know how long you think Simon will be here!'

The social-worker stood firm and pointed out that although Natalie might perceive Simon to be back to normal, he may have some subtle but significant problems that only the very well-equipped, Royal Rehabilitation Centre could help him with.

'But how will you know what these subtle problems are if you don't know what he was like before this? And how do you propose to cure him?' Natalie insisted.

She didn't get a straight answer, but was given a ray of hope when the social worker admitted that the doctor, who saw him earlier that morning, recommended that Simon get home as soon as possible.

Natalie thinks she's banging her head against a brick wall. The wheels of this place are turning very slowly, and people have no consideration for our situation.

When Natalie started talking about making some phone calls to find out if we could find better care for Simon, I agreed that it would be a good idea. She wanted to phone Byron hospital directly and ask what they could do for him. She's making plans to take some drastic action if things don't start to happen here soon.

If Simon can be based at Byron, at least we can get back to some kind of normality, even though it might not be the best place for Simon, it couldn't be much worse than what he'd experienced so far at Ryde.

I asked her to give this place a little time. I pointed out that we'd only been here two days and as Simon had a hospital appointment at the RPA on Monday to review his feet, we may as well stay until his casts come off.

She agreed to give the people here until Friday to get their act together. If nothing had happened by then, and if Simon hadn't had any significant therapy, and she had no definitive answers, then she was going to move heaven and earth to get him out of here.

Natalie phoned Simon to let him know how the meeting had gone.

He sounded disheartened, and Natalie found it hard to cheer him up. She was frustrated that she couldn't see him and talk with him in person. Natalie wanted to hold his hand and keep him company during these stressful, lonely hours, but she wasn't allowed to visit until after 3pm.

We took a walk into the local village of Putney and explored the few shops. We found plenty of takeaway food shops, a bottle shop and a supermarket. We bought some supplies and had lunch at a pavement cafe. We discovered a doctor's surgery and a pharmacy, and as I was almost out of my reflux pills, I made an appointment to see the doctor on Friday. Paul can't send my prescription pills from home without a lot of red tape. Even if he managed to get the export license he needed to send them, we didn't have a long-term address to mail them to. This was my only option. I hoped it wouldn't prove expensive for me to get my prescription here. Natalie had managed to solve her medication problem. She had spare contraceptive pills at home and brought some back with her from her trip north.

We took our time walking back from the village. It is an uphill walk, and the incline is very steep. We let Ruby walk most of the way, and we chatted about our options. Natalie was still talking about regretting the move to Ryde and was considering that the Gold Coast or Brisbane may have been a better alternative, but I pointed out that we had no way of knowing that either of those places would have been any improvement on Ryde, and we didn't have much choice anyway as all the decisions had been made for us.

It's Tuesday today, and we have to wait until Friday to learn how long we might be here. Simon has an appointment next Monday to review his legs. He needs the wire taken out and hopefully the casts will come off, and he can start physiotherapy in earnest. We hope this will happen next week as Simon's rehab will go much more quickly when he can start to walk.

We took Ruby to see Simon for half-an-hour at visiting time, but she didn't want to sit still. Simon was not happy and complained incessantly about the poor standard of treatment he was receiving.

'The physio talks to me like I'm a moron!' he told us.

'So tell her you don't want to be treated like a child!' Natalie told him.

'If I say anything, I'll know I'll blow a fuse! You know what I'm like!'

'Just ask her nicely to talk to you like an adult. You don't have to lose your temper with her.'

'The other blokes don't like her either! I don't know how these people get jobs!'

I played with Ruby, keeping her amused, distracting her from the anger in her daddy's voice. Natalie was trying to give him strategies to cope, planting ideas into his head and putting words into his mouth.

He did seem to be listening, but had the final say on the matter with, 'I'll just wheel myself out of here if they don't get their finger out soon!'

I took Ruby back to the villa for dinner, and Natalie came back shortly after. We had a hurried meal, and she went back down to Simon after Ruby was tucked in bed.

Fortunately, the brain injury unit is only a two-minute walk down the hill, and I have no worries about her safety in this quiet, enclosed, hospital compound. I do still worry that Simon is draining her emotions. He still seems to need her help and support for the tiniest of things, but she is more than willing to give him everything he needs.

I hope things start to move along soon with his rehab. This slowness is frustrating for all of us. Simon has so many therapists that need to assess and work with him, but they can't seem to get their act together. It feels as if they aren't talking to each other as one will say one thing that another will contradict. We were told the family meeting will happen on Friday, but then we were told that we might have to wait until his legs have been reviewed. Natalie is fighting to get Simon home as quickly as she can, but no one is listening to her yet.

DAY 39 Wednesday 6th August

At last it seems as if things are starting to happen for Simon. He has had a morning filled with assessments. He had visits from speech therapists and occupational therapists. He has been involved in some planning for various therapies that he'll be scheduled for.

He's been told that the doctors and therapists will meet tomorrow to discuss their findings. The family meeting will be held the following Thursday, when they have the results from his hospital appointment on Monday to review his legs.

We were hoping the family meeting would happen this week as we still won't know how long we need to be here until this meeting has taken place, but at last, we know for certain when it will be.

The neuropsychologist spent time with Simon this morning. He gave him a series of tests to assess his brain function. As expected, Simon didn't do well on the intellectual side because he has never been an academic. However, he was proud of his results in the practical skills tests. He did well in the creative thinking and problem solving. I don't know what was involved, but apparently he did amazingly well.

Simon's strengths lie in his practical skills. He's a hands-on kind of guy and is happiest when he has a practical problem to solve, something to build, or make. We were happy to know that these basic skills are still in place for him.

He was informed what he would have to do during the occupational therapy sessions. These are geared toward making sure he can look after himself independently, so he has to demonstrate that he can cook and clean, dress and do laundry, and all the other mundane tasks that we all take for granted.

He has to shop for ingredients to make a meal for the other patients in the unit at least once while he's here. He stressed about this, saying that Natalie does all the cooking at home, and he doesn't get involved.

Eventually, after some persuasion, he agreed that he did cook before he met Natalie. He remembered that he could make lasagne and agreed that he would be able to do that as part of his occupational therapy.

Natalie was able to see him for a few minutes this morning, to find out how he was feeling. When she came back to me midmorning she was happy that things were progressing. She told me that Simon would be involved in more therapy sessions until visiting time.

To fill in the time, we did some shopping and bought stir-fry ingredients for our evening meal. I'd found an electric wok in the cupboard, so I hope it works. We came back to put Ruby down for a sleep, and we did crosswords until she woke, and it was time to go see her daddy.

We took Simon outside to the grassy area opposite the unit, where he could watch Ruby while she played and ran around. Natalie played with Ruby while I stayed with Simon. He was rational, and although still desperate to get home, he does at last, seem to realise that the neuro people need to do some work with him first.

He told me that he took part in a social activity session with the other guys in the unit. Apparently, on Wednesdays they have news round, where each patient chooses a news item to present. After the presentations, they take part in a group discussion, and therapists watch and take note on how the patients interact with each other.

Simon is normally very opinionated and joined the discussion with gusto. However, he struggled to find the right words to express what he meant to say, and the therapist asked if he was having trouble remembering the word he needed.

Simon said, 'Yes, but I never can find the right word, even when I'm normal!'

'It's a standing joke with our friends,' Natalie told me as she joined us. 'He's always saying the wrong word, or asking me what the right one is.'

'What do you expect? I spent most of my life with French speaking parents, so English is virtually my second language!'

'How did you go with the speech therapist?' Natalie asked, knowing he'd spent time with her that afternoon.

'She asked me to name as many countries as I could, so I said Africa, but she wouldn't accept that. She said it was a continent and didn't count! Then I said Europe and that didn't count either! She seemed okay with Afghanistan, though.'

'Well, you wouldn't pass a geography test before the accident, so how can they expect you to do well in something like that now? It's so stupid!' Natalie leapt to his defence.

'That's what I told her! You ask me anything to do with my job, like the best joints to use for what materials and I'll give you the right answer, but if I asked you, you wouldn't know, would you?'

'You have a point, Simon.' I agreed with him. 'It's horses for courses. You know your own stuff in your own comfort zone. We're all the same aren't we?'

'I already told this speech therapist about Simon.' Natalie said. 'They know he's no academic, so why are they asking him these stupid questions?' Natalie said.

'He often uses the wrong word in the wrong place. He always gets the words, 'content' and 'context' mixed up, and he calls Velcro, velcrove. There must be lots of people who do the same kind of thing. It can't be so unusual.'

'I know. Your grandma, my mum, was always getting words mixed up.' I told them. 'We called her, Hilda Baker, she was so bad sometimes.' Natalie and Simon looked confused. 'Oh, Hilda Baker was an actress. She was in a sitcom in the sixties and was famous for getting her words mixed up.'

'Oh, I remember Hilda Baker,' Simon said, 'she's the one who said, "I must get a little watch for this hand".'

Natalie and I exchanged a glance and raised eyebrows at each other. How surprising that he could remember some obscure actress from the TV of his childhood, but can't remember many details about the last ten years of his life.

We took Simon back to his unit for dinner, and we came back to the villa. We enjoyed a couple of hours of domestic bliss, playing with Ruby, bathing her and then we had our meal. The electric wok worked fine, and we enjoyed some stir-fry with noodles. While we ate, we shared our thoughts about Simon. He had told Natalie that he wants to get out of here by two weeks on Sunday. That's the goal he set himself. I think it has a lot to do with the fact that the next Formula One race is being televised from Valencia on the 24th August, and he wants to go home to watch this on his own television in the comfort of his own home.

'I think it's more realistic to aim for the beginning of September.' I told Natalie. 'Judging by the slowness that things happen here, I can't see them letting him go much before then.'

'Simon doesn't see there's much for them to do, though.' Natalie said.

'It must be hard to be in Simon's position. Of course, he won't be able to see what's wrong, will he? Not like we can.'

'I think he's in denial, Mum. He knows there's something wrong with the way he thinks, but he's trying to block it out and make excuses. It's the same when I talk with him about going back to work. It's as if he doesn't want to go back to work. I think he might have lost confidence or something because when I mention it, he says maybe he could stay at home and look after Ruby, and I can go to work.'

'Maybe he feels he won't be safe to go back to work, and this is his way of dealing with those feelings. It wouldn't be nice for him to have to admit these thoughts, would it? It would also be better for his self-esteem if it were his decision not to go back to work, rather than wait for some therapist to tell him he can't.'

'I don't think he's capable of thinking it through in the same way we can. I think he's in denial, and that's okay, but it will be hard to deal with if he's also in denial about the treatment he needs.'

She then told me something worrying. 'I think he's trying to keep things from them too,' she began. 'He doesn't want the staff to know about some of his problems because he thinks they'll use them as an excuse to keep him here longer.'

'What other problems?' I asked.

'Oh, I told them he'd lost weight, and I was worried that he wasn't gaining it back. He told me off for telling them and said it was nothing to do with them.'

'Well, that's not too worrying. He'll gain weight when he starts eating your cooking.'

'Yeah, I guess. But he's keeping quiet about his eyes too, and he doesn't want me to remind them that he can't see properly.'

'But surely, they'll know about his eye problem from his medical notes.'

'Yeah, but I guess Simon doesn't realise that. He thinks they'll use any excuse to keep him here longer, and he doesn't want them to have any more excuses than they already have.'

'But surely, this is the best place to deal with his problems. He should be discussing them and getting them fixed.'

'This place is useless, Mum, and you know it as much as we do! It's nothing like they said it would be. They were supposed to be giving him intensive neuro rehab, and so far he's had nothing of any worth and the people aren't helpful...'

'To be fair,' I interrupted her. 'We have learned that most of the people are good. It's only the odd one or two who get his back up.'

'Yeah, I suppose. But that's all it takes. Just one bad member of staff and he'll fixate on that, and suddenly they're all bastards in his eyes.'

'What about that guy he saw today?'

'Yeah, he's really taken to Matthew.'

He's the neuropsychologist in charge of Simon's care, and he treats Simon with respect and tells him exactly how things are. Simon values honesty and this chap told him the truth.

'Then get Simon to focus on Matthew. He's the key to making Simon feel happier here,' I told her.

'Yeah, I guess he could be.'

'He won't try to fool Simon or give him false promises. If Simon respects honesty, you have to be honest with him about everything too.' I said. 'If he has to stay here longer than he wants to, he has to know how long it's going to be. If they want to keep him until he can walk again, you have to tell him. We have to live with that, and so does Simon. Don't hold any punches. You won't be doing him any favours in the long run. He has to know the reality of his situation then he can start to deal with it.'

'I am honest with him when I can be!' She protested. 'But he's doing so well. I know he'll be devastated if he has to be here for months. When I think of some of the stuff he'll have to go through, like learning to walk again, and maybe having to learn to drive again, wow! I can't tell him he has all that to come. It would be too much for him to take in. I don't want to upset him by dwelling on the negative side of things.

'He thinks that as soon as the casts are off his feet he'll be able to get up and walk. I have told him he'll have to have physio, and it will hurt, but he switches off. Sometimes I just don't know what to say to him.'

'I know what you mean. I've talked with him about getting a new car once or twice, and he's convinced that you'll need two cars by Christmas so he can be independent and go places without you. He doesn't think he might not be able to drive again.'

'That's a thought he couldn't handle. We won't go there yet.'

'Yeah, I see what you mean. Sometimes it's kinder to be economical with the truth, isn't it?'

'He is trying to be more tolerant, though.' Natalie changed the subject.

'I think it's helping that he has other patients to chat with and compare notes. Even if some staff are patronizing, at least they're patronizing to everyone and Simon doesn't feel it's just him.' I pointed out.

'Yeah and he's managing to keep his temper pretty well. But I don't know how much longer he can control it. He's been close to losing it a few times here already.'

Natalie left after Ruby was in bed and didn't come home until after 10pm. She stayed with Simon until he was ready for sleep, and when she came home I was ready for bed too.

DAY 40 Thursday 7th August

We were woken early when Ruby decided that 5am was a good time for breakfast. We don't mind our early starts. By the time we were all dressed and fed, Natalie decided to go for a run, and I did some yoga with Ruby. The gentle stretches help me keep mobile as age stiffens my joints and the exercises have helped me cope with the discomfort of the lumpy beds I've slept in here in Sydney.

Ruby joins me on the floor and loves to copy me as I do the poses. I part my legs and lean to the side, and Ruby widens her legs and leans until she falls over, giggling. Her favourite trick is to wait until I stretch my arms to the ceiling then she toddles up to tickle my tummy. When I bend to touch my toes she comes up behind me and peeks between my legs, giggling as she makes me lose concentration.

Natalie came back all sweaty and pepped-up after her run, and while she showered, I got Ruby ready for a walk. We intend to go down to the brain injury unit to see if we can take Simon out for lunch. He has an empty schedule today, so we can't see that it will be a problem.

SAME DAY next entry

We were able to collect Simon from the unit. They gave permission for him to leave until 3pm. They also asked if we had any plans to take him out at the weekend, which gave us something to think about. They intend to show Simon how he can transfer from the wheelchair into a car so we can take him somewhere in a taxi at the weekend. The zoo was mentioned as a possibility.

Today we took him down to the village. It was hard going on Natalie as she had to push him down then back up the steep hill, but she's fit and healthy and Simon helped by holding the brake on the descent and pushing the wheels with his hands going uphill on the way back. I can't say I was so lucky with Ruby in the pram. It's a heavy piece of equipment, and I was puffing like an old steam train by the time we got back.

We had lunch at the pavement cafe we'd found, and Simon told us about what he had been doing earlier. He'd had a session with one therapist where he had to read a passage about a blowfish then answer questions about what he'd read.

'They said I did pretty well, and I've never done anything like that before.' He was feeling quite pleased with himself and was in a good mood. 'Physio was too easy, though. I told her I could do lots more, but she wasn't interested.'

'Maybe they don't want you to overtax yourself.' I suggested.

'Ruby could do the exercises without breaking into a sweat! It's useless!'

As we chatted more, Simon began to repeat himself. When Natalie pointed out that we'd already talked about that topic, he got cross. This tendency towards anger is a normal part of Simon's makeup, but it seems he's quicker to rise now than he would have been before the accident.

He complained that Natalie had bought him a puzzle book. He used to enjoy doing crosswords and word searches, so she thought the book would be good for him. He complained the puzzles were too difficult, and he can't do them.

'I don't know why you got me a puzzle book. I never do puzzles.'

Natalie told me later that he did them all the time, and we realised that Simon's inability to process the information required to solve a puzzle, would be down to the brain injury. We hoped this would improve as it might mean that he would also have trouble following complicated instructions and functioning on all kinds of levels of normal, everyday life. Simon doesn't see it this way. He just thinks he can't do puzzles.

We took him back to keep his appointments with the neuropsychologist and occupational therapist, and I brought Ruby back to the villa.

Natalie stayed down at the unit for a little while because Bob, his colleague from work, was coming to visit Simon again. Natalie didn't want him to be turned away because Simon was busy with appointments.

Ruby and I played outside in the sunshine for a little while then I brought her back so she could have her nap.

SAME DAY next entry

Natalie and Bob came back to the villa shortly after Ruby went to sleep. Bob was amazed at the change in Simon since the last time he saw him. I suppose we don't notice the huge changes so much because we concentrate on the smaller ones we see from day to day, but to Bob, the improvement was vast. He couldn't stay long, but it was good to catch up and Simon appreciated seeing his friend from work.

Natalie had spent a good deal of time on the phone while Bob visited Simon. She was told that Simon's orthopaedic appointment at the RPA, to review his legs, had been changed to the following Friday.

She was not happy about this change as it meant putting things on hold for another few days and might mean she would have to reschedule the family meeting as that couldn't be held until the leg review results from the hospital were back.

She phoned Simon's case manager to see why the appointment had been changed and learned that the surgeon had asked for the change so he could do the operation to remove the wires in his foot at the same time. He operated on Fridays, so this seemed a sensible solution, which meant Simon wouldn't need to travel to the hospital twice.

Natalie asked if the surgeon could see Simon tomorrow as that was a Friday and amazingly, after a few more calls, the surgeon agreed to fit him in.

Within a few minutes of organising all that, Natalie was asked to go see the neuropsychologist, who told her that the team has agreed that Simon may be ready to go home by the 29th of August, which is only three weeks away, depending how the appointment goes tomorrow for his feet.

This is brilliant news, and we can't help being excited, though we know that a lot depends on what happens tomorrow.

DAY 41 Friday 8th August

Last night when Natalie came home, she told me that Simon opened up to her, at last. He's admitted that he's afraid to go back to do the job he's employed to do. He's seen so many accidents while working in various places. It is a dangerous job, and I suppose the car crash has made him realise that he's not immortal. He told Natalie that he doesn't want to do a dangerous job because he doesn't want to put her or Ruby through this again. It must have been a huge thing for Simon to admit his fear, but as always, Natalie supported him and told him that they would manage somehow.

Natalie puts on a brave front for Simon but is now worried about their financial future. What if they can't keep up the payments on the mortgage? What if she has to work full time to support them? Will Simon be capable of doing all the household chores, looking after the animals and Ruby while she works?

She told me she'd thought of asking to take a break

from paying the mortgage. Up until now, they had been paying more than necessary to get the loan paid more quickly, so this might be a realistic option for them in the short term.

'I'll have to see if I can talk to a financial planner. We have some savings and I can do more hours for my work, I suppose, but if Simon doesn't want to go back to work at all, I think we'll be stuffed!'

'He might be persuaded to go back to do light duties when he gets back on his feet. Then you'll get enough money with the government handout added to his wages, won't you?'

'Yeah, but Simon won't like counting nails! That's what they'll make him do. It's soul destroying, Mum. He has more self-respect than that.'

'He'll have to ditch his pride if you need the money, Natalie.'

I'm helping all I can while I'm here so they can keep hold of the money they already have and use it as a buffer in the lean times ahead. I buy most of our shopping on my credit card and Paul pays that off in UK. Paul transferred a good chunk of cash into Natalie and Simon's joint account, and I haven't touched that yet.

Natalie will need every penny over the coming months as she's not earning anything while she's down here in Sydney, and Simon is only getting the basic pay. He regularly topped that up each month with overtime and bonuses, but he won't be earning these useful extras for some time.

We had to get up early this morning as Natalie had to go with Simon, to attend the appointment at the RPA. I hope the surgeon will decide that his legs are healed enough to take the casts off. If Simon can start to weight bear, we'll be well on schedule for going home on the 29th of August.

Ruby and I did some chores while we waited for news from the hospital. We did some laundry and emptied the rubbish bin. I did some yoga and Ruby had fun tickling me. I have a doctor's appointment at 10am, so I'm trying to keep Ruby going without a nap this morning as I will have to take her with me. We've been singing nursery rhymes and doing all the actions to Twinkle, twinkle little star. She is so adorable.

SAME DAY next entry

I've been to see the doctor. After hearing why I didn't have time to fill my prescription before leaving England, she only charged me ten dollars for the appointment, which was a nice surprise. The pills cost me thirty-eight dollars, but at least I don't have to worry about getting my reflux problems now.

Natalie didn't get back from the RPA until mid-afternoon, and the news was bleak. Simon has to keep the casts on for another six weeks and can't weight bear at least until then. So he has to stay in the wheelchair.

Natalie doesn't think this is a huge blow to us, regarding getting Simon home. She'd been doing some thinking and come to the decision that we will be able to get things in place for him to enable him to manage at home in the wheelchair. It will just mean that she has to help him more.

I know she doesn't mind the hard work involved in looking after Simon. She'll do whatever it takes to get him home, even if that means she has to be his full-time nurse when they get there.

We also got a weekend pass for Simon. He can come and stay with us here in the Villa. He had to wait until he'd had his medications before he left the unit, so Natalie has just gone to collect him. We plan to have a takeaway for dinner this evening, and I'll have Ruby in my room so they can enjoy some privacy in the other bedroom. It will be the first time they've slept together since the accident. I know Natalie has missed being close to him.

Natalie told me the immediate plans for Simon while we waited to go to collect him. She told me he had another appointment on Tuesday at the RPA to get the wires out of his foot. They weren't able to do it today.

The surgeon spent time explaining the x-ray images to Natalie so that she would understand the extent of the damage and the reasons for Simon keeping the casts on. She said he skimmed over the technical stuff until Natalie started talking in medical terms too, and when he realised that she understood what he was talking about, he went into detail.

Natalie drew diagrams to show me what the x-rays had looked like, so she could explain the damage to me. Her drawings were simple, but they showed me exactly how badly damaged Simon's body was. The broken heel was pretty smashed up and will probably cause him pain and mobility problems in the future. His other foot was badly crushed, but all the bones were healing well.

His ankle was also badly broken and will affect his mobility too, which means he might always have a limp.

His thighbone had a spiral, splinter break, with a

floating section in the middle. The splinters damaged his muscles and the titanium rod that now holds the bone together, will stay in place forever. Natalie knows that Simon will be unpleasantly surprised when he starts to get mobile. He's in for a very painful time.

I asked how he'd fare in the long run. 'How will he cope with climbing scaffolding and doing his job? Even if he doesn't go back to the same kind of work, or any other kind of work. If he has to stay home, how will he manage the jobs around the property?'

'I can't think so far ahead yet, but Simon is strong and fit and I know he won't be beaten by this.'

'Well, he's done amazingly well so far. He's surprised us all with the way he seems to be recovering from the brain injury, maybe he'll do the same with all the physical injuries too.'

'Yeah I hope so.' She sighed. 'The doctors want to keep giving us the bad news and every time they do he proves 'em wrong, doesn't he?'

I hope he continues to prove them all wrong. I hope he's as strong as Natalie believes him to be. He'll need to be. He has lots of suffering to go through before he can learn to walk again.

DAY 42 Saturday 9th August

It was lovely to see Simon in the heart of his family last night. He was relaxed and happy as he sat with Natalie, cuddling Ruby in his lap and reading her a bedtime story. When Ruby went to bed, we ordered pizza from the village and settled to talk.

Simon told us about some things he'd been remembering, and we were pleased to note that some of his recent memories seem to be surfacing. He can remember showing someone Natalie's business cards and remembered being proud of his wife and her skills.

Simon remembered his plans to build a shelter for the horses and talked about completing the fire pit for their camp oven. They introduced me to outside cooking, the Australian way, around an open fire on a late summer evening when I came to see Ruby a month after her birth. Simon had constructed a small fire pit on the back lawn while I was there, but he had started making it bigger before the accident. To hear him talking of these small plans was so good and it's so nice to see him looking to the future.

He remembered starting to rebuild the fire pit and the light-hearted argument he had with Natalie about the positioning of it. 'I wanted it to line up with the veggie patch, so it would look neat.'

'He marked it out with string,' Natalie told me. 'But then it wouldn't line up with the pool, so I told him he would have to turn it a bit.'

'But then I told you it wouldn't be in line with the retaining wall for the hill at the back.' He chuckled.

'Then we talked about getting a telescope and lining it up with the stars!' Natalie giggled as she told me how the whole argument had disintegrated into silly banter between them.

I watched them laughing together and felt a warm glow grow inside me. It was lovely to see Simon remembering these small things. The gaps in his memory are filling up gradually, and it's remarkable to witness the evidence of his improvements. It's nothing short of the miracle we prayed for.

He still goes over the same conversation a lot, but aren't we all prone to repeating ourselves sometimes? I think he's still a little uncomfortable because I'm here. He can't totally relax with Natalie because his mother-in-law is constantly there too. I understand how he feels and know that he can't talk freely about things that might be on his mind while I'm in the same room. He doesn't feel comfortable discussing his deepest fears while in my company. I know he tells Natalie, though, and that's encouraging. She told me earlier that she felt he'd come out of the denial stage.

He talked about work but not in realistic terms. He was still thinking about what he used to do ten years ago before he met Natalie, when he worked on short term contracts in the outback for big money.

'I know I can spend three months away and earn a lot, and then I can stay at home for the rest of the year.'

Natalie and I know that would be highly unlikely to happen in the future, but we let it go, neither of us wanted to burst his bubble because he sounded so happy. Then he switched moods and began to talk about the dangerous side of the job. He told me that he had always planned to be out of construction work by the time he was forty.

'I'm almost thirty-nine, and I think this has made me think I should bring these plans forward. I don't want to be doing a job like this forever. I want to spend time with Ruby and the dogs and Natalie.'

'We'll be glad to see more of you too, honey.' Natalie encouraged his positive thinking and steered him away from the fear of returning to a dangerous job.

This morning, Simon was talking about being able to drive again. He really wants to reach that goal. I told him he'd have to wait until Christmas at least, because of the chance of fits, but even then, he will have to have full use of his legs and feet. Then there's the problem with his eyes. If he can't see properly, he won't be allowed to drive. However, despite all the problems he will have to overcome, Simon is still confident that he'll be walking and driving again by Christmas. He's very determined, and I know he'll work hard to reach his goal. It will be incredible if he manages to achieve it.

I know that although he is improving rapidly, his brain injury is a very severe one and to hope he emerges unscathed from this would be too much to expect. I can see hardships and difficulties ahead for them, and it will break my heart to leave Natalie to deal with it on her own. I am trying to be realistic, though, and realise that she wouldn't want it any other way. I know how much she appreciates my being here to help her through this worst phase, but she is eager for me to go home so she can have Simon to herself. They'll need space to work out the problems they will face, without me being in the way. I can respect that, but it would be so much easier if I were just around the corner and only a few minutes away if Natalie should need me.

At this moment, Ruby is asleep. Natalie has taken Simon down to the unit so he can shower and shave and have his medications. When they return we plan to order a taxi and go to the shopping centre. We discussed going to the zoo, but it might be too taxing for Simon to have such a big day out. A few hours looking for sunglasses might be a better idea.

SAME DAY next entry

We went shopping and had lunch out at a large shopping complex earlier, but it was very stressful for Simon. He got disorientated on the journey there and blamed this on the erratic driving of the taxi driver. The poor driver was doing nothing wrong.

We looked in every shop that sold sunglasses, searching for some that would suit Simon's needs, but he didn't see any that he liked.

We looked at children's books for a long time while Simon took ages to choose one for Ruby. After lunch, Simon was very tired and anxious, so we ordered the taxi to take us back. It hadn't been a successful day out. Simon was tetchy and argumentative when we got back, and Natalie took him back to the unit for his injection. (He still has to have anti-clotting drugs, and these are given daily by injection into his tummy.)

I took Ruby to play on the grass and waited for her mum and dad to join us. The sun was still warm and we picked clover flowers and dandelion heads, enjoying the peace and tranquillity after our stressful day out. Ruby led me to another four-leaf clover. I picked it and put it in my pocket. I'm not usually superstitious, but I made another exception with my second lucky find. I wished we could get Simon home soon.

We found some large logs on the ground, and I sat for a while, and Ruby climbed up to sit beside me. She thought it was a good game to shuffle her bottom backward off the log and fall on her back into the long grass with her legs in the air. She laughed and jumped up to do it again. She's a real adrenaline junkie and loves danger. She'll run headlong down the big hill outside the villa until she loses her balance then she continues a wobbly sideways run until she regains it! It's so funny to watch her stagger until she almost falls.

She also likes to spin around until she's so dizzy she bumps into everything. Occasionally she hurts herself, but she only has a few minutes of dramatic crying before she's off doing the same thing again and smiling. She must take after her daddy. She's as tough as old boots and has nerves of steel.

When Natalie and Simon joined us, Natalie took care of Ruby, and I talked with Simon. He explained to me about the dangers in his work.

I've seen the beautiful cabinets and furniture he made for their home, but he earns more money working on construction sites. The heavy and dangerous work is climbing scaffolding and working on roofs. Working on scaffolding in wet weather; sitting astride roofing beams to fix them in place, and then manoeuvring around to get the next beam in place is not easy. He said he didn't mind the danger; he loves his job and was happy to talk about returning to work. He was stressing to me how much easier it will be for him to go back to doing a job he is qualified for, than take on lighter duties that he would hate. It was good to hear him talking so positively about work at last.

We discussed the tests he'd done the day before, and he got really angry that he got a question wrong. He'd been asked to name pictures of household gadgets and called one a mixer, then changed his mind and called it a blender.

'But even Natalie said she might call a mixer a blender. Why can't they ask me questions about things I know? Why can't they show me pictures of hammers and wrenches? What do I know about kitchen gadgets?'

I thought he had a good point.

The rest of the day went by quietly. We took Ruby home for her supper and Simon read her a story from her new book while Natalie went to the village to get us a takeaway dinner.

After I had put Ruby to bed, Simon complained that his eyes hurt and said he was seeing double. He was still blaming the taxi driver's erratic driving for upsetting his vision, but I felt Simon's problems were due to too much stimulation. Driving through heavy traffic, followed by the distractions of a busy shopping centre, then another stressful drive back, would have been a lot for him to deal with after the peace and tranquillity he was used to in the rehab environment.

WEEK SEVEN: Frustrations & temper

DAY 43 Sunday 10th August

Paul rang earlier this morning, and it was good to tell him that Simon had a weekend pass and was spending time with us. We talked about me going home, and how it might happen sooner rather than later, if things continued to improve at this rate. He asked if I'd got my pills and was relieved that I had. We talked of normal family things and looked forward to seeing each other again soon.

Katy rang too, but as I was in the middle of changing Ruby's smelly nappy. I told her I would ring her back. I'll try to ring her later for our catch up call.

This morning, Simon seemed subdued. He stayed in bed until Natalie and I had showered and dressed. Natalie took him down to the unit for his shower and medications. We were hoping to go out somewhere today, maybe the zoo or the aquarium, but after Natalie and I had a small discussion, we decided to stay in the local area. Simon was so disorientated yesterday that we didn't want to risk setting him back by giving his brain too much stimulation again today.

Natalie suggested that as Simon should have a full schedule during the week with all his various therapies, we could always go to the zoo while he was busy. I told her I wasn't too worried about going anywhere. I insisted yet again that I wasn't in Sydney to be a tourist, and if she didn't feel like going too far away from her husband, that was fine by me.

SAME DAY next entry

When Natalie brought Simon back up the hill after his shower, I was outside playing with Ruby on the grass. They came to join me and Natalie headed for Ruby, leaving Simon in the shade of a tree. I saw that Simon was not happy just by the tense set of his shoulders and I went to speak to him.

He'd been given his schedule for the following week and was disappointed to find that he was only seeing the neuropsychologist for one hour on Wednesday. Tomorrow he has a four-hour block to go shopping. Thursday he has to cook a meal and Friday morning he has to make breakfast. He has a one-hour slot every day for computer time, and that's it.

After all the promises of a full schedule of intensive therapies, this was a very bitter blow.

Simon was kicking off big time about shopping and cooking. 'I don't go shopping for food unless Natalie writes me a list! It's not something I normally do, so why are they expecting me to do it now?'

I tried to calm him by stressing the positive angles for him. 'Maybe *you* can write a list, it's not as if you can't do it, is it? You know how to do shopping, and that's all they want to see.' I tried to simplify it for him.

'But they can't expect me to cook! I can cook! I can make lasagne, but I'm in a wheelchair! I can't reach the top of a cooker and I can't see to do anything!'

'Maybe they'll let you have some help.'

'I don't see what the rush is. Why can't they wait until I can walk and stand up? For fuck's sake!' he yelled.

'I don't know, Simon,' I said.

'I can't drive until Christmas, so what's the rush to

see if I can cook or shop?' He voice rose by decibels as he became more upset, and it was clear he was well out of his comfort zone with what they were expecting him to do.

'If they asked me to make a mitre joint or ask me what tools I use in the shed instead of showing me pictures of bloody blenders, I might have a chance!'

I could see his point. You'd think they'd target the tests to suit the patient's background. Women could be shown pictures of household gadgets and kitchen equipment, but most men are out of their depth in those areas. Surely tests could be tailored to the individual?

'And what's all this about computer skills?' He yelled. 'I don't know about computers. I know what I need to do to get my I-tunes, and I can look for stuff on the Internet, but I don't know anything else. What the hell are they expecting?'

'Maybe they're filing in time as they can't do anything else with you. You can't do physiotherapy until the casts come off and you passed all your neuropsychology tests, so they don't need to do anything more there. Matthew only wants to see you for an hour this week, so he must think you don't need much more help in that area.'

'So why do I need to be here at all?' He growled. 'Why can't they just let me go home?'

'Good point, Simon. I wish I knew the answer to that one.' I told him.

Natalie came to join us. She'd heard Simon's raised voice. I think anyone within a half mile of us would have heard him. I took Ruby and retreated to the villa, leaving Natalie to talk to Simon and hopefully try to calm him.

It's easy to understand why Simon can't see the point in being here any longer. He thinks that once he gets the wires out of his foot on Tuesday, we should be allowed to go home. I hope he's right, but I have an awful feeling that they'll want to keep him here for longer and maybe even until he can walk. I'd like to see what happens if they try to suggest that to Natalie or Simon. There'll be fireworks, and I can see Natalie signing him out and doing a runner!

Ruby was in bed for her nap when they came back to the villa. Simon was calmer, and it was clear that Natalie had managed to talk him down from his stressed state. However, conversation was stilted between them, tension filled the air.

When Ruby woke she was upset, and even biscuits wouldn't fix her tears, I guessed she sensed the tension and nothing would make her smile. She didn't want her omelette at dinner time, so I took her for a long and playful bath. We splashed and giggled and drenched the bathroom. I ended up wet through too, but I had succeeded in making her happy again.

I could hear that Natalie and Simon were talking on the phone in the next room. They had it on speakerphone, and I could hear Carina's voice asking him how things were going. I kept Ruby in the bath to give them some time to have a peaceful conversation.

I really enjoyed playing with my little angel, letting her pour water over the side of her baby bath then listening as it gurgled down the drain in the middle of the bathroom floor. The louder the water gurgled, the louder we giggled. She thought it was so funny, and I thought she was even funnier. Eventually, when her bath was empty, she was persuaded to get out and get dried and ready for bed.

After dinner, Natalie took Simon back to the unit as his weekend pass was expired, but he was reluctant to go. Natalie and I had found it hard work to look after him all weekend and keep him happy. It had given us a small insight of what might be in store for us when we finally got him home for good.

Natalie and I had a long conversation after she returned from taking Simon to the unit. We thought that this rehab situation had let Simon down badly. After being promised so much and expecting to see therapy sessions filling his days to help him recover more quickly, we felt disappointed and frustrated and so did Simon.

We discussed getting him home and what we might need to do to make that happen. Natalie remembered that one of her neighbours, Mary, worked in the offices at Byron District Hospital. Mary had rung Natalie a week or two back to ask if there were anything she could do to help. Natalie wasted no time in ringing this friend and asked if she knew how we could get Simon to Byron. After a brief conversation, Natalie ended the call, and she was smiling.

'She thinks if we can get him a wheelchair and everything we need to have him at home, they can't object to him being taken as an outpatient at the hospital. Mary gave me a number for one of our other neighbours. I completely forgot that Anita is an occupational therapist! They'd even been discussing Simon the other day, and said how good it would be to get him home so maybe Anita could work with him.'

'Hang on a minute, Natalie.' I interrupted her. 'Isn't that jumping the gun a bit too far?' I was just as excited about the prospect of taking Simon home, but there was a lot to organise and a lot of people to talk with before we could be sure it would be possible.

'Mary seems to think we can do it. I just need to make some calls tomorrow. I'll call Anita and the insurance people to make sure they'll pay for the equipment we'll need.'

'What equipment will we need for him? I know we need a wheelchair, obviously, but what about bathing and taking him to the toilet?'

'We can get a commode chair and the bathroom is like the wet room here at the villa, it has a central drain, so we can put him in the middle of the floor and hose him down if we have to.'

'That's a bit drastic.' I laughed at the image she had put in my mind. 'But I'm sure if it means we can get him home, Simon won't object.'

I was beginning to see that it was a real possibility, and allowed myself to feel a little excited at the prospect of going home.

Natalie would have to pull out all the stops and use her skills at persuasion, but I had every faith in my daughter to accomplish the miracle of getting Simon home very soon.

DAY 44 Monday 11th August

This morning, Natalie went to the brain injury unit as soon as the desk was manned to make an appointment to see the neuropsychologist in charge of Simon. She said she wanted to ask his opinion about taking Simon home, but I knew she would give him no choice in the matter. Her mind was already made up, and she wouldn't let anything stand in her way. She has the appointment for 12 noon.

When she got back to the villa, Simon phoned to let us know how he was doing. He'd had his computer skills therapy and told us it was a waste of time. A member of staff had taken him to a computer, logged him on and left him to it. Simon asked her what she wanted him to do, and she told him he could check his e-mails, surf the net and do whatever he wanted. She didn't even stay to make sure he knew what he was doing! What was all that about? What was he supposed to achieve with that? We had been right to assume they were killing time with him. The sooner we get him out of here the better. He could surf the Internet at home in comfort!

He then told us about the occupational therapist who called to see him to discuss recreational therapy. She asked what he enjoyed doing, so he told her he liked to go surfing. She then steered him toward something more realistic and suggested table tennis.

'Listen, lady,' he told her. 'I played table tennis at school, and I was a champion. You don't get to play at that level in a wheelchair and I'm not up for playing Ping-Pong!'

She was persistent, and asked if he were bored.

'Of course I'm bored! You're not doing anything to help me in here!'

She asked if he enjoyed doing jigsaws or played board games.

'Yes, I have lots of board games at home and people to play them with! Just get me home so I can pat my dogs and play with my little girl. That will be recreation enough for me.'

Natalie filled the morning making calls to put things in place for our return home. I did some tickly-tummy yoga with Ruby. She was full of giggles and cute as a button as she copied my moves. We had a lovely time, and when Natalie finished her calls, we went to the shops to get something for our dinner tonight. We let Ruby walk to tire her out, and now she's asleep in bed while Natalie makes more calls before her meeting with the neuropsychologist.

Anita proved very helpful. She asked Natalie questions about wheelchair access in the home and told her what kind of equipment Simon would need. She also told us that there is a team of occupational therapists who work in the Bangalow area, and they make house calls, so he wouldn't need to keep travelling into the hospital at Byron to see them, they would offer him therapies in his own home.

The outlook was getting better, and better. She said these therapists could deliver all the necessary equipment to the house with only a day's notice, in readiness for our homecoming.

Natalie then phoned the insurance company to make sure they would be willing to pay for the hire of all this equipment and the answer was positive. They even offered to arrange to have it delivered to the house for her. The next call was to the airline to see if they had seats available for us on Thursday and to ask about wheelchair access on the plane. There was a flight on Thursday afternoon, but Natalie knew she'd have to attend the family meeting here before they would allow her to leave with Simon. We wouldn't have time to make the Thursday flight, but there was another on Friday morning. Wheelchair access would be no problem, and the airline had a special hoist lift to get Simon into the plane.

When Natalie set out to keep her appointment with Matthew, the neuropsychologist, I sensed she was geared up for a fight. She had all the ammunition in place and all her arguments made sense. I just hoped the doctors would see it her way.

SAME DAY next entry

In theory, we should be good to go on Thursday evening or Friday morning. Matthew listened to Natalie's reasons for wanting Simon home, and she told him about the arrangements that were awaiting her final confirmation.

'Everything can be in place by Thursday for Simon so we can manage him at home. I just have to give the insurance people the go-ahead and book our flights.'

Matthew agreed with Natalie that Simon would do better in his own home, but mentioned there were still some issues that needed to be addressed and in his opinion, Simon would be better dealing with those here in the protected environment of the Brain Injury unit, but he also agreed that to keep Simon here against his will would be no good at all.

Finally, he said it was a decision that had to be made by the team. He would need to talk with the other doctors about arranging onward referrals for Simon's various problems, but he promised that he should have an answer for us by tomorrow afternoon.

Simon has to go for his surgery in the morning, to remove the wires in his foot, so hopefully, by the time he gets back, we will know something positive and be able to book our flights home.

We took Ruby down to see Simon at visiting time. One of his workmates from home was sitting with him. This chap was visiting family in Sydney and thought he'd call to see Simon. It was good to see them chatting about work and mutual friends. Simon was doing well with the conversation, and hardly made any mistakes with his words. He was vastly improved and I could see that he was now more than ready to go home.

Simon talked about the occupational therapy shopping trip that he'd been taken on earlier that morning, which had been a complete waste of time for him. He had been taken to the local supermarket with another patient. The other patient was doing some shopping from a list and Simon was asked, by the occupational therapist, to find some pine-o-clean, (same product as clean-o-pine in England.)

He wheeled his chair to the correct aisle, but couldn't find any. He then asked a member of the supermarket staff where it might be on the shelves, and found out they didn't stock it. That was the sum total of his shopping experience!

I guess, to be fair that the therapists would have been watching how Simon coped with the situation and would assess how he could process the information they gave him. They would have been looking at how he could follow instructions and achieve a goal. Simon might have had more respect for their methods if they had bothered to do some forward planning and made sure the shop stocked the product that they had asked him to find.

Simon's workmate left after an hour or so, and Ruby was getting restless. She'd already explored every inch of the communal room and wanted to explore more. I had to keep chasing her to stop her from toddling into private areas where other patients were sleeping. She's so inquisitive; I can't take my eyes off her for a moment. I was glad when it was Simon's dinner time, and we could return to the villa for our meal.

Ruby has been a dream today. She's played happily inside and out and splashed so much at bath time that I was drenched again! We enjoyed some cuddles while I was eating dinner and she happily swapped kisses for noodles. She knows how to win me over. After dinner, Natalie went back to see Simon for a few hours and Ruby was happy to sit with me for more cuddles before bed.

She feels so comfortable with me now, and I feel we have forged a special bond. It will be doubly hard for me to leave her when I have to go back to England.

Simon's sister, Helen, is coming to stay overnight with us tomorrow. Helen is a little younger than me and I'm looking forward to seeing her again. I met her once before at the wedding.

Helen knows that Simon is undergoing surgery, so she plans to arrive about supper time as we don't know how long Simon will be at the hospital. Natalie plans to be out of bed in the morning by 5am so she can go with Simon. His appointment is for 7am to have the wires taken out of his foot, but it's a block booking, and he could be seen at any time.

DAY 45 Tuesday 12th August
Natalie got up at some ungodly hour to go with Simon to the hospital. Ruby slept in my bedroom, so Natalie could get ready without disturbing us, but as Ruby had been awake a few times in the night, we were all tired this morning.

Just as Ruby and I were dressed and breakfasted, Paul phoned. He was staying with our friends in Middlesbrough while he was working in the area. It cheered me to talk with Wendy. She's been a friend for more than twenty-five years and has known Natalie since she was four-years-old. She sent her love to us and handed me back to Paul.

We discussed the possibility of us going home to Bangalow at the end of this week, and he was so pleased to hear this news. I explained that I wanted to stay on at Natalie's place for a few weeks to make sure Natalie could cope with Simon at home before I left her and he agreed that's what I should do.

We knew that the first few weeks at home would be stressful for Natalie as she would have to juggle appointments for Simon with looking after the animals and Ruby and doing all the normal household chores.

Paul and I postponed plans of an early reunion. We could wait a little longer.

DAY 46 Wednesday 13th August
I didn't get much time to write yesterday. Ruby was awake for much of the day and obviously knew that her mum was missing.

I tried to distract her from being grumpy by playing with her. It rained nearly all morning, so we were cooped up in the villa, but as soon as it stopped I took Ruby out for a walk.

We splashed in lots of puddles. She got thoroughly cold and wet, but we had lots of fun. I eventually coaxed her away from the rain soaked ground by suggesting it was time for dinner. Food won over fun, and I could bring her back to get her warm and dry again.

Natalie and Simon didn't get back from the hospital until late in the afternoon, and Helen was waiting for them at the unit as she didn't know where I would be and didn't have my number to call me.

After Simon had his dinner, Natalie asked if she could bring him to the villa for the evening so he could spend quality time with his sister.

He'd had the wires taken out of his left foot, and the cast has been taken off. He still can't weight-bear on either foot until the cast is taken off his other leg, but that won't happen until sometime in the next four or five weeks.

I made us girls some dinner of chicken and pasta in the wok while Helen played with Ruby, getting to know her little niece and talking with her brother. Simon was very tired after his long day at the hospital, but he enjoyed talking with Helen and playing with his little girl.

Natalie brought me up to date on the news from Matthew. He had sanctioned our release. We could go home on Friday. It was the best news! No wonder Simon was looking so relaxed and happy. We were one step closer to our goal of getting home.

Helen offered to take Simon back down to the unit and help to put him to bed. Natalie was tired after her early start followed by a boring day hanging around at the hospital. I knew she was grateful that Helen had noticed this and had offered to give her a break.

We talked more over a glass of wine after Simon and Helen left. We were so happy at the thought of going home. We had a lot to arrange, but Natalie was confident it would all be done in time. Helen came back to join us, and we bedded down for the night. I shared with Natalie and Helen slept in my bed. It's a good thing I'm getting used to bed hopping.

This morning, Helen left early, after one last quick visit to Simon. I rang Paul to give him the good news about our move home and Natalie called the insurance people to organise a wheelchair, commode chair and transfer-slider-board to be delivered to the house.

The insurance person wanted Natalie to answer a few questions about Simon's current medical status, but Natalie didn't want to waste time talking to them and told them they could get that information from his case manager.

SAME DAY next entry

It's been a quiet waiting day for us. After the initial flurry of phone calls to arrange things and book flights for Friday morning, we found ourselves with time on our hands. Simon had some therapy sessions, and we couldn't visit until later, so we went shopping for food for our lunch and dinner, played with Ruby and talked of the future.

Natalie is continuing to be concerned about their financial security. We had already discussed their options many times, but now, I think Natalie is facing them realistically for the first time. The possibility that

Simon might never work again is scary, but Natalie is prepared to face the daunting prospect.

'I can always go back to work full-time and let Simon be the house husband.'

'That would be a good solution if your income were enough to keep you. Would you be able to earn enough?' I asked.

'I'd have to ask for a raise, but I can make it worth their while. They know I'm a good worker and they know I'm committed to giving them good value for money. If Simon can be capable of looking after Ruby, this would be the way to go, I think.'

'You can't go back to work full-time until Simon's back on his feet, so what will you do meantime?'

'Manage.' She shrugged. 'We'll have to.'

I told her that Paul and I would help if she needed money. We had a nest egg saved for our retirement, but as we weren't planning to retire for a good few years, the cash was available should she need it.

We discussed some of Simon's ongoing problems. The conversation with Helen last night had highlighted a few memory issues that he still couldn't get to grips with. Helen had asked who cut his hair and Simon had said Emma had been to see him. It was Linda who visited with his mum, not Emma. He could remember that his mum had been to see him in hospital, but couldn't remember anything about the visit.

We talked about this memory problem and hoped it wouldn't be permanent.

'But, people live with short-term memory loss, and there are ways to cope with this.' I told Natalie.

'I know, and I'm sure we'll manage, but it makes me wonder what other problems might be lurking in the future for us.'

'It's no use worrying about what might lie in wait for you. Better to deal with problems as they come up, eh? That way you won't feel swamped by it all.'

'Yeah, but I'm not looking forward to when Simon has to do the psychology tests so he can work and drive again. He doesn't know that he'll have to jump through hoops before they'll let him near machinery again. He won't like having to do them.'

'Lets hope by the time he has to do the tests, he'll realise why he needs to do them, and it won't be such a big issue for him.'

'I hope he can pass them. He'll be so frustrated and angry if he can't. He'll feel like such a burden and he'll feel guilty and useless. Besides being angry, he'll get depressed, and —'

'One thing at a time, Natalie.' I interrupted her. 'You know all this will come, but you don't have to face it yet. You don't have to face it alone, either. I'll stay as long as you need me to. If I have to stay until Christmas, then that's what I'll do.'

'You need to get home to Dad. You two have been apart long enough, and me and Simon have to work this out for ourselves. We have to find a way to live our lives from now on. It's going to be very different, but we have to learn.'

'Well, I'll wait until you kick me out, or give me enough hints to know that it's time to leave. You'll need me for a while yet, though.'

'Yeah, thanks, Mum. It will be good to have you

around a bit longer, but I know Simon is looking forward to having some space at home.'

'And that doesn't include me being there. I know. I won't outstay my welcome.' I understood how Simon felt. I'd feel the same myself, but I know my daughter and granddaughter will have many more stressful times ahead, and I wanted to be there to help.

SAME DAY next entry

We went to Simon at visiting time. He was disappointed his session with the neuropsychologist hadn't gone well.

He'd been given a list of fifteen unrelated words and asked to repeat them. As the session progressed, he did other mental exercises and was asked to repeat the list of words at intervals between the other tasks. He could only remember nine of them by the end of the session. To be fair, I doubt that I could have done much better than that.

We discussed that he would probably be asked to do similar tests at the outpatient clinic at Byron, so they could continue to assess his progress.

'I was never any good at school. I barely made it to tenth grade! I'm as good as I'm going to get, but that still ain't good enough!'

'Simon, you can't say that.' I told him. 'You said the same thing two weeks ago, but look how much you've improved since then. You're getting better every day. You will get better at these tests. You will!' I insisted.

'They're testing me against the whole of Australia and they don't understand that I never was any good at tests, so how can I get good marks.'

'They're not testing you against anyone else, Simon.' I tried to explain. 'They are testing you against yourself. They'll compare these results with results further down the line, to see if you've improved.'

'Well, Matthew said I shouldn't be too worried as it's only six weeks since the accident and not even two weeks since I woke up to know what's real.'

'Exactly!' Natalie and I chorused together.

'You have a long way to go, Simon, but you'll still be making improvements for years to come!' Natalie said.

He looked confused, so I hastened to explain. 'We were told, at the beginning, Simon, that most of your improvements will happen in the first six months after the injury, and you're only six weeks into that time frame, aren't you?'

I watched him nod warily.

'Then they told us that with the type of brain injury you have, even after six months, your brain will continue to repair itself for up to two more years at least.'

'You had a massive injury, Simon. It will take a long time to get fully right, but I'm here with you and I'll help all I can.' Natalie took his hand. 'We don't know how good you'll get, but even if you don't get any better from how you are right now, I'll still love you and I'll still be here for you.'

'I won't say the same.' I hoped to lighten the atmosphere as I could see tears in Simon's eyes. 'I'll be leaving just as soon as you don't want me around anymore.'

Simon smiled at me, and Natalie laughed. 'Don't worry, Mum. We'll pack your bags for you when we're ready to give you the hint to go.'

We left Simon to his dinner and came back to the villa for ours. Natalie went back down for the last few hours of visiting time while I put Ruby to bed. I think we managed to convince Simon that he will improve, but stressed that it would take a long time. Natalie will have to reinforce this many times to make sure he understands it fully and to keep it fresh in his memory, so he doesn't lose sight of the hope.

My worry is that Simon, the real Simon, complete with memories and concern for others; will take a long time to turn up. I'm afraid of a future where Natalie will be left with a kind of half a Simon. One that is just as demanding and dependant as he is now. One who repeats himself; can't remember very well and so can't be relied upon.

Oh, I wish I could be as positive as Natalie. I really wish I could see a rosy future for them, but I'm too scared to look into the crystal ball for fear of seeing my worst fears lurking inside.

DAY 47 Thursday 14th August

When Ruby went down for her morning nap, we did some packing. We're trying to squeeze everything in and deciding what to leave behind is a problem. We have limited space in our bags and we have extra baggage with Simon's clothes and items. We'll leave the baby bath and most of the toiletries. We won't take the food or the magazines we bought. We'll need as much room in the suitcases as we can find.

When Simon had physiotherapy this morning, the girl asked if she could take off his bandages so she could see to work on his legs better. Simon refused to let her take off the dressings, telling her that it was only one day since he had surgery, and the surgeon had told him to keep the dressing on for at least a week.

He was so upset that he rang Natalie to check that he remembered properly what the surgeon had said. Natalie told him not to get upset and suggested that the physiotherapist was just nosey. This person clearly didn't understand Simon's case and hadn't read his notes! It was another little disturbing incident that reinforced our determination to get him home.

When it was time for Simon's computer skills session, Natalie went to join him so she could check her e-mails and make sure our flights home were booked and confirmed.

While she was there, the doctors asked if she needed training to give Simon his injections. He still needs the anti-clotting drugs while he is in the wheelchair. Fortunately this is something she has experience of due to her training at various animal clinics, so she didn't need to be shown.

'I know I've only injected animals before, but it's no different and at least these are into the tummy, and I don't have to find a vein,' she told me when she came back for lunch.

She's just left to attend the family meeting. It will be interesting to see what they discuss. We were holding out all kinds of hope for the future with this meeting when we arrived here. Now we see it as a waste of time as we're going home tomorrow, but they insisted that it still go ahead.

SAME DAY next entry

What a joke! The family meeting lasted ten minutes! Matthew spoke for all the therapists and said that the team had concluded that Simon might have ongoing memory problems regarding being able to retain new information, but it was only a few days ago that he told Simon that as he was only just out of PTA he couldn't really assess any ongoing problems.

What's poor Simon supposed to believe now? Basically, that is all that was said. Natalie didn't bother asking questions. Her questions could be asked of other specialists further down the line and probably answered with more accuracy.

She was told that referral letters would be prepared. She could pick them up in the morning. Medications would be issued for Simon, and she can collect them this evening. She stressed that our flight was early, and we'd be leaving here by 6am, but she was assured the letters would be ready for her.

Simon and Natalie had to wait until 5pm for the medications, but finally, Simon was released, to spend the last night with us in the villa. While I was waiting for them, I took Ruby for a long walk around the complex.

We found two more four-leaf clovers, in different parts of the parkland, so I have four in my purse; all with huge wishes riding on them. Simon's full recovery is the only thing I wished for with these two new ones. My first wish was granted, we are going home much sooner than expected, so I have every reason to believe I might be granted another big wish.

We watched a kookaburra sitting in a tree and Ruby giggled at the Indian Mynah birds that pestered it. They swooped low and chattered and squawked at the bigger bird to try to make it move, but the kookaburra stayed put, serenely ignoring the raucous pests. It reminded me so much of Natalie. No matter what anyone did or said to annoy or obstruct her, she would calmly and confidently stick to her guns and get what she wanted.

When we met with Simon and Natalie at the villa, we decided an early night was best for us all. Everything was packed and ready for our early start. Natalie ordered a taxi for 6am to collect us and soon after dinner we all retired.

DAY 48 Friday 15th August
We rose early at 5.30am and were ready when the taxi pulled up outside. Natalie returned the wheelchair to the unit and collected the referral letters. Our journey to the airport was uneventful, and we quickly got organised with Simon's temporary airport wheelchair. We cleared passport control and had a short wait to board the tiny plane. We were first on board as Simon had to use the hoist before all the other passengers could get on. Ruby took this journey in her stride. After a few sweets, she fell fast asleep on my lap and didn't wake until we landed in Ballina two hours later.

I left Natalie with Simon on the little aircraft and took Ruby into the arrivals building. Martin was waiting for us, and it was so good to see him. We hugged, and he took Ruby into his arms. She wasn't sure at first, but didn't complain to get down. She was happy to stay in Martin's arms.

'How is he?' Martin asked.

'He's glad to be getting home. We all are.'

'It's been a long time.'

'Yes. We didn't think it would be this long when I left you all those weeks ago, did we?'

'I guess it hasn't been an easy ride?' He raised his eyebrows questioningly.

'No, we've had our moments.' I told him. 'But it can only get better form here.' I didn't want to discuss how bad it had been. We had to look forward now, not backwards.

Martin helped to pack our luggage and pram into Natalie's car while I strapped Ruby into her car seat.

Natalie helped Simon into the passenger seat and returned the airport wheelchair. We were soon on our way, and Martin talked to us of normal neighbourly things until we neared the scene of the accident. Martin slowed and pointed it out to Simon, but Simon didn't look. We all fell silent, and Simon kept his eyes on the road in front. I felt he didn't want to acknowledge what Martin was saying, but I couldn't be sure.

When we arrived at the house, a wheelchair was waiting for Simon and Natalie wasted no time in getting him out of the car. Then she went up to the back lawn where the two dogs were tied up.

Within seconds of being released the dogs were fussing around Simon, almost knocked Ruby over in their excitement at seeing her, and greeted us all enthusiastically with tails wagging so hard their bodies were almost doubled in two.

We settled on the veranda for a little while after unpacking the car and Martin made himself at home by making us tea and giving us cookies. He pointed out the small ramps at the threshold of the main door into the house. Some friends of Simon had been around and worked hard to make the one-storey house wheelchair friendly.

He also showed us a wooden seat he'd brought over, to go across the bath so Simon could take a shower in comfort. He'd used it when he broke his leg a few years ago and brought it down from his shed for Simon.

Later, after Martin went home, I made omelettes for our lunch then Natalie went shopping for groceries. I took Ruby for a walk around the property while Simon relaxed on his own sofa, watching his own television.

Ruby wandered around, getting thoroughly dirty, playing in all her favourite spots. She loves to stamp around on the fallen twigs under an old knurled lemon tree. Then she reaches to pick the lower hanging fruits.

She loves to watch the chickens in their chicken house and feed them blades of grass. When she got tired, I brought her back down to the house and put her to bed. She went into her cot with no trouble, and I could sense her relief at lying on a comfy mattress after weeks of sleeping in the travel cot.

Simon's friend Richard stopped by for a short visit, and when Natalie came back with the shopping, Richard helped to unload the car, and I helped put the shopping away. We were enjoying some long awaited domestic bliss, doing normal things in a familiar place.

When Ruby woke from her nap she was very happy and relaxed. She played with the dogs, her long-lost friends, and seemed to be discovering them again. They are very tolerant of her and let her pat them and tug at their tails. They don't complain when she falls on them or chases them.

She played all afternoon very happily, and when bedtime came she settled really well in her cot. It's as if she knows she's come home.

Natalie treated us to a steak dinner to celebrate our homecoming after Richard had gone home and Ruby had gone to bed. We talked over dinner about how awful the past seven weeks had been. We talked of the ups and downs of the long road we'd travelled.

Simon got quite emotional when I told him how Natalie had fought his battles to keep him well cared for, how she'd stayed positive even when the doctors were giving her bad news and how she always believed that he would come back to her.

'I knew you'd come back to me, honey.'

'She never gave up hope of having you home again.' I told him, 'and here you are.'

DAY 49 Saturday 16th August

Ruby woke at 6.30am, and when I went to pick her out of her cot she was wide eyed with amazement. She looked as if she couldn't believe where she was. I took her into the lounge, and she had the same reaction. Her eyes were like saucers and her mouth formed a big round 'O'.

I made her breakfast, and when Natalie joined us in the kitchen, Ruby was chattering happily in her gobbledegook language. When Max came into the kitchen, Ruby giggled and ran towards him. She was like a different child. Although she seemed happy enough in Sydney, it is obvious that she is much happier at home.

'Did Simon have a good night?' I asked Natalie.

'Yeah, he slept like a baby till 4am. Then he woke

and said, "Have we got a plane to catch"? I told him we did that yesterday, and he was already back at home.'

'I guess he just woke up and was disorientated as usual.'

'Yeah, he remembered when I reminded him.'

We had a few more incidents of his memory problems throughout that first day home. He wanted to use his I-pod, but it hadn't been working properly, so he wanted to try to fix the problem and needed the manual. He was sure he kept this in his briefcase, but Natalie said the old briefcase hadn't been used to store things like that in years. They had a filing cabinet now, and the manual wasn't in there. Then Simon got quite cross, insisting that his briefcase was the only place it could be. He was obviously remembering how things were a few years ago.

We talked about going out for lunch tomorrow, and Simon suggested a place that he said they'd been to many times before. He couldn't remember the name of it but could describe it down to the last detail. Next to a river, tennis courts at the side, huge car parking area, over the road from an antiques shop. Natalie didn't know the place and couldn't remember it from Simon's detailed description.

He got very annoyed and yelled for a map book, believing that if he could show her where it was, she'd remember. Again, we decided this was another memory from long ago before Natalie was in his life, but Simon wouldn't accept that until he'd exhausted all the other possibilities.

I hate to see him get so cross and aim his anger at Natalie, but she handles him so well. She knows exactly what to do and what to say to rein his anger in and calm him down. If she can't calm him, she walks away so he can vent his anger on something other than her.

It's difficult to watch, but I don't interfere. Instead, I bite my tongue and walk away too, taking Ruby with me. They have to learn to cope with episodes like this. We know there will be many more upsetting incidents like this in the future. I know that Natalie is hurt by the anger he directs at her, but she returns the abuse with love and patience.

She knows where his anger is coming from and knows she is the only one he can direct the anger at. I hate to think how much longer he'll be like this.

WEEK EIGHT: Home at last

DAY 50 Sunday 17th August

We had a nice quiet day today with no dramas. Natalie and I left Simon for an hour or two while we did some shopping for items that Natalie had forgotten on her first trip to town and to give us some space away from Simon. We bought a shower curtain, so Simon can enjoy a shower and use the seat that Martin brought over. We got a book for him to read, new socks for Ruby, apple pastries for desert and some wine. (Of course.) We didn't stay away too long, but we had enough time to breathe a little easier for a short while.

Ruby enjoyed playing with the doggies again when we got home and discovered another playmate when Puddy, the cat, came to her for a cuddle. Ruby loves to pull his ears and tail, and the cat takes it calmly, allowing Ruby to be as rough as she likes.

Simon seemed much calmer today. He's been taking things easy and is more confident in his wheelchair. He can manoeuvre it better and can now get himself in and out of bed. He even managed to get his own breakfast and drink. All this independence is helping to build his confidence and gives Natalie time to do other things.

A few things bothered him today. He was convinced he had a ten-stack CD system in the ute and complained that it hadn't been collected from the wreck, but Natalie was sure it hadn't been in there. Sure enough, she found it in the shed and Simon had to concede he'd been wrong about that.

He thought he'd been reading a book before the accident and couldn't remember finishing it, so we had to turn the house upside down searching for the book. He couldn't remember the title or the name of the author, but said it had a picture of a spider's web on the front. We couldn't find the book, so we think it was another memory from way back in his youth. Simon was frustrated when we told him this because he feels he had been reading the book last week! These long-ago memories feel so recent to him, so real and clear that it must be awful to be told that he's wrong.

At dinner, we asked Simon some questions about what it feels like for him. We are trying to get a handle on his problems so we could help him more. He described it to us like this.

'It's strange for me to listen to you telling me I'm wrong about things that feel real to me.' Simon admitted. 'I don't remember any of the past few weeks. I know I've had a car crash, but I can't remember having it. To me, it feels like I woke up in Sydney two weeks ago, and the first clear memories I have, feel as if they happened only a few weeks ago, but you are telling me these memories are from ten years ago.

'I don't remember getting married, but I know I love Natalie, and she's my life.' He reached for her hand and had tears in his eyes. 'I can't remember Ruby being born, but I know she is my daughter, and I love her.'

'That's all we need to know, honey.' Natalie told him. 'That's all we'll ever need.'

DAY 51 Monday 18th August
I got up early with Ruby this morning so Natalie could have a lie-in with Simon. She was a little angel and played happily until her mum joined us two hours later.

She's learned to copy us when we give the dogs orders. One frequently given order is, 'Max, on your mat!' when the frisky Labrador gets too boisterous. Ruby shouts at Max, 'Aye! Aye! Mat!' and points to his mat. It's so funny when he obeys her and lies down without complaint!

It's been raining all night, and the gutters are overflowing. Everything is starting to feel damp and cold, and it's miserable being cooped up inside.

Simon is starting to try to do some ordinary household activities and can make himself a cup of tea, but struggled to work the toaster.

'How does this work?' he had to ask.

He saw one of Natalie's new kitchen gadgets, a pasta maker and asked, 'What does this do?'

She'd had it a few months and he'd seen her using it lots of times. He also can't remember where everything is kept and has to keep asking things like, 'Where do we keep the cereals?' or 'Where is the sauce?' and, 'Where do we keep the bread?'

His mobile phone had a minor fault, and Simon wanted to try to fix it. He asked Natalie to explain to him what needed doing. Of course, she didn't know and told him so.

He exploded and yelled at her at the top of his lungs, 'You must know! Don't we have a manual?' He banged his fist on the wall. 'Get me the fucking manual!' he shouted.

Natalie walked away from him, scooped Ruby into her arms and went outside. I followed her and we left Simon to calm down. We stood in silence under the veranda, watching the rain bouncing off the ground. I put a hand on Natalie's shoulder to offer some comfort. I couldn't speak and neither could she. We endured a tense few minutes before Simon called out to us. It was, for him, as if his temper tantrum had never happened. He called to us in a very happy voice, 'I think I fixed it, it's working now.'

I called Paul on Skype this evening. He is going to be working in Dundee for the next few days and will go to his sister's birthday party at the weekend. I wished I could go with him. I miss him so much, but Natalie will need me for a while longer here. Simon is still dependent on her, and I don't want to leave her to cope alone just yet. She always puts him first, and poor Ruby always comes second when Simon needs Natalie. I can understand how my daughter feels, after all, she almost lost him, but I think she should be encouraging him to be independent instead of running every time he calls her. I can't interfere, I know it wouldn't be appreciated, but I have started to hang back when Ruby needs attention. Natalie has to start to be her full-time mum again, and if that means making Simon wait a few minutes, then Simon will have to learn to cope with that.

Simon has a doctor's appointment tomorrow, so I hope the visit will go smoothly. I hope the building has wheelchair access, because if it doesn't, I have visions of Simon erupting like a volcano.

DAY 52 Tuesday 19th August
I wish I could say we'd had another quiet day, but Simon has been ranting big style about the smallest things. He expects Natalie to respond to him in seconds, and when

she doesn't he shouts and swears in his loudest voice. I'm sick of hearing it, but I bite my tongue. Natalie is handling it well. She walks away when he gets too bad, leaving him to stew. It's hard, though. It's hard for all of us to live through this.

I was enjoying my morning shower later than usual. Ruby was back in bed for her morning nap, and all was quiet in the household. The rain was still pouring outside, so we couldn't go anywhere or do anything. We enjoyed a lazy relaxing morning until Simon started shouting about something from the computer room at the end of the hall. His yelling woke Ruby and Natalie was not happy.

Simon yelled even louder, and she went to him and whispered, 'I'm not talking to you until you can be more reasonable.'

I finished my shower then stayed in my room until things calmed down. They left to go to the doctor's appointment soon after we put Ruby in bed for her afternoon nap, and I called Paul. I needed to talk with someone sane who wasn't living through this daily round of abuse and anger and tension.

Paul is concerned for us all and frustrated that he can't help us, but admitted that he would just lose his temper with Simon and that would be no help at all.

While Ruby continued to sleep, I did some laundry, lit a fire and brought some wood down from the shed.

It's not cold, but the constant rain makes it feel chilly, and everything feels damp, so a log fire helps to make us all feel cosy and happy.

Tonight over dinner, Natalie discussed that it might be good for me to be back home for my birthday. This came as a shock as my birthday is only two weeks away and I couldn't see that she would be ready for me to go by then and I said so.

'I thought you would need me until Simon is mobile. How will you manage with Ruby and the pram and the wheelchair when you need to go to appointments with Simon?'

'He might not be mobile for another two or three months, Mum. I can't have you here so long, it wouldn't be fair.'

I sighed deeply. 'I know,' I agreed, realising that she and Simon must have discussed this while they were out. 'You need your space to work things out, I know, but I don't want to leave when things are still so difficult for you.'

I tried to discuss Simon's difficulties, but she insisted she would be able to cope and assured me that it will get better. I know it will, but not as soon as we hoped.

When Natalie was bathing Ruby, I talked to Simon, asking how the doctor's visit had gone, but I couldn't understand his answer as he went off on a tangent and began talking about the new car that he wanted.

I steered the conversation back to his treatment and asked what was planned, but he didn't know.

I tried another subject, a sensitive one and asked him if he could try to think about Natalie's feelings. I pointed out that his constant demands on her were tiring her out, and she had other things to do now that they were home.

Surprisingly he acknowledged that he had been hard on Natalie, but in the next breath he said that it was her fault he got so cross because she shouldn't leave him alone to struggle when he's asking her for help.

'She only walks away when you get cross with her,' I pointed out to him, gently.

'But she only does half a job.' His voice raised an octave. 'If she doesn't want to help me, why doesn't she just say so!'

'She does want to help, but you make it so difficult for her.' I explained calmly.

'I don't mean to.' He sighed. 'It's just that I don't know anything anymore. Things aren't the same as I remember.'

I know it's going to get better. The good times are surely just around the corner, and I know they'll come through this terrible stage and emerge stronger on the other side, but it's not going to happen overnight. Tonight, as I'm writing this in my room, they are cuddled up on the sofa together, talking quietly and calmly about nothing in particular. Just like a normal loving couple. I hope it lasts.

DAY 53 Wednesday 20th August
At last it stopped raining, and we could go out and enjoy some fresh air and sunshine. Natalie and I took Ruby to the nearby town of Lismore to do some supermarket shopping and left Simon alone all morning. He coped really well and was calm and happy when we got home.

This evening I broached the subject of me going home and asked how they'd feel if I looked into changing my flights to an earlier date. Natalie still needs me, but I know from last night's conversation that she now feels ready for me to go. Simon's response to my question made it clear that he wants me to go home too. It isn't always easy to understand as his sentences get very mixed up, but when he started talking about how it would be up to Natalie, but that he would be more comfortable in some respects if I went.

Then he said, 'As long as she understands that she has to leave me a torch where I can get it,' and added, 'if I can reach things I need it'll be okay.'

From these few short sentences, I got the impression that Natalie had primed him for my leaving and told him that he would be left on his own a lot more if I were to go home. She had obviously reassured him that she would make sure he would have everything he needed before leaving him alone.

I smiled at my daughter and told her I would look into re-arranging my flights in the morning.

We enjoyed some television together in the evening and watched a memorial programme about Steve Irwin, the famous Australian wildlife personality who had tragically died a couple of years ago. Simon was shocked.

'When did he die?'

He couldn't remember. Simon had been a big fan of Steve Irwin, and he and Natalie had been frequent visitors to his zoo, which is only a few hours drive from their home in Bangalow.

Later that night there was something on TV about the British Royal family, with some archive footage of Princess Dianna.

'You'll be telling me next that she died too.' Simon joked, but the smile soon left his face when we told him that she had. He was so shocked.

317

We then tried to think of other world and personal events that had happened over the last few years, giving him clues to see whether he could remember.

'Twin towers terrorist attack?'

No memory.

'Sydney Olympics?'

Nothing.

'Katy and John visiting last Christmas?'

'Who's Katy?'

We had to explain and then he seemed to remember that she is Natalie's Sister.

How strange it must be for him. All our recent history is fresh in our memories, but for Simon, his recent memories are the ones he made more that ten years ago. He must feel so disconnected from our reality.

DAY 54 Thursday 21st August

I rang my airline today and was told there were no available flights until the 24th September and my booking was for the 25th, so I can't go home early. I asked if I could get on a waiting list for any cancellations on flights from Brisbane on the 4th to 6th September. There are no guarantees, but I'll keep checking my e-mails.

Natalie was invited to go to the local yoga group, and I tagged along with Ruby in her pram. Natalie had been along to some sessions before the accident, and it was good to see her chatting with all her friends.

One of the ladies had a sister who suffered a brain aneurysm a year ago and suffered similar brain function problems to Simon. She encouraged Natalie by telling her of her sister's recovery and assured us that improvements happen quite quickly once you get the patient home in familiar surroundings. She had a good understanding of what Natalie is going though, so she could be a good source of support in the future.

The neighbours have been discussing how best they can help, and the yoga session was a good excuse to ask Natalie what she would like them to do for her.

The men want to organise a working day at the property to mow the lawns and maintain the paddocks. The neighbours want to cook, clean, bake, babysit, or do anything else that Natalie might want them to do. They made it clear that Natalie wouldn't be left to cope alone, once I had left, and it was so good to hear. I don't feel so guilty for wanting to go home, now that I know these good people will be around to help.

When we got home, Simon had been invited to a barbecue over at his work's depot, so Natalie drove him there, stayed for a while, did some shopping and collected him after an hour or so.

He was very talkative when they got home. He has thoroughly enjoyed his outing and seeing some of his work pals has helped to slot more memories into place for him. He can remember incidents from work that happened a few days before the accident. He remembered people he worked with and details about their families too.

As our chat progressed, Simon's sidetracks got more pronounced. He started talking about injections in the middle of a discussion about work schedules. Then when we were talking about car accidents he switched topic again to mention that computer games are dangerous.

To be fair, I think he was trying to communicate that kids play computer games, drive fast cars on screen and crash with no consequences, so when it came to driving in real life, they feel invincible. He didn't say it so coherently, but I think I got the essence of what he meant.

While they were out, I had a call from Paul, and he was disappointed that I wouldn't be home for my birthday, but we agreed that at least the end was in sight, and I would be home soon.

I also went for a walk with Sally from next door. We took Ruby and the dogs with us along the country lane that runs the length of both properties. Sally had walked Max and Sasha every day in our absence, so she was keeping up the favour to help Natalie.

Sally has a good heart and is the best neighbour in the world. I don't know how Natalie would have managed the last couple of months without her help.

She's looked after the animals, kept an eye on the place and befriended the house-sitter who came to help. She seems to understand Natalie's situation too.

'If ever she needs to get away for a while, tell her to come to our place. Even when we're not in, she can come over and make a cup of tea to escape for a little bit. No one locks doors in this area. There's no need,' she explained.

Sally also gave me some good advice to pass on to Natalie and Simon. She knew the Insurance people were sending someone to see them in the next couple of days, but I didn't know what the visit would be about. Sally explained that this person would be asking them if they needed more help and whether there was anything else the insurance company could provide for them to make life easier.

'When Martin broke his leg a few years back, they came to see us too.' She explained. 'At the time, I wasn't prepared for questions and didn't ask all that I wanted to or should have. I could have had a cleaner to help with the chores as I still worked full time while looking after Martin because he couldn't do anything for himself at first.'

'Thanks, Sally. I'll bear it in mind and tell them to make a list,' I told her.

'How about babysitting services, they might need to think about that? Help with the land, the animals, maintenance about the house and things like that. The insurance has a duty to provide anything that Simon usually is able to do but now can't.'

'Wow, it seems a very comprehensive insurance.'

'Well, I guess there are various levels, and it will depend on what level Simon has, but usually work-cover is pretty good.'

While we talked, Ruby chased the dogs and the dogs foraged around in the verges for interesting smells. We had a good long walk, and although I had to carry Ruby most of the way home, it had been lovely to chat to someone about normal things in a normal, stress free environment. I had enjoyed my walk.

DAY 55 Friday 22nd August

I booked my flight home this morning! I leave two weeks from today. Paul e-mailed to ask whether I'd thought of trying for a flight from Sydney. I rang the ticket office and got a flight for the 5th September. It's only three weeks earlier than my originally booked date, but I feel I'm ready to go now. It meant arranging an internal flight from Ballina, and an overnight stay in a hotel, in Sydney, but I managed to do all that on the Internet with no problems.

I arranged everything while Natalie and Simon attended a physio appointment in town and Ruby napped, so I looked forward to them getting home to give them my news.

I was up in the backyard with Ruby when they got home. We had armfuls of lemons and oranges that Ruby had harvested. I managed to save some from her squeezing fingers and sharp teeth. She loves to eat them right off the bush, doesn't even wait for them to be peeled. Luckily, the lemons here are so sweet that she doesn't get a mouthful of sour juice.

Simon was happy with his visit to the physio. He's seen the guy before, after his bike accident. The chap took the time to assess him, working out the best way forward. He recommended things for Simon to do in preparation for the cast coming off. He can work on strengthening his muscles in readiness for getting back on his feet.

They were both pleased to hear the news about my flights, though I think my news threw Natalie into a panic. She would have so much to organise before I left, but at least having a date to work towards would help her focus on what needed to be done.

Natalie and I took the dogs for a walk this evening, with Ruby in her pram. She told me again how grateful she was that I had come over to help. She was glad I was going home, but more for my sake than hers.

She knows how difficult it's been, on me and Paul, to be apart for so long, but she couldn't have managed without me here. It's nice to be appreciated, but I told her for the hundredth time that I only did what I felt I had to.

'You are my child, and you needed me. I'm glad I was able to come. So many people wouldn't have the same good fortune to be able to drop everything as I could do.'

'I'll never be able to thank you enough, Mum.'

'I don't need your thanks. I just want some reassurance. I want to know you'll be okay when I'm gone.'

'I can't promise you that. You know what it's like. But we'll cope, Mum. You don't have to worry about us.'

'I know, but I'll still worry. You have to promise me that you'll ask for help if you need it. I can be on a flight in no time if you can't cope with Simon's tantrums, and we can transfer money if you need help in that way.'

'Oh, Mum. You've done enough. I can't ask any more from you and dad.'

'You'd better! I'll worry all the more if I think that you're struggling. You have to e-mail me every chance you get. I want to know all the details of Simon's recovery and how you are coping with his moods, his temper and his demands.'

'I will, Mum. I promise.'

'And I want regular photos and updates on my little angel. I'm going to miss her so much.'

'I think she'll miss you too, Mum. You've been amazing with her.'

'She was the easy bit in all this. I've loved every minute of looking after her.'

'Even the dirty nappies?' Natalie grinned at me.

'Well, maybe not everything about her is angelic!' I laughed.

When we got home, Simon was enjoying a beer on the veranda with Richard who had called to visit. We joined them, and Natalie got some burgers out to grill on the barbecue for dinner. I made salad and prepared the bread buns and we had a calm evening, sitting around the pool, listening to the frogs croaking and cicadas chirruping. I was going to miss Australia so much.

DAY 56 Saturday 23rd August

I had a busy day house cleaning today. Richard called around this morning to introduce his girlfriend and Martin came to see how we were doing. We were enjoying a normal day, full of ordinary weekend family activities.

Simon has been pretty quiet today, except for a couple of incidents. This afternoon, Natalie prepared to inject Simon with his anti-clotting drugs. She stuck the needle into his tummy, just as she has done every day since we got home, and Simon yanked the needle out and threw it across the room before she had the chance to push the meds into him.

'Didn't you hear me gasp?' he yelled, loud enough to burst eardrums.

'You always gasp!' Natalie pointed out.

'Didn't you read my body language?' he asked and followed this by more swearing and cursing.

'I'm not psychic, Simon! If I hurt you I'm sorry.'

Natalie was close to tears, but she straightened her shoulders and handed him another syringe. 'Maybe you can do it yourself in future?'

Simon took the syringe and injected himself.

He reacts like a little boy to most things now, but with an adult vocabulary and much more aggression than a small boy would have.

He asks Natalie to watch him while he does his exercises to make sure he is doing them correctly. She sits with him willingly and encourages him lovingly. Nothing is too much trouble for her.

It is difficult for me to watch them work out the realities of their life now. Simon is totally dependent on Natalie. He is moody and depressed and abusive most of the time. Natalie handles him very well. She is patient and understanding. She knows this behaviour is because of the brain injury, and is very forgiving of his insults and nastiness. When his abuse becomes more than she can stand, she walks away and lets him stew.

I hope he can get help soon with his behavioural problems. I feel I will be abandoning Natalie to manage as best she can when I take the child care away. She will have to care for her family, run the house and look after the animals. It will be such a lot of work, on top of running around with Simon to take him to all his appointments. I can't stay here forever, but I really don't want to leave just yet.

Simon seemed to get agitated over dinner. He never stopped talking and went off on tangents all over the place, but I was too tired to interrupt him to set him back on the right conversational path and Natalie seemed to feel the same, so we let him ramble. It was easier than trying to shut him up.

Paul phoned after dinner. He was overjoyed to know I'd managed to change my flights. He's arranged time off work so he can meet me at the airport, and I told him I can't wait to see him. He asked if I had anywhere in mind to go away for a holiday as he could take a few weeks off work. I told him that I'd rather wait until I get home and see how I feel. I wasn't in the right frame of mind to enjoy a holiday, but I didn't have the heart to say so when he was so excited about having me back home.

Carol and James rang to say they would be in the area for a few days and asked if they could come to visit. We expect to see them tomorrow afternoon.

WEEK NINE: Objections & arguments

DAY 57 Sunday 24th August

The sun shone today and lifted all our spirits. It is lovely to see clear blue sky again. Carol and James arrived at lunchtime, and we enjoyed an afternoon of family chatter. They brought us photographs of their travels and had some interesting stories to tell about their trip to the outback a few years ago.

Carol is older than me by four years and is a retired nurse. She is well aware of Simon's problems and memory issues and knows how difficult it's going to be for Natalie in the coming months, but she doesn't live locally, so can only support from a distance, on the phone. Emma is closer, only a three hour drive away, but she has a family of teenagers to look after and won't be able to make the trip too often. I explained about the neighbours being kind and pitching in to help where they can, but Simon got stroppy about that.

'I don't want all and sundry calling around here doing stuff with my tools.'

'I think they'll bring their own, Simon.' Natalie smiled at him nervously.

'Yeah, well, I don't want them in my shed.' His voice grew louder. 'You tell them not to go near my stuff!'

Carol took her younger brother's hand and got his attention. 'No one is going to take advantage of you, Simon. They want to help. Natalie can't do everything that needs doing. You should be grateful that there are so many people willing to give up their time to do these things for you.'

'Yeah, well. I am.' He spoke in a calmer tone. 'But tell them not to touch my stuff!'

Natalie shrugged. I shook my head and sighed. James took Ruby up to the fruit bushes to escape the tension.

'Tell me about Sydney.' Carol asked Simon and Natalie and I groaned.

'You'll regret you ever asked that question.' Natalie raised her eyebrows at Carol and went to make a start on dinner.

'Need any help,' I asked and went to join her.

We could hear Simon's monologue from the kitchen. He clearly enjoyed telling his big sister about all the negative incidents that he fixated on during his hospital and rehab stay. It made me very sad to listen to him being so negative. I wish he could let them go. We'd heard them hundreds of times, but he had a fresh audience and Carol was making all the right comments of agreement and sympathy. She was the perfect distraction for us, and the perfect conversationalist for Simon.

Later that evening when Carol and James had gone back to their lodgings in Byron Bay, Simon decided to phone Emma. The conversation was a repeat of the one with Carol. The phone call started at around 8.30pm, and I have come to bed to write my journal to escape. The time is now 9.45pm, and I can still hear the conversation continuing. He must have told poor Emma the same stories over and over, but she still listens patiently to her little brother. He has a good family. His sisters care deeply about him. I wished they lived closer so they could be more help to Natalie when I'm gone.

Richard is coming over soon to watch the Formula One racing with Simon. They'll stay up late and enjoy a man-only evening into the small hours, watching the live footage from Valencia. It's not good for Simon to miss sleep, but I'm sure he'll enjoy the race.

DAY 58 Monday 25h August

Simon got up toward lunchtime, and seemed none the worse for his late night.

We drove to the park in the centre of Bangalow and met with Carol and James. We enjoyed a picnic lunch and the dogs swam in the river while Ruby played on the swings and slides. When it started raining, we packed the picnic away and came home. Carol and James came with us, and we had a barbecue dinner this evening.

Throughout the day, Simon's conversation was quite good. He slipped off topic a few times and began to ramble about his fixations, or talk about unrelated things, but we steered him back, with help from Carol and James. They seemed to understand Simon's new idiosyncrasies. Natalie and I could enjoy some normal conversation, and it was so refreshing.

DAY 59 Tuesday 26th August

I'm not writing so much now. Each day feels like a repeat of the one before, so there's not much to write about. Simon fluctuates between obsessive conversation fixating on past issues or flying into a rage at minor frustrations. He's very difficult to live with, and I worry about leaving Natalie and Ruby with such a bad tempered man.

The work cover insurance lady came today and talked of things that can be provided. From commodes to bath hoists, she discussed everything. Child care is a possibility, an odd job man to call once a week might be another, but Simon is not happy. He doesn't want strangers in his house or on his land. He kept his cool until the lady left and then launched into a diatribe of jumbled objections.

'I don't want a shrink coming round here telling me how to run my life!'

'That's not...' Natalie tried to interrupt.

'I don't want strangers coming to clean the house while Natalie isn't here and asking me if I need my bum cleaned!'

'But Simon...' I tried to stop him.

'If they think they're gonna use my tools...! I paid a lot of bucks for my stuff. You think I'm gonna let just any old drongo into my shed?'

'They won't...' Natalie tried to interrupt him.

'We don't need anyone! I don't want strangers using my stuff!'

His voice boomed across the paddocks, and it was easier to let him rant than to try to stop him. He'd got hold of the wrong end of the stick and wouldn't drop it.

We waited for the storm to pass, and when he eventually calmed, Natalie took his hand. 'Listen, honey. We don't have to accept help from anyone. But who do you think is going to have to do everything if we don't have help?'

'I'll be right soon. I can do all that stuff.'

'Simon, you won't be able to do those things for a long time.' I told him.

'You won't be well enough to mow the lawns or tidy the paddocks for a few months, Simon, and the veranda roof needs repairing. I can't clean the house well enough and look after you and the animals and Ruby. I can't take Ruby with me to work, and I have to go back to work soon, so we'll need to organise some childcare.'

'You have to go to work?' He seemed confused.

'We talked about this, honey. I have to go back to work soon, if only for a few hours a day. We need the money.'

His eyes went glassy as they filled with tears. 'I should go back to work soon. You have enough to do.'

'You will, honey. When you're well enough.'

DAY 60 Wednesday 27th August

It has been another beautiful sunny and warm day today. I helped Natalie take some things to the tip and generally tidy up outside.

Simon was invited to the neighbour's house for a beer with the blokes. He was tipsy when they brought him home, and very talkative. He drove us mad with his incessant monologue.

I tried to get a word in here and there, but that just set him off on tangents and he didn't make a lot of sense. So I asked about the appointment he has for tomorrow with the occupational therapist who had arranged to call here at the house. I hoped to get him to focus on something other than his obsessions.

Poor Simon began to stress about the visit. He got quite agitated and angry and began to rant.

'You don't know where these people are coming from!' he yelled. 'You can't trust them!'

Natalie and I tried to interrupt him, but he didn't hear us.

'Will she want to talk to me?' he asked. 'I don't have anything to say to her!' He rushed on, 'When these people get you in your own home, they can...'

'Oh stop stressing and shut up, will you!' Natalie shouted at him.

Amazingly he did just that! We were able to enjoy a nice pizza dinner in a calm atmosphere.

DAY 61 Thursday 28th August

The occupational therapist didn't arrive until mid afternoon, and Simon stressed about the visit all morning. He got really wound up.

His main problem seems to be that he doesn't trust anyone. He thinks this person's job is to get him back to work as quickly as possible, which it probably is, but no one is going to be sending Simon back to work anytime soon.

Poor Simon doesn't understand that, though. He thinks that as soon as he is able to sit comfortably, they will make him go back to do office work and he will hate that. He doesn't realise that even office work will be beyond him for quite a while, due to the brain injury problems.

Thankfully, when this person arrived, Simon was calmer. They chatted on the veranda, and I took Ruby for a walk around the paddocks.

This evening, Simon complained that his leg was hurting quite badly. He confessed that it had been itching, and he'd poked a stick down between the cast and his leg to scratch it and get some relief. He thought he might have damaged the skin on his leg and he said it hurt like hell.

Natalie sighed and shook her head. She loaded him into the car, and they have just set out to the local hospital A&E department to get it looked at.

DAY 62 Friday 29th August

Simon had a small part of the cast removed to enable the doctor at the hospital to see the damage on his leg. It was a minor graze and won't cause problems.

Natalie took him to physio this morning, and he returned with a round board with half a ball on one side of it. He has to use this balance board to do some gentle exercises to help strengthen his muscles in readiness for when the casts are taken off in a few weeks' time.

Simon does not like to do his exercises, and Natalie has to cajole, tempt and badger him to do them. He always finds an excuse. He's too tired, has too much pain, or says he can't see how it will help!

It is an uphill battle for Natalie. He's acting like a spoilt brat.

DAY 63 Saturday 30th August

Same old, same old. The days revolve around Simon's tantrums, monologues, fixations, obsessions and paranoia. He's wearing us out. I'll be leaving in a few days, and I'll be so glad to leave the stress behind, but I'll feel very guilty for leaving Natalie and Ruby in the thick of it.

Natalie assures me that she is confident that Simon will improve quickly, especially once he starts to get mobile. She has lots of good friends who have offered to help with childcare, so she insists that they will be fine and I shouldn't worry.

It doesn't matter how much she tries to reassure me, I know it will still be a struggle for her.

I desperately want to stay. My heart is breaking because I don't want to leave my daughter to cope with this alone. I want to help. I want to ease the burden for her, but I know she wants me to go home.

Simon wants me to leave too. I can understand. I know he wants to have Natalie to himself, and I'm in their space. I try to give them time alone, I come to bed early to write this diary, and leave them to talk in the lounge. It's not the same as having the house to themselves, though.

We've been invited for dinner at Sally and Martin's house tomorrow, along with some of the other neighbours. I hope we can enjoy a pleasant evening.

WEEK TEN: Promises of help

DAY 64 Sunday 31st August

We went to Martin and Sally's dinner party this evening. A few of the other neighbours were there too, and it was good to hear more offers of help for Simon and Natalie.

The dinner conversation was a little strained as Simon monopolised the table with his monologues. We did try to steer him towards conversation that didn't involve the hospital, but of course he had a new audience that hadn't heard about his terrible treatment from unsympathetic morons.

Simon seemed to be in his element and enjoyed being centre stage. The neighbours were enthralled with his stories until Simon started telling them the same tales for the third time without a break or pause for breath.

The older children helped to keep Ruby happy, and I was able to join in with some ordinary adult conversation eventually as Simon grew tired and quieted.

Some ladies were concerned that I was leaving shortly. They had first-hand knowledge now of how Simon had changed since the accident, and I had seen one or two sympathetic glances aimed at Natalie during the evening. At the end of the night as we were saying our goodbyes, Samantha from the cattle farm next door came to give me a hug. She whispered in my ear, 'Don't worry about Natalie. We'll look after her for you.'

It was just what I needed to hear, and I thanked her. She wasn't the only one to reassure me that Natalie would not be left alone to cope with the difficulties she faced. A few of the ladies has made encouraging comments to me so I felt a little more confident about leaving.

During the evening, someone asked Simon what it felt like not to be able to remember things properly. Simon's reply was a very simplified version of the whole story.

'Apparently I was only 5 minutes away from home when the accident happened, but the first thing I know about it, I wake up in Sydney five weeks later, to be told that the clearest memory I have of my yesterday, was actually from ten years ago.'

Author's note: As nothing of any significance happened between Sunday and my leaving date, I decided to end this account of my time in Australia here, but it's not the end of Simon's story. The following few pages bring Simon's recovery journey up to date.

NOVEMBER: Five weeks on

I flew home on 5th September, three weeks after getting Simon home to Bangalow. It was a wrench to say goodbye to them, but we knew it was time for me to leave.

They'd found their feet and were getting on with life, fitting into a new routine that revolved around Simon's therapies and appointments. I was needed less and less, and neighbours constantly reassured me that they would be around to help Natalie when she *did* need someone to help.

Saying goodbye to Natalie was difficult. Leaving my child in a state of flux was so hard, when every beat of my heart was telling me to stay, to help, to support, to love, but my head was telling me to go. Natalie was strong, and she was patient. She loved Simon beyond words. I knew they would be all right.

Saying goodbye to Ruby was something else entirely. My darling baby girl who'd made me laugh out loud with joy at her antics and cry with sympathy when she hurt herself or was ill.

How I miss her little wriggling body. How I miss her ready smile, her tiny hands reaching out for me. My little angel. My adorable grandchild. I'm heartbroken that I can't hold her close and keep her safe.

As I'm writing this in November, it is more than five months since the accident. Simon is working hard to regain his independence. He is beginning to take his first few steps with a walking frame.

He works out on a new exercise bike that the insurance company provided, and does hydrotherapy in the pool. He hopes to be walking unaided by Christmas. I feel sure he will achieve this ambitious goal.

I talk to them regularly and we see each other on the computer screen on Skype as often as we can. My little angel blows me kisses, and I can see for myself how the family unit is coping. Simon sits next to Natalie in his wheelchair and Ruby toddles between them as we talk.

The effects of his brain injury are still causing lots of problems, but Simon is slowly coming back to us. His improvements continue, and Natalie is happy with his progress, so I have to be happy for them.

Simon is still working on his happy ending. Natalie is still supporting him every step of the way. Nothing is certain yet about their future or what it might hold. Who can be certain of the future?

Life can change in an instant and never be the same again. A momentary lapse of concentration, a freak accident; that's all it takes to set us on a new path, a path we don't know how to travel, but with love and patience, even the hardest roads can be navigated.

My time in Sydney, with my brave and patient daughter, taught me that love and positive thinking can work miracles.

POST SCRIPT: Five years later

More than five years have now passed since the accident. I'm so happy to report that Simon has made an excellent recovery. He describes himself as ninety-five-per-cent of what he used to be. Considering how badly his brain was damaged, we are all over the moon with this result.

He still has lots of problems. One is poor short-term memory, so he keeps a pocket notebook to remind him of the basic day-to-day things he has to remember. He has regained his physical strength and has returned to work full-time and supports his family financially. Natalie has her own thriving business and, as she puts it, 'Is working hard whilst living the dream.'

I can't say the last few years have been easy.

Natalie and Simon lost many good and close friends in the first few years. Even the closest of friends and neighbours couldn't cope with the realities of Simon's altered personality. The anger outbursts, the paranoia, the yelling and inappropriate comments are all typical symptoms of brain injury, but can alienate even the most kindly and sympathetic people.

Paul and I travelled to Australia as often as we could, and we paid for them to make the trip to England, but the visits weren't easy. Simon's distorted character, his dependency on Natalie, his antagonism, mistrust, obsessions and fanatical behaviour were hard to cope with, and most of our family and friends could not spend more than a few hours in Simon's company without losing patience with him.

When I received an e-mail from Natalie one day, about two years after the accident, to tell me that she had asked Simon to move out, my heart broke. After so much time trying to make it work, my daughter had reached rock bottom. Lots of phone calls followed her revelation. We spoke daily, and somehow, she got through the pit of despair. They both agreed to try counselling. They did this jointly and individually, and eventually they made it through and found the strength to continue.

They still came very close to separation. The strain of living with brain damage does that to couples. The statistics make for sober reading. Some reports say that one in three marriages end in divorce within four years after one partner suffers a brain injury. After witnessing the results of brain damage, I can fully appreciate why so many couples don't make it.

Forgiveness is a word that my daughter uses when describing how she got through the worst times. She didn't confide the details to me until the most terrible times were behind them, but I know now that she suffered distressing verbal abuse from Simon, especially during the first two years.

She describes being crippled by mental cruelty and pain at times, but somehow, through all the nastiness, she managed to remember that the offensive person she lived with was not to blame for his actions. She filled her mind with memories of the real Simon, clearly focusing on his love for her. In this way, she could forgive the brain damaged Simon, and move toward a future that she tried to keep sight of, a future where Simon would be whole again.

I'm absolutely sure that another, very emotional and harrowing story could be written about how they came through those first few years, but that's not my story to tell. I only know that their love for each other was very powerful before this trauma, and now that love has grown even deeper and is stronger than ever.

Simon works hard to ensure his ongoing brain problems don't impact his family, and Natalie supports his endeavours with love and encouragement. Their home is filled with laughter and love where once it held angry words, resentment and despair. I'm just so happy that their relationship survived and they have arrived at this happier, more secure stage in their lives.

Right at the beginning, in the first weeks after the accident, Natalie told Simon to imagine walking on the beach with his dogs and Ruby, giving him something to focus on as a goal for him to work towards. They now live close to the beach and walk there often with Ruby and the dogs, and their new daughter, Amy, who was born a little more than three years after the accident.

Life *can* be good again after brain injury, if you're willing to put in the hard yards, have patience, give it all the love you have got and then give more. My daughter and son-in-law did just that, and I'm so proud they achieved their goal.

THE END

ABOUT THE AUTHOR

Pearl A. Gardner lives in West Yorkshire, England.

She has enjoyed some success with short story fiction, winning some national competitions. Her articles and stories have been published in popular magazines, both fiction and non-fiction, but she is concentrating on full length works now.

Pearl has a wide ranging and eclectic author list that includes many genres from chick lit romances to science fiction, which she writes under the author name of P.A. Gardner

The following is not a comprehensive list, so if you really would like to see more work by Pearl A. Gardner, simply search for her name in Amazon.

MORE PUBLICATIONS by Pearl A Gardner

The Scent of Bluebells – In spring of 1939, life seems full of promise for the young girl from a northern mill town. War is brewing. For Amy, and for many women like her, it would change her life forever.

Through the following five years of turmoil, Amy endures heartache and loss. Just as she is about to give birth, Jimmy, her husband, is reported missing in action and presumed dead.

After more than a year with no further news of her missing husband, she slowly begins to enjoy freedom and independence like she'd never known before.

The war continues with no news of Jimmy, and she dares to love again.

Will this new love survive the war?

Will Jimmy be found?

Pushed on the Shelf – a romantic comedy. Forty-something Trisha is reeling from the shock of being dumped by her husband, Alan, aka DISCWIFF (Dick in Sports Car With Foot Fetish.) Trisha now has to support her two children financially, as DISCWIFF has set up home with TITSNOBB (Tits no Brain Bimbo) and left her in a pile of debt.

With no qualifications or experience, the job market looks bleak, but she is determined not to go under. As Trisha struggles to hold together all the threads of her unravelling life, her emotions get in a tangle when the owner of the local flower shop takes a keen interest in her, and she agrees to a date with him.

Trisha feels like her life is being lived inside a pressure cooker that's ready to blow a gasket. Something has to give, but what?

Books by P. A. Gardner
They Take our Children book one The Truth Revealed –
Soft science fiction / family saga about alien abduction. Courtney is an astonishingly beautiful teenager. She is also a brighter than average young woman but is otherwise as ordinary, happy and well adjusted as any other girl her age.

On her sixteenth birthday, Courtney's neurotic mother, Helen, calls her a monster in a fit of rage. The teenager runs off, causing panic in the family. Courtney's father, Gavin, has long suspected something sinister hiding in his wife's history, but nothing could have prepared him for the truth. Helen's father, George, tries to reveal what he knows about the mystery but the family find it hard to accept his far-fetched version of events as realistic.

Weaving between past and present the facts about Courtney's shocking alien origin are exposed and the search for the whole truth begins.

They Take our Children book two Taking Control – The second book in the two book series about alien abduction.

Courtney's family is drawn into the murky world of ufology experts. Subterfuge and concealment become part of their everyday lives as they search for the secret to open the gateway to the second dimension. They hope to cross the gateway and search for Courtney's cousins and meet face to face with the aliens who abducted them.

Talk of government agencies and 'above top secret' organisations make them fearful, but when they discover how much information has been covered up about the alien abductions, they become even more determined to take control and find the missing children.

CONNECT WITH THE AUTHOR

Discover more on the web site
www.pearlagardner.co.uk

On Goodreads
https://www.goodreads.com/author/show/7350328.Pearl_A_Gardner

On Facebook
https://www.facebook.com/pearlagardner

On Twitter
https://twitter.com/PearlAGardner

Dear Reader
I really appreciate that you took the time to read this work of non- fiction. I hope you enjoyed it.

It would be lovely if you could leave a review of the book on Amazon, Goodreads, or any other place that will accept your comments. Reviews help authors in lots of ways. Good reviews help to convince more people to read the book. The not so good reviews help the author to understand how they might improve the work.

If you have not enjoyed this book, or found faults with the work, please feel free to contact me to let me know how I may be able improve your reading experience of this novel.

With very best wishes from the author,
Pearl A. Gardner

It's Penguin Shooting Day

9860890R00193

Printed in Great Britain
by Amazon.co.uk, Ltd.,
Marston Gate.